THE LAW OF THE SEA

THE LAW OF THE SEA

Current problems

by

René-Jean Dupuy

Secretary General of the Hague Academy of
International Law
Professor at the University of Nice
Member of the Institut de Droit International

OCEANA PUBLICATIONS INC. – DOBBS FERRY, N.Y.

A. W. SIJTHOFF–LEIDEN

1974

ISBN 0-379-00217-5 (Oceana)

ISBN 90 286 0354 9 (Sijthoff)
Library of Congress Catalog Card Number: 74-79800

Printed in the Netherlands.

to Wolfgang Friedmann
my friend
in memoriam

PREFACE

It is generally accepted that the law of the sea is in the process of drastic change. The third United Nations Conference on the Law of the Sea will have to reflect this evolution, and it may therefore seem unrealistic to devote a book to such a dynamic subject before the future Convention has been adopted.

The aim of this work, however, is not to give a description of the whole range of positive law but to analyse a number of crucial legal problems raised by the new uses of ocean space so as to indicate to the reader the changing structure of the law of the sea.

The rapid progress achieved in off-shore drilling technology has made the exploitation of hydrocarbons commercially possible at greater depths than could be reached, or were ever thought of, fifteen years ago. It can be foreseen that deposits of manganese nodules lying on the deep sea-bed will be exploited in the very near future. These activities, hazardous by their very nature, in combination with the increased danger resulting from the recent trends in maritime oil transportation (supertankers) will create serious risks of pollution to the marine environment.

All these factors, which initially appeared as technological phenomena, are aggravated and made even more complex by a set of legal and political problems which have also arisen.

The process of decolonization has introduced into the international scene a large number of coastal and landlocked and otherwise geographically disadvantaged States. The oceans are becoming areas of potential conflicts. As far as the law of the sea is concerned, it is necessary, as the late Wolfgang Friedmann said, to go from the law of mere coexistence toward the law of co-operation.

The questions examined in this book constitute a series of examples of the ways in which widely accepted needs might be met.

In the introductory chapter of Part I, we attempted to demonstrate that the present stage of the law of the sea is characterized by the opposition of the classical principles established within the framework of a law of movement and various new rules which appear on the basis of a law of appropriation. This dialectical method shows that no chaos reigns in the law of the sea if we concentrate on this main opposition between the traditional and the new uses of the ocean space.

Then we shall probe into the concept of common heritage of mankind, wondering if it is a myth or a reality.

At the very time when the United Nations in 1970 were proclaiming that the sea-bed and the ocean floor were prohibited to national sovereignty and private appropriation, many riparian States, following a movement which had been in progress in South America for several years, extended their national jurisdiction over large areas of the oceans. One of the main problems of the third Conference on the Law of the Sea is precisely that of delimitation between the international zone and the national zone. Furthermore, for the latter, which in all likelihood will be fixed at 200 miles with the agreement of the majority of States, a choice will have to be made between two legal solutions as to the scope of the jurisdiction which the riparian States would have over this national area: either full and entire sovereignty, assimilating this zone to their waters or only, as seems more probable, a projection beyond these national waters of specific and exclusive economic rights for the purposes of development.

In Part II, we shall be dealing with various sea-bed legal problems connected with the broader issue of peace and development. We shall consider successively three themes which presently appear to be the most important for ensuring the peaceful uses of the sea-bed and the rational exploitation of its living and mineral resources.

In Part III, we shall be considering some regional problems showing the insufficiency of purely national legal approaches to promote some particularly significant patterns of struggle in answer to the challenge raised by pollution. Moreover in the Mediterranean and the Caribbean sea a certain trend can be noted towards vital co-operation among the riparians in view of the development of their region.

In fact, if the law of the sea has to enunciate universal rules in the interest of all peoples, it must also provide for a certain amount of decentralization to take regional situations into account.

The law of the sea has become a significant part of the international law for development, it is also, like the latter, a situational law–which should satisfy specific needs which flow from local conditions having their influence on the process of development.[1]

1. The following chapters of this book have been prepared in view of specific meetings.

Chapter two of the second part, chapters one and three of the third part have been prepared in their first version for the Pacem in Maribus meeting, convened by Mrs. Elizabeth Mann Borgese and the Center for the Study of Democratic Institutions in Malta, from 1970 to 1973.

Chapter three of the second part has been prepared for the United Nations inter-regional Seminar on the Mineral Resources of the Continental Shelf (Port of Spain, Trinidad and Tobago, April 1971).

Chapter two of the third part, dealing with national legislations relating to water pollution in five mediterranean countries, develops a study devoted to the legislation of four of these countries, and published in the book: *The Pollution of the Mediterranean Sea,* edited by Lord Ritchie-Calder, Herbert Lang, Bern, 1972.

We wish to express our gratitude to Mrs. Elizabeth Mann Borgese, to Lord Ritchie-Calder and to the United Nations Secretariat for having allowed us to publish these different studies.

TABLE OF CONTENTS

First Part

General problems

Chapter I

CONTRADICTIONS IN THE LAW OF THE SEA

The law of the sea has developed over the centuries around the notion of freedom of navigation and the aura which attaches to the word has tended to hide the expansion of maritime empires which it has permitted. The idea of free communications between peoples, rich in images of large ships opening the way to exchanges with far off lands, justifies placing the sea at the disposal of all; however, in historical reality, only the great maritime powers were able to make use of it. Freedom of the seas has been akin to "Freedom of Labour" in the Industrial Europe of the 19th century: in effect the right of the great was licence, that of the poor was submission.

It is to be expected that the great movement in the world towards demand for equality will extend to the law of the sea thus placing in question the foundations of this law. That this did not appear sooner is because maritime technology has evolved very slowly since the growth of technology has permitted a multiplication of the uses of the marine environment and the exploitation of its riches, and we have witnessed various actions on the part of maritime powers such as the developing countries which have upset traditional practices and the law which governs them. While in the past the sea was the subject of political and military rivalry, and economic considerations were only of secondary significance, it has become a coveted area today because of the riches of its waters and its bed.

Two opposing principles have come into conflict in the attempt to develop a new régime with respect to the seas and the oceans which takes into account the economic objectives of States. The coastal State has tended to extend its domain by appropriating maritime zones beyond a limit undreamed of in the recent past,[1]

1. W. Friedmann, "Selden Redivivus– 'Towards a Partition of the Seas' ", AJIL, Oct. 1971, Vol. 65, pp. 757-770

while on the other hand, the desire to establish the marine environment as part of the public international domain for the equal benefit of all peoples, provokes the demand for a collective management based on the notion of "The Common Heritage of Mankind".[2]

(1) The movement towards appropriation began with the Truman Proclamation of 1945 on the continental shelf, this act being inspired by the American fear of a shortage of hydrocarbons. One could hardly be astonished that this demand by the leading industrial power in the world should be followed immediately by those of the developing countries, beginning with the Latin American countries who have large continental shelves off their Atlantic coast. From this beginning, the subjects of appropriation grew ever richer, the seabed and the subsoil thereof, then the adjacent waters up to a distance of 200 miles from the coast and finally, on the western side of the continent, an identical distance in waters lacking a continental shelf but rich in biological resources.

Without adopting these latter claims the Geneva Convention of 1958 placed the shelf under a simple and coherent juridical régime, and has been able for a dozen years to calm the appetite for appropriation at least for the sea bottom.

(2) This situation would appear to be compatible with the advent of an opposing tendency following the adoption by the General Assembly of the Pardo proposition which in 1967 characterized the seabed, the ocean floor and the subsoil thereof, beyond the zone of national jurisdiction as the "Common Heritage of Mankind", and as such, devoted the peaceful uses in the interest of all peoples with or without sea coasts, and especially for the benefit of the developing countries. Resolution 2750 (XXV) of December 17, 1970, by which the General Assembly decided to hold a conference planned for 1973 with the aim of revising the law of the sea, demonstrates the consciousness, not only of the necessity for reform but also for legislation concerning the new domains of international law and the Declaration of principle of December 17, 1970, outlined for the seabed the fundamental norms of this fu-

2. G. Scelle saw the sea thirty years ago as in the public international domain. This view, then premature, is becoming accepted today.

ture régime based on the exclusion of all sovereign property on the seabed.

However, if the States of the Third World applauded this revolutionary process designed to create an international mechanism which in the final analysis would manage the resources of the seabed and its underlying strata for their benefit, numerous were those among them who wanted to extend their appropriation unilaterally.

Naturally enough the proclamation of "The Common Heritage of Mankind" aroused, dialectically, a renewal of the movement towards appropriation of the seabed as well as of the waters.

With respect to the former, they were encouraged by the juridical uncertainty which leaves the continental shelf without precise limits, taking into account the duality of the criteria, denounced so often, in the first article of the 1958 Convention. Until the third UN conference on the law of the sea puts an end to this ambiguity, it was tempting to carve out, with the justification of exploitability, an "undersea territory beyond the depth of 200 metres".

And why wouldn't this territorial appropriation, in certain countries confronted with the needs of development, include a demand for waters beyond the continental shelf when these waters offer rich fishing grounds to the fishing fleets of foreign powers, which for months, without touching shore, undertake massive expeditions without benefiting the riparians and with no other limit than the destruction of the species subject to their greed. The principle proposed by the United Nations of the "sovereignty of peoples over their natural resources" serves as a basis for this response by the riparian States, despite the fact that the question remains unresolved of how far their rights extend. They intend to capitalize on the possibilities for their development which contiguity may bear.

Thus, an unusual cacophony reigns over the seas and the oceans: while the maritime powers invoke the age-old freedom and the principle of agreement as the basis of international law, the coastal States rely on the right of development and the duty to protect living species in order to preserve the ecological equilibrium, a concern justifying recourse to a unilateral exercise of their jurisdiction. However, it does not appear that we should despair before this discordance. As in all periods of upheaval resulting from the advent of new technological or economic factors, contradictions are exaggerated, but it is possible to isolate the principles of dialectical tension which activate them. We see four:

– the law of the sea was unidimensional, it is becoming pluridimensional;

– it was essentially a law relating to movement, more and more it is taking its place as a law relating to appropriation;

– for the most part it was a law of a personal character in which the notion of sovereignty has little place; today on the contrary it has become territorial law with the juridical consequences which that implies;

– a law of a universal nature and function, it now gives effect more and more to regional situations.

These four principles should be understood, as always in a dialectical analysis, as portraying not phenomena of substitution but sources of tension; for each principle, the second alternative does not replace the first; it only confronts the first alternative obliging the first to take account of it without succeeding in destroying the first.

I. FROM A UNIDIMENSIONAL LAW TO A PLURIDIMENSIONAL LAW

Classical law of the sea had only one dimension: essentially a law of navigation on the surface, it was scarcely concerned with the underwater environment. The warships which moved there were affected neither by the law of war, except by reason of their activity with respect to surface vessels, nor by the law of peace, except for the obligation not to use foreign territorial waters except in surface navigation in order to benefit from the presumption of innocent passage.

Questions relating to the régime of the seabed took on a theoretical character in the absence of technically feasible economic uses. Recourse to Gilbert Gidel's book is enlightening in this regard. It examines the problem of sedentary fisheries on the high seas with admitted difficulty, "considering that freedom of the high seas and sedentary fisheries are not compatible as notions of the same weight and the same rank".[3] He concludes that they

3. G. Gidel, *La mer territoriale*, p. 500.

should only be considered as an exception to the principle, which has the effect that, in case of doubt, the principle prevails.

Similarly, according to Gidel, it is because "all work executed on the seabed has necessary repercussions more or less pronounced, but inevitable, on the use of the high seas", that he poses the rule that activities on the underlying strata are only legal on condition that they have no appreciable repercussions on the seabed. For the same reason, he considers all work on the subsoil illegal which does not commence on the land territory of the State which undertakes it, to the exclusion of that initiated in the adjacent waters and on the seabed of the high seas. Gidel is led by these principles to envisage, notably, the proposed tunnel under the English Channel.

All juridical reasoning on the seabed, the subsoil, or on the waters thus found itself dominated by the essential consideration given to the surface.

Today, on the contrary, international law has taken note of its pluridimensional character. It entered this path with the 1958 Convention on the continental shelf following, it is true, a traditional approach founded on the recognition of the sovereign rights of the riparian State, which meant extending to the continental shelf the reasoning on which the régime relating to territorial waters is based, with the result that the State can dispose of the seabed since that falls within its sovereignty, the only condition being the obligation to respect inoffensive navigation on the surface.

We have come today, it being possible to exploit the seabed, not only to think of its régime as not including the notion of the sovereignty of the riparian State, but also excluding all appropriation of an area hence forward to be considered the common heritage of mankind. That is why the universal expression "ocean space" tends, in specialized American circles, to supplant the words "sea" or "ocean".[4]

The progressive increase in man's knowledge of the seabed,

4. Resolution 2750 (XXV) of December 17, 1970, deciding to call a conference for 1973 on the law of the sea includes in its preamble the following article: "the General Assembly . . . conscious that the problems of the marine environment are closely linked to each other and should be examined in their totality". Cf. the text in our book *Le fond des mers*, A. Colin, editor, 1971, pp. 21-24.

which represents a great discovery comparable to that of an unknown continent, has thus restored dimensional unity to the oceanic environment. At the same time its fundamental unity is restored; the fundamental unity which for Gidel involved only the surface, but which today one is led to consider as involving also the seabed and the adjacent waters. Ocean space tends to be governed by the law relating to each of its elements without any of these being privileged. If, for the present, the surface and the principle of freedom which reigns there still maintains its preponderance at the theoretical level, it is not affected by the régime governing the other dimensions.

This phenomenon is particularly valuable with respect to the struggle against pollution. The ecological interdependence of the seabed and the surface renders vain any action limited to a single level of the marine environment. In point of fact negotiations in progress concern a treaty which will regulate the transport and discharge of waste on the high seas; the same necessity to act at the horizontal and vertical level appears for other forms of pollution, such as that originating from the seabed following a leak from an oil well.

Consequently, surface navigation, like the exploitation of the seabed, should be governed by specific and complementary regulations.

This interaction of problems is born whether one takes a stand in favour of extensions of the competences of riparians or in favour of setting up an international system.

(1) In the former case, we have already noted, within the framework of the Geneva Convention that in spite of the declaration of respect for the freedom of navigation the rules relating to the continental shelf have led to certain cases of regulation of this freedom. However, it is in the case of the demands of riparian States, especially of the developing countries, that one notices the dialectic of the seabed and the surface: it should be remembered that, although the Truman Declaration of the United States over the continental shelf thus left the adjacent waters as high seas, that of Argentina, on October 11, 1946, claimed both. Other Latin American States did the same, notably Brazil, Uruguay, El Salvador and Nicaragua, up to a limit of 200 miles. To be sure, these countries always recognized the freedom of navigation and overflight but they intended to reserve for themselves the biological

resources such as those of the seabed and its underlying strata; they did not understand why rights should be recognized with respect to the former but not with respect to the latter.

(2) If we envisage the zone to be under international management (the boundaries of which remain to be defined), the phenomenon is comparable. The authority of the international mechanism in charge of it should include certain powers to be exercised at the surface in order to protect the biological resources and from the surface in order to ensure the orderly use of the seabed.

Here we see clearly the tension between traditional law and the law which is tending to take its place: the régime of freedom of the high seas still proclaimed must come to terms with those increasingly important uses which conflict with it.

II. FROM A LAW OF MOVEMENT TO A LAW OF APPROPRIATION

The sea is a passage way; it is essentially under this guise that the geopoliticists, notably, André Siegfried, have studied it; wars took place to block maritime routes and political strategies attempted to protect them.[5] The law of the sea was thus logically conceived as destined to govern activities involving movement. Today it is tending to double as a law which applies to fixed installations as well.

A. The sea has always fulfilled two functions, that of a path for navigation and that of a reservoir for riches. But the latter were essentially living resources. Fishing was included as one of the two objects of navigation, the other being transport. The latter moreover has not ceased to grow in importance. It must be recognized that it relates not to the riches of the sea, but to those of the land. The value of the sea consisted only of the path which it offers for contacts between lands. The liaison which exists between the idea of non-appropriation and that of community of the sea, which is one of the facets of the idea of liberty was very clearly emphasized by Vittoria: "with the world was born the community, since

5. It is to be noted that in his major book (droit international public, Themis) appearing for the first time in 1958, Paul Reuter studied it fairly in a chapter entitled: "Communications Maritimes".

originally, there existed no other régime and all was in common, freedom of communication was equally a reality. Later, men established themselves in diverse parts of the earth: part of those things which, in the beginning were common, were appropriated, but the transformation was not total. The stationary existence could not modify that which, by nature and distinction, was common. Among those things which remained common over man's evolution in his relational existence, must be included that right possessed by all men to establish communication between themselves".[6]

As for fishing, it was localized along coastal bands well supplied and protected by the régime of territorial waters. Large-scale fishing remained an adventure at the peril of the sea, a race after migratory species. To be sure, in the case of certain seas of relatively limited size and heavily fished by ships of different flags, such as the North Sea, competition posed certain problems in the "fishing fields", an expression which suggests a certain degree of establishment. However, the conventions which attempted to resolve them appeared as exceptions to the principle of liberty and that of November 6, 1887, concerning floating taverns which aimed at forestalling an alcoholic use of the freedom of the seas, takes part in the folklore that the law of man has always provided for its most austere servants.

Bertrand de Jouvenel[7] has admirably demonstrated that the economic exploitation of the sea has remained, up to our time, the province of individuals behaving as nomads. These, he points out, have always played two roles with respect to sedentary people: carriers and merchants or pirates and conquerors. From the latter point of view, it is evident that 20th-century man has retained "the habits of the hunting tribes of the 4th millenium B.C.", abandoning themselves to hunting and not to raising the living species of the seas which, though it covers 71 per cent. of the surface of the globe, furnishes only 2 per cent. of man's food. Despite the modest level of this harvest, it is destroying the biological resources because of the primitive methods employed which exclude any concern for rational culture.

6. Cited by Gidel, *op. cit.*, J.1, p. 140, No. 3.

7. Report to Pacem in Maribus III, June 1972, International Ocean Institute, Malta.

These observations made from an economic point of view can be transposed to the juridical plane where they illustrate the character of the law of the sea, a law of movement. The nomadic character of the subjects of this law explains the growth of maritime law, that of carriers and merchants, as well as the important place occupied by pirates, privateering, the slave trade and the law of war at sea in the classical manuals.

It is true and perfectly natural that the maritime powers constitute the principal, if not the exclusive, users of this law of the sea, the essential norms of which inevitably only interest those who have the means to navigate over long distances.

On the other hand, this law was of only minor interest to riparian States lacking large fleets and as a result being restricted to coastal fisheries, which more often than not satisfied them; for them, the presence of foreign fleets three miles off their coasts was less than preoccupying given the inexhaustible character ascribed to the resources of the sea. It was only for special reasons such as the shape of coastlines or the importance of fishing to the economy of the country that any resistance to freedom of the seas ever occurred. Ironically enough it was for the protection of British fishermen at a time when England was not yet a great maritime power, that Selden defended the thesis of the closed sea.

The development of English fleets lent a contrary orientation not only to London's politics but also to the law of the sea in general which gave the not incorrect impression after the event that the law was established by the great powers and the developing States readily take exception to it on these grounds today. To be sure, it could not be otherwise since custom is created by the behaviour of the predominant users.

Consequently, the entire law of the sea has been constructed around the notion of freedom of navigation, that is to say the freedom to move on oceans. The régime of innocent passage can thus be explained: the presumption of innocence only benefits a foreign ship in territorial waters as long as it does not stop; if not it is suspect.

Maritime juridical practice has always been dominated by the concern not to hinder navigation. One is reminded of the emotion caused by the judgment in the *Lotus* case which threatened to produce this result. Similarly, certain other facets of the law of the sea can be understood from this point of view; for example, the régime relating to straits which connect two parts of the high seas or lead to the high seas and the responsibilities incurred as a result of an inopportune or unfounded stopping of a ship.

It is evident that these rules are not condemned to disappearance today, at a time when maritime transport continues to increase in volume; it is only necessary to recognize that they will have to take into account the limits imposed, more and more, on the principle of liberty, the tradition on which they are based by the appearance of new uses based not on movement but on acquisition.

B. The law of the sea should, hence forward, regulate activities established at a given point on the surface, the seabed, or the adjacent waters, and arbitrate the resulting implications for navigation.

As a result of large-scale industrial fishing, the notion of domination of a fishing ground has taken on a significance until now unsuspected. At the present time, on certain stretches of the North Sea, English and French fishing boats are unable to withstand the appearance of a massive Soviet fleet before which they are obliged to make way.[8]

Even when competition is not so keen between them large fleets establish their quarters on fishing grounds situated beyond traditional limits (3 or 6 miles) of coastal States, remaining there several months, not only with no advantage to the latter, where they never set foot, but also to the detriment of the species fished or hunted without any restraint. It is understandable that when hunger is rife in the nearby countries, they have the feeling that they have been subjected to pillage even though it takes place on the high seas; its proximity appears to them to hold promise for their development. To be sure, they are not at all ignorant of their technical deficiencies and the impossibility of their exploiting the resources themselves. Also their demand, of an economic and social inspiration, is above all juridical; it involves a jurisdiction conferring on them the power to legislate concerning the zones adjacent to their territorial waters for the purpose of organizing a rational exploitation of the living resources there and not only

8. The Soviet Union has 49 per cent. of the world total sum of fishing ships of more than 100 gross tonnage.

concerning the granting of monopoly preferential fishing rights for their nationals.

In addition marine farming, which presupposes a certain localization, offers them a promising perspective. To be sure, this can be pursued on their continental shelf which, even reduced to its uncontested limit the depth of 200 metres, can constitute a considerable area. However, the possibility can be foreseen in the near future of working at greater and greater depths further removed from coasts. Experiments have been successful in taking waters rich in nitrates and phosphates from a depth of over 800 metres and drawing them towards the surface in order to enrich the phytoplankton and at the same time provide nourishment for more intensive biological life, thus reproducing a sort of "Humboldt current", this latter being Peru's reason for extending its jurisdiction up to 200 miles in 1947.[9]

It is obviously the exploitation of the mineral resources of the seabed which will lead to the development of a law of acquisition. Although the exploitation of manganese nodules, because of their quantity and their rapid reproduction, will depend on harvesting and thus lend itself to a continuation of the nomadic activity of the users, hydrocarbons, on the other hand, require a durable or permanent installation.[10] If it is recalled that the underwater production of petroleum has attained the level of the total overall production in 1948, the growing volume of this harvest can be appreciated. It is true that, for the present, it is taking place on the continental shelf at depths which are still modest; however, the technical means exists to drill at much greater depths in the zone envisaged by the United Nations as being outside the limits of national jurisdiction, when those are finally defined.

This leads us to another area of the tension which gives rise to the contradictions in the law of the sea; in the face of classical law which had little room for territorial jurisdiction, we are now witnessing the development of the basic premises of a juridical

9. Sainte-Croix experiment reported by Bertrand de Jouvenel, *op. cit.*

10. Diverse proposals, presently at the theoretical stage, foresee the fertilization of deep water which does not appear to be attainable for several decades. It is not impossible that the exploitation of floating brine in the red sea can be achieved by means of a pump feeding a pipe-line placed on the seabed. A pumping system from ships could also be used.

system dominated by the consideration of the apportionment of space.

III. FROM A PERSONAL LAW TO A TERRITORIAL LAW

Classical law of navigation is above all a system of "carrying along one's law" (personalité des lois): the monopoly of the flag, a consequence of the freedom of the high seas, expresses this projection of international juridical order. A State has a ship and here it is floating on the sea. [11] The notion of sovereignty occupied only a modest place: uncontested for internal waters, but until the convention of 1958, it was debated in doctrine and sometimes denied in internal positive law [12] with respect to territorial waters. The colours prevailed over the flag.

Two great winds have never ceased to blow over the seas: the wind from the open sea, that of freedom, and the wind from the land, that of sovereignty. The former, for a long time has been predominant: reigning over the high seas it enters territorial waters in the form of innocent passage. It is only internal waters which are sheltered from its gusts: it enters ports with the freedom of access proclaimed by the Geneva Convention of 1929.

It is only since the Second World War that the wind from the land shouldered the eager sovereignty and carried the authority of States to distances further and further removed from their coasts. Here the contradiction attained its most dramatic level for it leads to a collision of political philosophies and economic interests.

The rule of non-appropriation of the high seas is based on the supposedly inexhaustible character of its resources. Grotius explains this: when the land community comes to an end by reason of insufficiency of the products of the land for the satisfaction of the growing needs of man, the sea remains inexhaustible: "I say

11. By this, we do not mean to reawaken the old theory of territoriality of ships; it should be recognized that this phenomenon can best be explained using an unpolished formulation.

12. French jurisprudence, both judicial and administrative, does not recognize territorial waters as being part of national territory (at the level of judicial divisions) not as being subject to the public domain (Cass. civ. 26 Nov. 1918, Proux c) Courcous, DP 1923-I-103; C, E, 24 mai 1935, Sieur Thiriaut, s. 1936-3-1 avec note).

that the sea, whether taken in its totality or confined to its principal parts, cannot be possessed, firstly for a moral reason, it is because for the renunciation of common property has not occurred here, the sea is so vast that it is sufficient for all the uses which all peoples can subject it, whether they want to draw water, fish or navigate".[13] It should be recognized that this reasoning can still be applied to the régime relating to the resources of the sea and the ocean beds. They are portrayed for us as inexhaustible in the case of certain things, among them nodules, and quasi-inexhaustible in the case of others, at least for a forseeable future, and in fact the United Nations declared in 1970 that they were not susceptible to appropriation, pledging them to a régime of international management. From the opposite point of view the threat to the living resources serves as justification for the generalization of the phenomenon of appropriation; the coastal States engaging in this practice explain that it is the sole means of protecting them. It should be noted that it can just as well be argued, perfectly logically, that this peril leads us to consider these living resources as part of the common property of humanity, in which case those who exploited them could only do so according to the norms established and enforced by an international organization. These two theses come into conflict as we know, but the most remarkable thing is that, no matter what solution is adopted, the problem is one of spatial definition of jurisdiction whether the seabed or the surface is considered.

If we examine the position of the coastal States the "territorialization" of their jurisdiction appears to be of considerable scope on the bed of the seas and the oceans. The minimum dimensions of the continental shelf (up to a depth of 200 metres) represent 5.5 per cent. of the surface of the earth. It it were decided to extend it up to 600 metres it would equal the surface of the moon.[14]

13. *Le droit de la guerre et de la paix*, transcribed by Barbeyrac, Liv. II, ch. III. Vattel demonstrates the same reasoning: "Those who navigate or fish on the high seas have nobody, and . . . the sea in these two respects, can meet the needs of all men. Nature gives man no right to appropriate for himself those things whose use is innocent, inexhaustible and sufficient for all". *Le Droit des Gens ou Principes de la Loi Naturelle, appliquée à la conduite et aux Affaires des Nations et des Souverains*, 1758, T.I., p. 243, cited by Bertrand de Jouvenel, *op. cit.*, p. 37

14. The Truman Proclamation resulted in an extension of the territorial

Sovereignty is also extending over the surface: even if the claims of the riparian States do not go so far as to include the appropriation of a 200-miles zone in full sovereignty, they take the form of special jurisdiction rights, which until they are qualified in functional terms, necessarily include as part of their definition a spatial element.

Thus, we have witnessed the birth, on the initiative of Mexico, Colombia and Venezuela, confirmed on June 7, 1972, by the Declaration of Santo Domingo concerning the Caribbean of the concept of a "patrimonial sea". This formulation posits the continuance of the régime of territorial waters, a zone of limited sovereignty up to 12 miles, beyond which the riparian State will dispose of an economic jurisdiction over the high seas up to a distance of 200 miles. In the patrimonial sea, the above described zone, it can reserve for its nationals the living resources as well as the mineral wealth of the seabed and the subsoil thereof.[15] This zone, moreover, could be further extended where the continental shelf extends beyond 200 miles, which is frequently the case in Latin America: the criterion of depth in the 1958 Convention can extend the limits of the patrimonial sea to considerable distances.[16]

The proposals for an international régime presented to the United Nations since 1970 all interpose the territorial dimension to which they attribute figures or which they leave blank pending subsequent negotiations. The American proposal is the clearest in this respect in carrying out zones in the sea and ocean beds: the first zone up to a depth of 200 metres in full sovereignty, the second zone up to the "continental margin" which, it appears, is

---

jurisdiction of the United States of 2 million square kilometres, which is equal to the area of the nine countries which are presently members of the European Community.

15. J. Castañeda, "Les positions des Etats latino-américains", in *Actualités du droit de la mer*, Colloque de Montpellier de la Société Française pour le Droit International, 1972 (to appear in a Pédone edition). R. Zacklin, "Latin America and the Development of the Law of the Sea", *Annals of International Studies on Hydrospace in International Relations*, Geneva, Vol. 4, 1973.

16. The patrimonial sea can be distinguished from territorial waters in that the freedom of navigation is recognized there, while in the case of the latter, where the prerogatives of sovereignty of the riparian State are operative, foreign ships have only the more limited rights of innocent passage.

the base of the precontinental slope, under the trusteeship of the riparian and the third zone, an abyssal plain, entrusted to an international mechanism. [17]

Also, anybody can see that the law of the sea will be constantly confronted with this problem of territorial delimitation, even if, in certain zones, the rights of the riparians do not take on a sovereign character. As to the constitution of an international mechanism it will not be able to avoid the problem; it will be necessary to determine its spatial area of jurisdiction. It is quite evident that it will be limited to what has not already been taken by the riparians. Its size will still be enormous but its economic value will decline as depth increases so that the important question is how long a continental shelf zone will be attributed to coastal States. It appears that negotiations should concentrate on the slope between (200 and 3,500 metres on an average) in order to set the limit from which the common heritage of mankind begins. Beyond this, on the slope (3,500 and 5,500 metres) and *a fortiori* on the abyssal plain, the economic interest (exception in nodules) is likely to be minimal, since the hydrocarbon resources are located inside the continental margin. [18]

The question also arises whether the common heritage of humanity will effectively extend to all seas or whether joint appropriations, undertaken at the regional level, will eliminate it completely from certain seas.

IV. FROM A UNIVERSAL LAW TO A REGIONAL LAW

To be sure, the law of the sea has always had a place for regional particularities, especially in the area of the economic use of the high seas: the fishing régime in the North Sea (Conventions of May 6, 1882, and February 9, 1964), the regulation of Flounder

17. On these proposals, cf. Alain Piquemal, *Le fond des mers, Patrimoine commun de l'humanité*, Institute for the Law of Peace and Development, Nice, CNEXO 1973, p. 226 and J. P. Levy, "La troisième conférence sur le droit de la mer", *AFOI*, 1971, p. 704, 832. The French Government, in turn, accepts the limit of 200 miles with respect to the seabed (cf. the French declaration to the Committee on the Seabed, Doc. A/AC.138/SCII/SR-27, p. 39) which would result in a partition of the western Mediterranean.

18. Cf. J. Polvèche in *Le fond des mers, op. cit.*, pp. 97-124.

and Plaice fishing in the Baltic (Convention of Berlin, December 17, 1929). Certain among these instruments, such as the Convention of Washington of February 8, 1949, relating to the conservation of fisheries in the Northeast Atlantic, involve vast zones.

The Mediterranean (Agreement of Rome, September 24, 1949) and the Indian Ocean (Bagnio Agreement of February 26, 1948) have in this manner been provided with Fisheries Councils, while bilateral treaties regulate fishing in smaller seas for several species or for a single species. All that is well known. However, these special régimes which amount to special policies arranged by interested States do not threaten the fundamental bases of the law of the sea which rests on principles of a universal nature. The freedom of the high seas and the size and the régime of territorial waters remain untouched. Where the Scandinavians were conspicuous with sovereign waters of 4 miles, most countries were content with three.

Already the Convention of 1958 on fishing and the protection of biological resources had valorized the notion of region and assigned rights to the riparians of regions and to those States whose nationals fished in those regions (Art. (*b*)). Did it not still remain at the level of general law since it was a convention with a universal vocation which foresaw the possibility of regional arrangements?

Today we have gone beyond this framework. Some fear even that it is destroyed. Unilateral declarations by individual States or by groups of States in Latin America have created a region which clearly has a characteristic law of the sea.[19]

Also on other continents, notably in Africa, other juridical worlds are breaking away from the former universe inherited from classical times.

Finally, in Asia, the archipelagos require a régime which recognizes the economic unit they constitute.

These appear to sketch broadly the coasts of under-development. Yet we must deal at greater depth with this image and apply a corrective.

In the first place the demands of riparians which are parallel when they face vast oceans, are convergent in partially closed seas which they tend to monopolize by means of partition or joint

19. The Declaration of Montevideo of May 8, 1970, issued by 9 States.

possession. It is here that we must correct the general observation which led us to believe that only the third world engages in maritime appropriations. Firstly, sometimes, nature automatically hands underwater territory to riparian States. Thus 95 per cent. of the continental shelf of the Baltic being at a depth of less than 200 metres, the Geneva Convention permits its total appropriation.[20] Similarly, the shelf of the North Sea has posed only problems of the limitation between States who have agreed to divide it among themselves. Furthermore, on the waters themselves, common interests often become established. A regulation of the EEC[21] lays down the principle of freedom of access of fishing boats flying the flag of one of the member States in the maritime waters falling within the sovereignty or jurisdiction of other member States. Here, community spirit has achieved on water what nature granted on the shelf.

More inovative are the cases of joint or collective appropriation affecting levels or zones of regional seas. Thus the decision of the countries of the western Mediterranean to extend their rights over the seabed to 200 miles effecting a partition of the Mediterranean.[22] It seems that a distinction is emerging between oceans whose bed, beyond the limits of national jurisdiction, forms part of the common heritage of humanity and the "Mediterraneans",[23] seas which are partially closed, creating close links between their riparians and thus forming a regional or sub-regional community.

Such is certainly the case of the Caribbean Sea, which, in the bosom of Latin America saw its particularity recognized by the Declaration of Santo Domingo of June 7, 1972. The following is

20. Agreement between Finland and the USSR concerning the limits of maritime zones and the continental shelf in the Gulf of Finland–May 20, 1965–(United Nations *Treaties Series,* Vol. 566, pp. 32 to 37). Agreement between Finland and the USSR on the limit of the continental shelf in the north-eastern part of the Baltic–May 5, 1967 (*ibid.*, Vol. 640, pp. 112 to 115). Treaty between Poland and the USSR on the delimitation of the continental shelf in the Gulf of Gdansk and the south-eastern Baltic–August 29, 1969 (*RGDIP*, 1971, No. 2, pp. 603-604).

21. Regulation No. 2141/70, Art. 2, section 1; *Official Journal* of the European Community, Book 236 of October 27, 1970.

22. The French Government accepts in principle the limit of 200 miles with respect to the seabed (cf. the declaration of the French representative to the Committee on the Seabed, UN Doc. A/AC.138/CS. 27, p. 39).

23. The theory of "Mediterraneans" was advanced in 1968 by Italy at the first Committee on the Seabed, cf. UN Doc. A/AC.135/I, a22.9.

to be found in the preamble: "The countries of the Caribbean Region by reason of their special situation need special criteria with respect to the application of the law of the sea". To be sure, the Declaration proclaims that the seabed of the Caribbean, beyond the patrimonial sea and the continental shelf not covered by the former are the common property of humanity; however, diverse States envisage the joint possession, if not of the sea, at least of the seabed between the countries which border on it, involving the constitution of an agency or enterprise entitled to exercise any technical, industrial or commercial activity relative to the exploration of the zone and the exploitation of its resources.[24] At the same time, the scope of the notion of common heritage would be changed to the extent that humanity would become the Caribbean people groups around the "Matrimonial sea". When the completely new notion of patrimonial sea is defensive, it appears to be productive,[25] designed above all for the common organization of use with a view to the development of the region.

These special régimes in the course of being defined should not surprise us; they express a solidarity which cannot be misunderstood.

The problem at the future conference on the law of the sea will be, precisely, to find the necessary conciliation between the rules subjecting the seas and the ocean to a universal régime and those giving effect to regional particularities which, since the law is established at the economic level and is devoted to development in the final analysis, take on an irreductible value.

However, the notion of regionalism should be combined with other grouping phenomena.

It is often fitting to talk about sub-regionalism, the position of the Latin American countries is not exactly the same at the south of the continent as in the Caribbean; the Africans are still less united if only "because of the fact that several of them are land-locked countries".

24. These proposals are inspired by the proposal presented to the Committee on the Seabed by various Latin American States. Cf. Art. 33, UN Doc. A/AC.138/49.

25. Interpretation given by Mrs. Elizabeth Mann-Borgese to the preliminary conference at Kingston (Jamaica), October 25-28, 1972, organized by the International Ocean Institute of the Royal University of Malta.

The discovery of the seabed had had as a result the promotion of the position of countries without coastlines. This paradox is explained by the designation of the seabed as the common heritage of mankind, a notion which admits of no discrimination between peoples, no matter what their situation with respect to the sea. This egalitarian thirst today, leads to a desire to correct all disparities including those resulting from nature. Enlarged by the shelf-locked States, the land-locked States form a total of 40 States who could have the "blocking" one-third of the votes at the conference on the sea. [26]

It is remarkable to note that this heterogeneous collection of States (although most are developing, certain ones are industrialized countries) distributed among the divers parts of the world, has caused the break-up of regional groups, the identity or community of interests being substituted with respect to the sea for a geographical grouping. Thus the contradictions of the law of the sea are multiplied by those of interest, to the extent that the latter are not always clearly perceived by all; certain States consider at length and hesitate to adopt a position either for lack of maritime experience or because of the diversity of their preoccupations, sometimes very diversified, depending on the problems envisaged. [27]

Is it to say that the jurist, if not the politician, is condemned to

26. This group was powerful enough at the last General Assembly to have passed the resolution of December 18, 1972, 3029 B XXVIII, Doc. A/8949, requesting that the Secretary-General establish "a comparative study of the extent and economic importance, from the point of view of resources, of the international zone which would exist in relation to the different proposals concerning the limits of national jurisdiction which have been presented up to now to the Committee on Peaceful Uses of the Seabed. This resolution was passed by 69 votes to 15 with 41 abstentions and underscores the rupture of the "Groups of" in its confrontations with respect to the problems of the seas. The counterstroke came in the form of a resolution initiated by Peru, (3029C) instructing the Secretary-General to research the effect on the interest of coastal States of each of the proposals concerning the limits of national jurisdiction. Part A. of the resolution envisages a conference on the face of the sea to be organized at the end of 1973, during the session of the 28th General Assembly, and will meet in April and May 1974 at Santiago, Chile.

27. A country like Canada with respect to certain problems (archipelagos) takes a position similar to certain Asian countries, while with respect to others its position is nearer to that of the Netherlands (shelf-locked to the north) without prejudicing special questions posed by regions blocked by ice (ice-locked countries).

venture without dividers or compass on a sea disturbed by opposing winds? Is it possible to perceive the dawning of calmer waters?

It does not seem impossible to foresee the basic outlines of the current trends among the Family of Nations. At this very moment there is agreement on the existence of a zone of national jurisdiction much larger than territorial waters, which themselves are being extended more and more to 12 miles, and on the existence of a public maritime domain under the jurisdiction of the international community. Although the essential problem of delimitation of these two worlds is not yet resolved, the dominant outlines are appearing of an image which is still imprecise, but which is being illuminated by the positions of States.

At present, States have acquired the following:

(i) In the case of coastal States the right to control the resources of the sea over a varying area, which in the case of the developing countries can be up to 200 miles, a limit of Peruvian origin which today is reflected and copied throughout the world and in particular in the People's Republic of China. There has been a resulting decline in the importance of the concept of the continental shelf because the appropriations are not limited to the seabed but rather relate to the totality of the marine environment whose unity with the land has been proclaimed. "We are an island", as the Chileans say.[28]

(ii) For all States, with or without coastlines, the right to derive a profit from the resources of the zone situated beyond the limits of national jurisdiction and thus under an international regulatory system which, it can be foreseen, will not be unitary but rather will be very dependent on whether the seabed or the adjacent waters are involved. The bed of the seas and the oceans which the United Nations has declared to be the common heritage of mankind should be so treated and an international mechanism should be created with jurisdiction and control over this area, if not the management of it.

Over the waters beyond the national jurisdiction, States should in general retain their exclusive organic competence, but with respect to the exploitation of living resources, limits will be im-

28. The United States, without recognizing Brazil's rights concluded an agreement on May 9, 1972, under which they agreed to pay a levy in order to fish in the Brazilian zone.

posed by the exactment of fundamental norms imposing a rational system of management and by the obligation to States to foster among themselves improved co-operation facilitated by fishing commissions, perfected to a greater degree. However, freedom of navigation will retain primacy, except it will be regulated in order to prevent pollution.

The notion of the high sea is thus tending to dissolve into that of an international zone: on those parts of it adjacent to coasts, the riparian States will exercise a functional jurisdiction in their own interest and in the interest of the community of peoples (custodial theory) and on the part subject to an international régime, there will be an organized system of control over the exercise by States of their jurisdiction. Thus we are moving from freedom of the seas, formerly conceived as a law permitting States to act without impediment, everyone for himself, to a concept of organized freedom exercised in the general interest.

This conceptual framework appears to resolve the contradictions which plague the law of the sea. However, the States, divided by two different visions of the sea, that of a means of communication and that of maritime territory rich in diverse resources, must work hard to overcome the conflicts at Santiago, and perhaps at Vienna over the next two years if they truly have the will to create a régime relating to ocean space which will assure navigation for all, the development of mankind, and the survival of waters.

Chapter II

THE COMMON HERITAGE OF MANKIND FOR DEVELOPMENT

As applied to the seabed and the ocean, the concept of the common heritage of mankind proclaimed by the Declaration of Principles of the General Assembly (Dec. 17, 1970)[1] seems to necessitate a change in a considerable part of the law of the sea. If the reference to humanity appears expressly in the treaty on space, and if the International Telecommunications Union makes comparable use of the notion of a common prerogative of all mankind in dealing with the spectrum of frequencies, it is certainly since the United Nations began grappling with the problem of the seabed that the common heritage of mankind has come to the fore, as much to affirm the principle of purely peaceful use of the seabed and its substratum as to distribute the resources common to all people having particular regard for the developing nations.

The application of the notion of common heritage in the maritime setting appears to offer more immediate possibilities of economic exploitation than does a spatial approach. According to Mr. Pardo, father of the idea of common heritage, "it is impossible to reduce the principle of inequalities that exist between nations in the contemporary world without creating profound changes in the existing international order".[2] The new concept should permit precisely this new approach to the problems of development. It would appear that the new approach must be made in two directions.

(1) The common heritage, involving as it does the principle of non-appropriation, is going to increase the mass of disposable resources; it imposes two correlatives: on the one hand the partici-

1. Resolution 2749 (XXV).

2. Thirty-sixth sitting of Sub-Committee I of the Committee on the Seabed. A/AC.138/SCI/SR.36, p. 49.

pation of everyone in the administration of the zone of common property and on the other hand, the equal sharing of advantages between all countries, with particular consideration of the needs and interests of the developing nations.

(2) Constituting an area reserved exclusively for humanity, the common heritage calls for a plan for the exploration and exploitation of its resources, with the main goal being the growth and stability of those societies that have been the most unfortunate. The concept of common patrimony is thus commonly represented by its advocates as a particularly revolutionary means of development, as opposed to national appropriation. In the latter case, development is planned by each coastal State and territorial application of the principle of sovereignty over natural resources is applied in order to appropriate maritime regions. It follows from this that instead of a multiplicity of actions dispersed between States, often in pursuit of short-term profit, it is possible to organize the exploitation of the common patrimony according to national programmes that encompass both global appropriation of resources and regulation of their distribution.

At the moment, however, this scheme remains theoretical and it must be questioned to what measure the notion of the common heritage of humanity risks deteriorating to the level of myth, always proclaimed, but factually contradicted by concrete diverse tendencies which are expressed by the claims of the coastal States.

The choice is crucial: if the development of all for all, that is, the common heritage, is to be realized; increasingly restricted in area, will it give place to traditional practices of bilateralism or regional multilateralism?

I. THE COMMON HERITAGE OF MANKIND, MODEL FOR DEVELOPMENT

The Declaration of Principles of December 17, 1970, like other resolutions of the General Assembly and the majority of proposed conventions of the United Nations [3] affirms that exploration of

3. For example, Article 1 of the United States proposal, Article 4 of the Tanzanian proposal, Article 1 of the proposal of the 13 Powers (A/AC.138/49), Article 66 of the Maltese proposal, Article 1 of the Canadian working document (A/AC.138/59), etc.

the international zone of the seabed and the exploitation of its resources should be carried out for the profit of all humanity, independent of the geographic positions of States, taking particular account of the interests and needs of the developing nations.

These countries have, in fact, greeted this concept with some enthusiasm, precisely because it was presented as having development as its actual end product. While equally accepted, the principle of purely peaceful use of the seabed was presented as being in the interests of all, the exploitation of its riches was dedicated essentially to the growth of the less fortunate nations. This movement of the common heritage toward development appears all the more attractive in that it is based on the implementation of two principles: the cumulation of natural resources and the globalization of development.

A. *The cumulation of natural resources*

The cumulation of natural resources allocated to development results naturally from the fact that there will be available a fund of profits of different types which will be allocated directly to development, rather than originating from individual States as in the traditional approach to development.

(*a*) The exploitation of the seabed should make a considerable and unprecedented contribution to development, as much from the value of the resources of the seabed and its substratum themselves, as from the importance of the implications implicit in the exploitation, particularly scientific research, which have a real, although indirect, influence on the level of growth.

(1) "According to United States experts, the benefits to developing countries should amount, as a minimum, to several hundred million dollars a year by the time the international resources agency is functioning".[4] This statement of Arvid Pardo's appears to be confirmed by the remarkable figures advanced by the United States on several occasions concerning the resources that can be recovered from manganese nodules.[5] The aluminium reserves of

4. *New York Times*, August 3, 1970, p. 7.
5. According to new methods of detection, the nodules cover 25 per cent.

these nodules would be about 48 billion tons, which, by reference to the world consumption in 1960, assures 20,000 years of use, while the earth's reserves will last no more than 100 years. Similarly the nodules' reserves of other minerals can be estimated:

–Manganese	:	358 billion	(400,000 years as compared to 100 years of earth reserves)
–Copper	:	7.9 billion	(200,000 years compared to 40)
–Nickel	:	14.7 billion	(150,000 years compared to 100)
–Cobalt	:	5.2 billion	(200,000 years compared to 40).

Important reserves of hydrocarbons are known to exist in certain oceanic basins.[6] The different studies done by the United Nations lead us to anticipate the possibilities of exploitation in the foreseeable future. On this last point, some industrial countries have expressed reservations. Japan and France particularly have drawn attention to existing gaps between exploration and commercial exploitation. However, the American representative recently declared to Sub-Committee I of the Seabed Committee (March 22, 1973) that "techniques applicable to the seabed have progressed to such a point that commercial exploitation of manganese nodules will begin in three to five years", which necessitates, according to this delegate, the establishment of a juridical régime and of a temporary mechanism.[7]

The contribution to development which might be made by a fiscal levy should not be neglected. As early as 1970, the conference "Pacem in Maribus", organized in Malta by the Santa Barbara Center for the Studies of Democratic Institutions, recommended an ocean development tax of 1 per cent. on all maritime activities. The Maltese proposal is also inspired by this maximalist approach; it taxes all exploitation of biological and mineral resources, while other government projects are limited to the latter. We may wonder if the common heritage is not likely to surface in the same way as in the national jurisdiction of certain Latin American countries the national demands have left the seabed to surface in the adjacent waters. Given the total notion of development it would hardly be acceptable to the poor countries to limit the

---

of the seabed to a volume of 600 billion tons, the distribution and the metal content varying from region to region.

6. F. S. P. Levy, "Les Ressources Minérales des fonds marins internationaux", *Revue française de l'energie*, 1972, pp. 417-427, no. 243.

7. Doc. A/AC.138/SCI/SR.64, p. 11.

exploitation of the resources of the seabed. The dialectic concerning the seabed and the surface does not seem to come into play as inevitably as for the international zone. The rights acquired in respect to fishing, already being encroached upon in coastal areas, would likely be more easily defended on the high seas above a common heritage.

However, even restricted to products of the seabed and its substrata, the tax levied to finance development, whether it be operated by an international mechanism or by the States which would contribute to a common fund,[8] would constitute a contribution all the more important in that it would be complemented by the other advantages to be derived from the exploration and exploitation of the seabed.

(2) The expansion of scientific research will of necessity affect the whole programme of development when the General Assembly declares in different resolutions that the exploitation of the seabed should be realized for the benefit of all humanity, the affirmation should be of an extensive nature; beyond the reparation of financial profits, the members of the international community have an

8. Doc. A/AC.138/27, 4th part; taxes. The Maltese delegate to the Committee on the Seabed presented a system for financial levies involving the coastal States and the international community: up to 100 miles from the coast no contribution would be paid by the coastal State. From 100 to 150 miles, the mechanism would receive 25 per cent. of the receipts from exploitation, then 50 per cent. in the zone from 150 to 175 miles, 75 per cent. from 175 to 200 miles and 100 per cent. beyond that.

According to the calculations of Mr. Pardo, assuming the creation of the mechanism in 1974, the international community would receive each year, beginning in 1979, approximately 600 million dollars from fish products, 200 million dollars from the exploitation of hydrocarbons and 100 million dollars from manganese nodules, or, after the deduction of administrative and personnel expenses a net amount in the order of 800 million dollars (57th Session of the Committee–March 23, 1971, A/AC.138/SR.57, p. 182).

With the goal of furthering the possibilities for development flowing from the common patrimony, but remaining non-committal concerning the limits of the international zone, Canada proposed to coastal States that they pay to a temporary mechanism a "fixed percentage of total revenues that they derive from the part of the bed of the seas and oceans which they claim outside of their territorial waters". On the basis of a payment of 1 per cent. of these revenues, several millions of dollars would be turned over to the international community. "A contribution of this type would be a form of international tax paid voluntarily on account of development" in anticipation of a permanent régime (cf. 58th Session of the Committee on the Seabed–March 28, 1971, A/AC.138/SR.58, p. 214).

obligation to participate fully in the exploration and exploitation, which involves a common pooling of the results of scientific research carried out in the international zone, the training of technicians from underdeveloped countries, and the sharing of the different technological processes related to oceanography.[9] On this basis the report of the Committee on the Seabed at the 24th General Assembly was able to declare that "the needs and interests of the underdeveloped countries are an essential element of the structure of the régime, which must keep in view not merely a simple equality of opportunities but also the equal and effective sharing of the advantages which will be gained from the exploitation and exploration of the seabed".[10] As the delegate from Nicaragua declared, at the 73rd Committee Session on March 10, 1972, "The principles of equality must be considered as early as the stage of determination of the possibilities of participation in the advantages; in this sense, it is best to give attention to the limitations that human resources, knowledge and techniques impose upon countries, as much as the difficulties resulting from possible economic restraints. Thus when it is a question of the common patrimony, that is, the sea, the considered criteria should aim not only at the allocation of the final benefits but also at the factors that determine the volume, methods and nature of the benefits".[11]

Thus we see that the financial profits and the various scientific

9. This broad interpretation falls within the framework of the options applied in other areas by the organs of the United Nations promoting the transfer and the applications of science and technology for development. The international seabed, however, favours such a policy even more by reason of its being devoted to humanity; a moral obligation could be transformed into a juridical obligation.

10. *Official Documents of the General Assembly*, 24th Session, Supp. No. 22 (A/7622, p. 30).

11. Declaration of the delegate from Nicaragua to the 73rd Session of the Committee on the Seabed, March 10, 1972 (A/AC.138/SR.73, p. 27). This approach is particularly interesting because it foreshadows, perhaps, a new conception of development as a whole: international co-operation should promote the participation of States being aided in their development, notably by means of transfers of technology. This action should not be conceived of as the stage following monetary aid, but rather in conjunction with it, for these two approaches are complementary: the flow of money, in isolation, only has a short term effect, while its association with technological capital has the effect of creating wealth which feeds on itself after a certain level of development is reached.

advantages flowing from exploration and exploitation are complementary and together support development.

This volume of contributions to development, totalising the commercial fiscal and technological products, becomes all the more significant if one is conscious that, thanks to the common heritage, the United Nations will dispose of natural resources.

(*b*) "The acquisition of natural resources by the world organization resulting from the role that it could be directed to play in the exploitation of the resources of the seabed would have incalculable consequences. The autonomy which would result for the system of the United Nations and the new élan which would be given to its activities would once again change its character."[12] This very apt observation by Michel Virally illustrates the new significance of development undertaken on the basis of the common heritage: it will no longer depend on grants but will result from the allocation of a property of humanity to the less-fortunate countries.

At present, the participation in development by the wealthy nations is based on a moral duty rather than a juridical obligation. The recommendations of the different organs of the United Nations determine the goals and proposals for aid to be accorded by the industrialized States, but the absence of any means of enforcement seriously limits the establishment of what was conceived, in the French terminology, as a public service fed by autonomous resources.[13]

That is precisely why the common heritage should be used for development; this allocation of a property would lend a revolutionary significance as much from the point of view of the specificity of resources reserved for development as the type of methods of utilizing them.

(1) The standard governing allocation posed in the Declaration of Principles of December 17, 1970, at first follows in a negative sense from the impossibility of the international zone being the

12. Mr. Virally, *L'organisation mondiale*, Armand Colin, 1972, p. 406.

13. To this effect, see the article by Guy de Lacharrière, "Identification et statut des pays moins développés" (*Annuaire français de droit international*, pp. 461 to 482). He observes that the industrialized countries have always refused to reduce texts on development to treaty form despite the attempts of the developing countries, for example, at the conference of New Delhi or in the strategy for the decade of development.

object, by any method, of appropriation by States or by individuals or corporations, and from the fact that "no State may demand or exercise sovereignty or sovereign rights over any part" of the seabed. Such a prohibition of all individual appropriations leads to a positive guarantee of the autonomy of the resources in question. The Peruvian delegate declared at the 36th Meeting of Sub-Committee I: "Humanity is the only owner of the zone and its resources . . .; it follows that the relationship between the subject of the law, that is, humanity, and the object of the law, that is, the zone and its resources, exhibit the characteristics of exclusive ownership without the necessity of it being placed in the same category as the notion of sovereignty. This fact in turn implies that the international authority to be created should have the power to exercise–in the name of humanity as its representative–an exclusive jurisdiction over the common patrimony". [14] Such an analysis shows that in the traditional framework of aid for development, the resources come from States which furnish aid in the bilateral as in the multilateral approach; the common heritage on the other hand places a mass of autonomous resources at the disposal of development.

(2) Also it is scarcely surprising that the developing countries are generally–in spite of their attachment to the principle of national sovereignty–in favour of an international facility provided with broad powers to recover unused resources. Thus the Tanzanian proposal provides that the net revenues of the authority will be

14. The existence of a zone free from national sovereignty creates a financial autonomy which is highly novel. When the imposition procedures of CECA are cited as a supranational example, the difference is noticeable, for this European plan provides for activities carried out within the territory of member States. On the other hand, the international seabed is a source of monetary profits and as a result the international community has the right to obtain a certain proportion of them.

To this effect, the delegate from Peru declared at the 36th Session of Sub-Committee I: "Humanity is the sole proprietor of the zone and its resources and as result it is impossible for any State or any physical or moral person to exercise a property right. It follows that the relationship between the subject entitled to the rights, that is to say humanity and the object of the right, being the zone and its resources, has the characteristics of exclusive property without it being necessary that this involve the notion of sovereignty. This in turn means that the international authority to be created must have the power to exercise–in the name of humanity as its representative–an exclusive jurisdiction over the common patrimony" (A/AC.138/SCI/SR.43, p. 55).

placed at the disposal of the member States for their development, which position is also supported in the proposal of the Thirteen countries (A/AC.138/49). However, if in the appropriation of the interest of humanity, one goes beyond the national framework to a global approach, the utilization of resources can be envisaged according to an action exercised by an organ of the international mechanism as is the case in Chapter 1, Article 5, of the United States' proposal. Given this approach, the planning of development appears more integrated. Different proposals, like that of Malta, envisage the use of a portion of the benefits for the development and protection of the maritime milieu.

Rather than review the numerous governmental projects, we will outline the main institutional models possible, from the most integrated to that which involves the intervention of States:

– We begin with a system of exploitation managed by an international authority which would gather and sell the resources and would redistribute profits to the developing countries.

– A joint-venture might also be envisaged, the investments being made by private enterprise and a portion of the benefits being deducted by the international authority for development.

– It appears that we are turning more toward a régime based on concession accorded by the international authority either directly to the enterprises which will make proportional or contractual payments to it or to States, on condition that a portion of the profits which the enterprises pay to them will be returned to the mechanism.

It is clear that, even in the latter hypothesis, which is closed to the French and British proposals, the principle of the autonomous resource is safeguarded, although to a lesser degree than in the more integrated models. Even when a State should, in effect, pay a portion of a benefit to PNUD, it is a question of a budgetary contribution and not payment of an amount fixed by the State.

These different schemes, which are covered in various national proposals, show the opposition between the developing countries, most of them favourable to direct exploitation by the mechanism, and the industrial giants, notably France and the Soviet Union, favourable to a non-operational mechanism. Certainly this disagreement essentially rests on the role of the State in the future international organization, but in regard to the problems of development it relates more to the level of economic efficiency and equity. For the USSR and the eastern countries, these two questions are related: the existence of a direct supranational mechanism for exploitation can only result in a hand-holding with the capitalist societies which would preclude any prospect of development consistent with the interests of humanity.

On the contrary, the proposal of the 13 developing countries (A/AC.138/49) is based on the following reasoning: "the international community, being owner of the zone and its resources, has the right to participate directly in their development until it acquires the technical and financial means to exploit them itself on its own account. Nothing can justify a system of exploitation which attributes the role of spectator to the legitimate owner" (Declaration of the Mexican delegate at the 40th Session of Sub-Committee I, A/AC.138/SCI/SR40, p. 131). For the developing countries there is a direct and necessary link between the common patrimony and direct exploitation by a mechanism, a notion which is contested particularly by France and the socialist countries.

The industrial countries justify their dislike for a system of exploitation exercised by a mechanism on considerations of economic efficiency; they feel that there would be serious problems in the financing of it. Moreover, the international authority would have to save revenue from licensing to amass the necessary capital, which would for many years suppress any hope of a financial contribution to development flowing from the common patrimony. [15]

The developing countries, particularly the Latin American ones, are not apprehensive of a long-term plan. The Colombian delegate categorically affirmed that they "would gladly make the sacrifice of postponing the distribution of profits (a large part of which would be returned to them) in order to strengthen the common patrimony. It is only by making this sacrifice that the developing countries can ensure that the great powers do not continue to appropriate that which belongs to all". [16] The system of common enterprises applied for example to the exploitation of hydrocar-

15. To this effect, see the declaration of the delegate from the United Kingdom to the 41st Session of Sub-Committee I (A/AC.138/SCI/SR.41, pp. 141, etc.).

16. Forty-fifth Session of Sub-Committee I (A/AC.138/SCI/SR.45, p. 211). This postponement of profits in order to strengthen the common

bons could provide an answer to the problems of financing. In any case, it is not a question of the pursuit of rapidly acquired profit, but rather of launching a rational system in order to achieve a global approach to development.

B. *The globalization of development*

The common heritage of mankind should be embodied in a global approach to development, and should attain the most highly integrated and perfected effort made so far during the decades of the United Nations interest in this area.

(1) The global strategy of development undertaken from the common heritage approach, should, more than that resulting from inter-State aid, pursue long-term objectives in the interests of all humanity. Humanity is, in effect, responsive to a global notion of time and space. It involves all peoples, more than all nations, poor or rich, totally interdependent in spite of economic or social disparities, in a developmental work that is of concern to all and which affects their common future on the planet on which they all live. Humanity, as opposed to nations in the past-oriented analysis of Compte or Renan, for whom the legacy of the past is just as important as the present, is tomorrow more than today. The international consciousness of this prospective reality has coincided with an awareness of threats to the survival of future generations. In this context, the common patrimony of the seabed appears less as a heritage received by man than as a promise made to men by nature; its Messianic significance is striking. As such, it should permit a global approach to development more naturally than does the international strategy, which also attempts this but with difficulties that result from the divisions among States in the origin of the resources offered for development as in the definition of goals.

The global pursuit of development requires rational economic management, not only at the level of the developing countries, but also at the level of the world economy. The United States delegate

---

property involves a certain contradiction given the large extensions of national jurisdiction which have a very limiting effect on the common heritage and which are based on a short term perspective.

to the Committee on the Seabed recalled in this regard that the international régime "aimed at protecting not only the interests of the developing countries but also those of the developed countries, by creating a climate of security for financial and technological investment".

This global development, which, in the decision-making process takes into account every situation, posits total international co-operation. It satisfies perfectly the preamble of the Declaration of Principle of 1970, which advocates the regulation of production, commercialization and distribution of resources extracted from the seabed in such a way "as to promote the healthy development of the world economy and the balanced growth of world trade and to reduce to a minimum all the unfavourable economic consequences of fluctuations in the price of primary products".

We are touching here upon an area in which the need for a rational approach to development is clearly evident. UNCTAD discussions on the regulation of markets for primary products express the need for harmonious development. However, the common patrimony, in this regard, runs the risk of exerting a wider influence: intended to further the needs of humanity, the exploitation of the international zone will contradict this principle if it should provoke a decline in prices. On several occasions, each time considering new facts revealed by the rapid evaluation of technology, the United Nations Secretariat has endeavoured to determine the possible repercussions on world markets of the exploitation of the mineral resources of the seabed beyond national jurisdiction.[17] These studies have not put an end to the controversy that separates the industrial and the developing countries in this regard.

The industrial nations conclude from Parts I and II of the Report of the Secretary-General (A/AC.138/73) that repercussions from this exploitation on the sales of minerals would not be

17. Cf. Doc. A/AC.135/14, A/AC.138/36 (summary of the report in the official documents of the General Assembly, 26th Session, Supp. No. 21, A/8421-Suppl. II-1, p. 222) and A/AC.138/73. See also the conclusions of the economic and technical work group (General Assembly, 23rd Session, Doc. A/7230, pp. 33-35), the declarations of the representative of UNCTAD (A/AC.138/SCI/L.5 and A/AC.138/SCI/SR.48, pp. 9 to 10) and of the Assistant Secretary-General for economic and social affairs (A/AC.138/SCI/SR.48, pp. 6 to 9).

great: [18] enough new mineral deposits continue to be found on land that it is unlikely that scarcity of minerals will account for much increase in their price. It is difficult therefore to imagine that the metals extracted from nodules will serve any purpose other than helping to supply the increasing world demand. With the possible exception of cobalt the exploitation of the manganese nodules of the seabed would not lower the price of metals and would not as a result have any unfavourable effects on the countries presently exploiting the land deposits. [19]

The developing countries, however, regard the risks of declining prices seriously, [20] and they are calling for establishment of regulatory controls.

A solution in principle is given by the Declaration of Principles of 1970, which provides for "rational management of the zone and its resources". There have been several proposed techniques, notably, a fixed level of production, a fixing of prices at the international market level, compensatory arrangements in favour of the developing countries, a tax levied on each ton of metal produced, or a tax paid by the consuming nations, proportionate to the lowering of market prices relative to a price fixed before the start of the exploitation of nodules, etc.

An analysis of these different approaches points to a distinction between "preventive" methods supported by nearly all of the developing countries and "indemnity" methods which are most frequently favoured by industrialized countries.

Without going into detail of the economics of these proposals, their effect on the problem of development requires comment: the

18. See, for example, the declaration of the delegate from Japan to the 49th Session of Sub-Committee I (A/AC.138/SCI/SR.49, p. 22).

19. Declaration of the delegate from the United Kingdom to the 50th Session of the Sub-Committee I (A/AC.138/SCI/SR.50, p. 29).

Similarly for the United States, "the metals contained in the manganese nodules have limited markets. The predictions with respect to the growth in world demand for the principal metals which they contain, in particular nickel, would lead one to believe that the rate of growth in production can be only rather limited. The two studies by the Secretary-General regarding the economic ramifications permit us to draw the conclusion that the markets for available resources are so limited that it will be a long time before more than an infinitesimal fraction can be exploited commercially". (Sub-Committee I, March 22, 1973, A/AC.138/SCI/SR.64, p. 15).

20. See, for example, the declaration of the delegate from Chile to the 49th Session of Sub-Committee I (A/AC.138/SCI/SR.49, pp. 19 and 20).

system of "indemnity", by analogy to the agreements on agricultural commodities, poses problems of application; however, the "preventive" approach, given its *a priori* nature, runs the risk of restraining the development of the underwater mineral resources which, in the long run, would be prejudicial to the interests of the entire international community.[21]

In its proposed constitution for an international authority governing the seabed, Tanzania proposed in Article 35, section 2: "in determining the price to set and the quantities to sell or make available, the office (of stabilization) should consider simultaneously the needs of the international community for the commodities in question and the necessity of stabilizing the economies of the producing countries especially when the developing countries number among the latter".

The Tanzanian proposal substitutes a qualitative form of development for the traditional quantitative form of development based on the goal of maximization in all areas. This is a qualitative type of development because of the fact that global commodity needs are not the sole point of reference: an equilibrium is achieved with the stabilization of the economies of the developing countries, which could lead to a lower overall growth rate, but which would avoid the anarchistic disequilibrium in the level of economic activity in certain countries.

This proposal demonstrates that, for the developing countries, "prevention" requires that broad regulatory powers be given to an international mechanism, the forecasts of which would integrate the entire market for the commodities in question whether their source is the sea or the land. The common patrimony would thus be used in a fashion leading from the particular to the general, from the management of the marine resources to a rational approach to economic development.

As well, the global approach to development flowing from the common heritage takes in not only economic problems but also those related to the protection of the common patrimony; in particular, the struggle against pollution is integrated in the process of development.

It is to be noted that the prospective nature of the notion of

21. To this effect, see the declaration of the delegate from Japan to the 49th Session of Sub-Committee I, *op. cit.*, p. 23.

humanity is very much in evidence: the imperative of rational management should permit generations to come to benefit from the common heritage. Each generation does not, truly speaking, have proprietary rights over the international zone; humanity, a transtemporal concept, only permits it a rational use which involves the conservation of the source of the common riches. In this sense, all of the proposed conventions presented to the Committee on the Seabed provide that activities in the international zone be governed by a concern for the conservation and protection of natural resources, living or animal.[22]

The principle of demilitarization of the seabed, for the present limited by the treaty passed by the 25th General Assembly to denuclearization, is of course founded on the preoccupation that the zone be devoted to peace and development.

Globalizing this latter goal, this strategy renewed by the common heritage, in its scope leads to a closer integration than that achieved up to the present on the general level.

(2) The integrated strategy of international action for development has already been broached in the United Nations at the level of operational aid.[23] It has not as yet been able to overcome the difficulties resulting from a persistence in traditional errors. The notion of aid, bilateral or multilateral which persists, is contrary to the strategy which supposes the integration of programmes in an increasingly coherent manner.

In a system of aid the financial resources available for development come from the different industrial States which agree to participate, and the integration appears only at the level of distribution the concept of the common heritage of humanity would appear to permit, in the area of the seabed, the establishment of a model or integrated action for development. The exclusion of national sovereignty from the international zone and the imperatives of rational exploitation should lead to the control and promotion, by the mechanism of the exploitation of the riches and their allocation for the purposes of development. Consequently, the integration of multilateralism, which, as we have seen can vary in

22. See, for example, Articles 9, 23 and 25 of the proposal of the United States, Article II of the proposal of the USSR, Article 6 of the proposal of the 13 countries, Articles 74 and 80 to 83 of the Maltese proposal, Article 11 of the Canadian document and Article 10 of the Japanese proposal.

23. Mr. Viralli, *op. cit.*, pp. 396-400.

degree itself, could lead to a modification of the perspectives of development which, when based on the common patrimony, rather that the general strategy, should more readily benefit from possibilities of long-range planning, permitting the revision of policies at the opportune stage in the process. We would thus pass, in the area involved, from co-ordination of development to regulation of development.

The conceptual model, as outlined, could be impressive were it not to a serious degree contradicted by various phenomena flowing from contrary considerations.[24]

Is the concept to be relegated to the status of a myth?

II. THE COMMON HERITAGE OF MANKIND, MYTH FOR DEVELOPMENT?

Since the bed of the seas and oceans was proclaimed the "common heritage of humanity", there has been a tendency on the part of coastal States to extend their national sovereignties out from their coasts in order to appropriate economically important parts of it. While the developing countries have applauded the appearance of the new concept, they have not slackened the pace of the extension of their jurisdiction over larger coastal zones. Their attitude can be well explained: the affirmation of the common patrimony affronted dialectically the national patrimony. The uncertainty concerning the extent of the common heritage leaves open to the great powers a broad range of possible actions with respect to the seabed situated beyond the territorial waters of the continental shelf restricted to its minimum area, up to a depth of 200 metres. The gap between diplomatic time and technological time poses the risk that the industrial States will impinge on the common heritage in spite of the moratorium imposed by resolution 2574 D (XXIV) of the General Assembly and reiterated by resolution 52 (III) of UNCTAD. On March 22, 1973, the delegate from the United States to Sub-Committee I did not exclude the possibility, given the development of techniques of exploitation of the seabed, of interim national legislation if the Conference planned in principle

24. Cf. R.-J. Dupuy, "Les contradictions du droit de la mer", *Revue française de l'énergie*, February 1950, No. 250, pp. 186-196.

for 1974 did not take place as planned or if it failed to elaborate an acceptable juridical régime.[25]

Thus the haste of the great powers to drag or drill on the seabed and that of the coastal States to reserve development zones shows that the common patrimony of mankind is confronting, today, the competition of two new patrimonies: the patrimonial sea and the matrimonial sea.

A. *The patrimonial sea*

The patrimonial sea is the juridical expression used recently to characterize the more or less general tendency to extend the zones of national competence.

The delegate from Peru to Sub-Committee II at the 1973 March Session, prepared a table recapitulating the tendencies towards extension of national jurisdiction over the last two years: "the events which have taken place in this area over the course of the past two years have clearly confirmed that, given different approaches, the 200-mile principle has gone beyond the framework of Latin America and that, despite differing ideologies and degrees of development, countries on five continents subscribe to it today. This principle has, in fact, received the support of a considerable number of countries in Africa, Asia, Oceania and even certain developed countries in Europe.[26] It also received the support of the majority of the jurists who participated in the Afro-Asian juridical consultative committee, of the 10 Latin American countries represented at the Santo Domingo Conference, of the African States who participated in the regional seminar held at Yaoundé and of the Inter-American Juridical Committee which was unanimous in its decision".[27]

The People's Republic of China and Cuba also support this position. This leads us to the conclusion that no international agreement could be concluded which did not involve the 200-mile

25. Doc. A/AC.138/SCI/SR.64, p. 13.

26. France has in effect embraced the extension of national jurisdiction over the seabed to 200 miles (cf. 27th Session of Sub-Committee II, March 27, 1972, Doc. A/AC.138/SCII/SR.51, p. 3).

27. Session of Sub-Committee II, March 14, 1973 (A/AC.138 SCII/SR.51, p. 3).

limit of national jurisdiction. Different economic studies as well as the declaration of certain countries (the United States and the USSR particularly) indicate that the generalized 200-mile limit could even be exceeded in the case of certain continental shelves. As a result the common patrimony will, in the short and medium term, be deprived of, on the one hand economic interest and, on the other hand, of the ability to assume a real contribution to development.[28]

In fact, since 1972, the notion of patrimonial sea has been consistently affirmed. Conceived for the purpose of protecting coastal waters up to 200 miles against the intrusion of foreign fishing fleets accused of pillaging the fishing resources, it appeared acceptable to several States, who held, moreover, moderate conceptions of the law of the sea, because it maintained the distinction between territorial waters, a zone of full sovereignty and the part extending beyond these up to 200 miles from coasts over which, in the words of Garcia Amador, there is "a projection of specialized sovereign rights". The latter permits, notably, the protection of national fishermen while this patrimonial sea remains open generally to free navigation and does not subject foreign ships to the more restrictive rules of innocent passage.

It was inevitable that this concept of a patrimonial sea should be applied to the seabed and in the proposed treaty deposed, on April 2, 1973, with Sub-Committee II by Colombia, Mexico and Venezuela, we find Article 4 which provides "the coastal State exercises sovereign rights over renewable and non-renewable natural resources found on the seabed and its subsoil in a zone adjacent to the territorial waters and designated by the name patrimonial sea".[29]

28. This movement has been strengthened by positions recently adopted, notably by Canada and Argentina, which envisage an extension of their competence over the seabed up to 200 miles as far as the edge of the abyssal plain even where it begins well beyond this limit. Similarly, for Senegal, "Geologically and physically, the continental shelf does not stop at the edge but rather at the foot of the slope and the prolongation of territory under the sea ends there, where the plain of the seabed begins" (51st Session, March 1973, of Sub-Committee II, A/AC.138/SCII/SR.51, p. 9). Similarly, Norway advocates an extension of sovereign rights beyond 200 miles up to a depth of 600 metres for States whose continental shelves extend beyond this limit (cf. 54th Session of Sub-Committee II, A/AC.138/SCII/SR.54, pp. 2 and 3).

29. Doc. A/AC.138/SCII/L.21.

We thus observe that there is a certain disaffection regarding the common heritage, not to say a certain disaffection on the part of the latter in this passage from patrimony to patrimonies.[30]

The common heritage, however, has not lost all of its attraction for the coastal States, but this tends to be limited to States situated in the same region around a partly closed sea which belongs, as a result, to the community of nations involved rather than to humanity.

B. *The matrimonial sea*

The exclusion of the common heritage of humanity from partly closed seas is now in progress. It is being effected by the convergence of riparian appropriation leading itself to a joint or collective appropriation of "Mediterraneans". This is typified by the case of the Caribbean Sea rich in petroleum and manganese nodules.[31] A co-ordination of demands is attractive because of the possibility of optimal exploitation which it presents. The meeting of ministers at the special conference of the countries of the

30. These tendencies towards appropriation by riparians arouse resistance on the part of land-locked States as well as those whose continental shelf is limited by shape of their coastline; these groups are partisans of the common heritage which they consider to be beneficial for them. These tensions were evident during the 27th General Assembly where they split the traditional regional groups in favour of interest groups, cf. our article cited below and the resolutions. The group of land-locked and "shelf-locked" countries was powerful enough to have adopted on December 18, 1972, resolution 3029 B (XXVII), Doc. A/8949, requesting the Secretary-General to make a comparative study of the extent and economic importance, from the point of view of resources, of the international zone depending on its size given the application of the different proposals concerning the limits of national jurisdiction which were presented to the Committee on the Seabed. This text, clearly directed against the riparian demands, with its goal of denouncing the amputations which they constitute at the expense of the common heritage, was passed by 69 votes to 15 with 41 abstentions; this points up the sundering of the "group of 77" in its approach to the problems of the sea.

The coastal States responded by passing, on the initiative of Peru, resolution 3029/C requiring the Secretary-General to make a similar study concerning the economic importance for the coastal States of each of the different proposals regarding the limits of national jurisdiction.

31. See D. D. Arden, Jr., in "Petroleum Perspectives in the Caribbean Area", UNESCO-FAO Symposium, ERm/R/71-1, pp. 205-211.

Caribbean region on the problems of the sea, held on June 7, 1972, confirmed these preoccupations in the Declaration of Santo Domingo which provided for a "patrimonial sea" of a maximum of 200 miles and dispositions concerning regional co-operation. [32]

Given this approach, if we attempt an analysis of the geographical positions of closed seas, we arrive at two types of solutions for the coastal States but, in both cases, the notion of common patrimony of humanity loses all of its substance:

– where the geographical and geological data are sufficiently simple, the coastal States can divide the seabed by bilateral or multilateral agreements. The Mediterranean fits into this context and it is easy to visualize that a generalized extension of national jurisdiction up to 200 miles would completely eliminate the common patrimony in this zone;

– where the geographic aspects of delimitation are revealed to be complex, by reason of the presence of a multiplicity of islands, in particular, physical constraints could lead to the birth of a system of undivided property among the coastal States, there would thus be individual and common property, but it would be limited to the riparians of the partly closed sea. The Caribbean Sea falls into the framework and it is significant that the coastal States on this sea proposed the notion of the "matrimonial sea", characterized juridically by an undivided property among coastal States and economically by the formation of an agency, associated in joint ventures and capable of engaging in technical, industrial and commercial activities relating to the exploration of the zone and the exploitation of its resources.

Whilst the notion of patrimonial sea is defensive, that of matrimonial sea appears to be productive, designed essentially to effect the communal organization of use with a view to the development of the region.

It appears that the idea of a matrimonial sea is tending to break out of the framework of partly closed seas in order to answer the need for regional associations grouping the countries bordering on an ocean. Thus, the community of interest among riparians has led certain Latin American States to propose a regional organization to exploit the seabed devoted to "the economic, social and

32. The text of this declaration is reproduced in UN Doc. A/AC.138/80.

cultural development of the peoples of Latin America".[33]

Some countries, such as China and certain African countries, go so far as to envisage a conciliation between the interests of riparians and land-locked countries, at least in certain cases, where the two groups are neighbours geographically and of a comparable level of development; this would involve an association under which the latter benefited from the patrimonial sea of the latter. Thus we would have the concept of a matrimonial sea among peoples brought together by region and by underdevelopment.

In conclusion, it would appear that at the very time when the notion of the common heritage of humanity is practically no longer contested in principle at the United Nations, its economic potential is being progressively diminished by extensions of national "jurisdictions".[34] This situation points to the significance of the proposal of the United States to the last Session of Sub-Committee I, in the spring of 1973, that preparations be undertaken immediately with a view to bringing into effect, on a provisional basis, provisions for a régime and an international mechanism to permit the rapid exploitation of the common patrimony "within the framework of international measures".[35]

The supporters of the common heritage thus have to contend with the tendency towards regionalism as well as with the impatience of those who are preparing to exploit the resources of the seabed. At the same time there appear to be difficulties in applying a truly global strategy of development based on the international zone.[36]

33. Proposal by Uruguay to the 47th Session of the Committee on the Seabed, A/AC.138/SR.47, p. 35.

34. It follows from the economic studies that: "if an Ocean Régime controlled the dispositions of all resources beyond the traditional three-mile limit, it would possess billions of dollars of assets, even under existing technologies of recovery. If, on the other hand, its authority began 200 miles or more from every coastline, the present economic value of its resources would be negligible" (*Pacem in Maribus,* Royal University of Malta Press, 1971, Vol. 1, p. 2).

35. Cf. 64th Session of Sub-Committee I, March 22, 1973, A/AC. 138/SCI/SR.64, pp. 11 to 17. The delegate from the United States pointed out that temporary provisions concerning situations of the same type had already been taken in the case of the Convention on International Civil Aviation or are applied by organizations such as WHO, the Preparatory Commission of the International Refugee Organization, the IAEA and the International Telecommunications Consortium (INTELSTAT).

36. It is significant that during the last session of the Committee on the

However, it would be an exaggeration to present a totally negative perspective. Even if the Conference on the Sea should confirm the reduction in the international zone to the abyssal plain, it would not mean that the entire treasure was engulfed. Certainly, the exploitation of mineral resources will, in the near future, be concentrated, for obvious reasons of profitability, on the continental slope which is richer in hydrocarbons than the abyss and often well stocked with nodules, but in 15 or 20 years, at the most, the entire bed will be more readily exploitable in light of technological progress.[37]

The common heritage of humanity retains then the capability, far from negligible, of being a fruitful myth, harbinger of a deferred reality.

Seabed, at New York in the spring of 1973, with respect to a system of exploitation, there was an affirmation of the tendency to favour an authority directed particularly to avoid any discrimination in the granting of permits relating to hydrocarbons, reserving the right to receive these permits to States only. This system, presently the most realistic, is the least integrated.

37. Cf. on the petroleum potential of the oceanic basins, the article of J. P. Levy and the report of the Secretary-General on the mineral resources of the sea, April 26, 1971, Doc. E/4973.

Chapter III

NATIONAL APPROPRIATION OF MARITIME AREAS*

On March 24, 1971, the representative of Turkey to the Committee on the Seabed observed that "The General Assembly had referred the examination of questions concerning marine areas, not to the International Law Commission composed of jurists, but to the 'Committee on the Peaceful Uses of the Seabed and the Oceans', which has an eminently political composition. The decision of the Members of the United Nations to not consider questions which arise concerning the law of the sea as subjects of law corresponds to the imperatives of modern life where political, economic and social factors have a strong influence".[1]

This declaration, unjust though it is with respect to the Commission emphasizes the complex consciousness of the "environment" accompanying the contemporary aspects of the law of the sea affecting all of the authors of proposals at the risk of arriving at abstract constructions.

The quasi "pluri-disciplinary" approach in the marine domain is particularly characteristic of the delegations from the developing countries to the Seabed Committee. The developed States should take account of this situation in order to establish a dialogue rather than two monologues,[2] a position already revealed by the different economic underpinnings of a law of development now in its infancy.

* This chapter has been written with the very useful collaboration of M. Alain Piquemal, Research Assistant at the Institute of the Law of Peace and Development of the University of Nice.

1. Declaration of Mr. Tuncel at the 69th Session of the Seabed Committee, March 24, 1971, UN Doc. A/AC.138/SR.59, p. 229.

2. This cleavage, based on economic considerations, was developed by Mr. Espinosa, delegate from Colombia to the Seabed Committee: "the divergencies of views are a function not of the ideologies which divide the world but of the degree of development, and reflect a cleavage not between East

Consequently, the new perspectives offered by the marine environment should be invoked in order to discern the future juridical mutations which will interpret them. But the evolution of the law of the sea cannot be reduced to a struggle for the equation of law to economic evolutionism. The political perspective translating the demands of coastal States[3] constitutes a second opening which jurists should accept as a parameter of the new equation for the law of the sea to be submitted to the conference foreseen for 1973: the wind of history is presently from the land towards the sea in favour of the coastal State, to the detriment of the sea wind, the symbol of freedom of the seas extolled by the great maritime powers.

The rapid evocation of the historical evolution of demands, recalling the successive appearance of the forces present will better allow us to situate the contemporary perspective of the dialectical movement of appropriations.

A. *New perspectives offered by the marine environment*

If national appropriation has characterized the law of the sea since the Second World War, this evolution can only be appreciated in comparison with the principle of freedom of the seas, expressed especially with respect to the role of the ocean as a means of communication and the practical impossibility of encroachment into the maritime domain.

(1) *From the sea, means of communication, to the sea, reservoir of riches*

The oceans, covering 70 per cent. of the surface of the earth, have constituted for classical jurists the preferential support for "jus communicationis". As a result, the principle of freedom has done

---

and West but between the industrial and maritime powers of the North and the vast underdeveloped South, resolved to participate in the progressive development of law and committed to the abolition of systems which accentuate the inegality between countries, 59th Session, UN Doc. A/AC. 138/SR.59, p. 221.

3. This political perspective is, moreover, linked closely to economic considerations, often giving voice to them as we will see later.

no more than to give juridical force to the principle of Vittoria.[4]

Biological resources represented the first aspect of "reservoir of riches", but the most complete expression of this tendency came into play only a few years ago with the perspectives of exploitation of the mineral riches of the seabed.[5] This evolution leads many States to give priority to the appropriation of these assessable material riches, rather than to the principle of freedom, the value of which is uncertain for the purposes of economic development.[6]

A few statistics demonstrate this evolution.[7] Thirty per cent. of Japanese coal production comes from under the ocean, the figure is more than 10 per cent. for the United States. But oil production has the most promising future, proven offshore reserves have tripled and represented in 1971, 21 per cent. of the total world reserves.

This economic weath, although unequally distributed, is present in a large proportion of the oceans; geological and geophysical explorations are presently in progress along the coasts of 75 countries including all of the continents except the Antarctic. In fact, the studies have already shown that there are zones off nearly all coastal States favourable to the presence of oil.

These new perspectives offered by the marine environment

4. It is evident that the principle of free communication includes in its broadest sense ideas as well as people or merchandise.

5. On the ambivalence concerning the use of the oceans and the results of it, Bertrand de Jouvenel, "Man and the Sea: Developing Problems". Working paper for "Pacem in Maribus", December, 1970. See also on the evolution of interests linked to the sea, the declaration of Mr. Beesley (Canada) at the 63rd Session of the Seabed Committee, August 5, 1971, who portrays the evolution of the law of the sea with reference to the conflict between coastal and maritime interests, "The present crisis flows from the intensification of this conflict following the intervention of new facts of a technical and political nature which have upset the traditional equilibrium". UN Doc. A/AC. 138/SR.63, p. 35.

6. This is particularly true in certain cases; freedom, even when restrained by resolutions of international organizations, can lead to abusive practices provoking the intervention of coastal States. On this problem, with the whale as an example, cf. declaration of Mr. Arias Schreiber (Peru) at the 46th Session of the Seabed Committee, March 15, 1971, UN Doc. A/AC.138/ SR.46, p. 19.

7. The following examples are taken from the report of the Secretary-General of the United Nations, "The Mineral Resources of the Sea", April 26, 1971-E/4973.

could give rise to the fear of a geographic extension of national appropriation resulting from the existence of oil, not only to the continental shelf and the upper part of the continental slope but also to the small oceanic basins[8] and perhaps even to the large oceanic basins.[9]

Consequently, one can only subscribe to the existence of a "direct encroachment, in fact, on the formulation of the law"[10] revealed also by the possible encroachment on the maritime domain.

(2) *The possible encroachment on the maritime domain*

For Gidel the material reasons which militate in favour of the freedom of the seas are essentially the necessity to ensure world trade and the physical impossibility for man to occupy the maritime domain.[11]

Technical progress has since intervened to remove the latter obstacle and it appears that the search for oil in deeper and deeper waters will lead to the installation of permanent bases on the ocean floor.[12] This submarine appropriation is equally foreseeable for military installations, while adjacent waters are also involved

8. The Gulf of Mexico, the Caribbean Sea, the Mediterranean, the Black Sea, the Bering Sea, the Okhotsk Sea, the Sea of Japan, the South China Sea, the deep basins of the Indonesian archipelago.

9. For example in the abyssal regions and the pre-continental slope of the Atlantic near Newfoundland and north of the Cap Vert Islands.

10. Charles De Visscher, *Les effectivités du droit international public*, p. 65, Pédone, 1967.

11. G. Gidel, *Le droit international public de la mer*, p. 208. This analysis only perpetuates the tradition of 18th-century jurists, such as Ortolan: "The impossibility of property in the sea results from the physical nature of this element which is such that it cannot be possessed and which serves man essentially as means of communication" (cited by Gidel, *op. cit.*, p. 201). In the same vein, cf. de Martens, *Précis du droit des gens modernes de l'Europe fondé sur les traités et l'usage*, Vol. I, Gattingue, 1789. This doctrine has found acceptance equally by chiefs of State: in 1580, Queen Elizabeth of England declared that no people and no person could have rights to the ocean "because, neither its nature nor its public use can permit its occupation or its possession".

12. For example, the experiments "Conshelf" (French), the Soviet project "Bentos 300", the German project "Helgoland" in the North Sea, the Canadian station "Sublimos" in Lake Superior, the "Aegir" station off Oahu Island (Hawaii) and the American station "Hydrolab" off Florida, UN Doc. E/4973, p. 50.

from the point of view of the construction of artificial ports and drilling platforms. [13]

Freedom of the seas has thus lost an important material trump with the new economic use for the sea. Consequently, a historical review is shown to be necessary in order to better trace the development of appropriation over a long period of time and thus to judge the present situation from its proper perspective.

B. *The historical evolution of demands*

We do not propose to retrace the entire history of national appropriation in the maritime domain but to bring to light certain significant facts.

(1) First, "The ancient conceptions 'Mare Clausum' and 'Mare liberum', like the notions 'res communis' and 'res nullius' applied to the high seas, have always varied according to the interests of the great maritime powers". [14] When maritime trade was limited to trade between several powers, the division into zones of influence constituted the most profitable solution for these States (Treaty of 509-508 and 306 between Rome and Carthage, claim of Genoa to the Ligurian Sea, of Venice to the Adriatic, etc.). The most perfect expression of this tendency is given by the Bull 'Inter Coetera" of 1493 dividing the Atlantic between Spain and Portugal.

The movement after the 16th century in favour of the freedom of the seas does not break with the tradition favourable to the maritime powers but, on the contrary, accentuates it by adding the free competition, mercantilist underpinning to the principle of freedom of the seas. Consequently a new form of appropriation was able to develop, much more difficult to condemn because it was based on a material reality. [15]

13. Among other examples, a private project has been proposed to the Belgian Government providing for the construction of an artificial port for supertankers 27 kilometres from the Belgian coast, UN Doc. A/AC.138/35.

14. Declaration of Mr. Alcivar (Ecuador) at the 56th Session of the Seabed Committee–March 23, 1971, UN Doc. A/AC.138/SR.56, p. 150.

15. This first approach underlines, at this early date, the complex and ambiguous nature of the notion of appropriation. It appears necessary, for a thorough understanding of the parties involved, especially the developing

(2) However, the historical account of the blooming of the principle of freedom of the seas, over the centuries, does not culminate in the elevation of the 3-mile rule to the status of a universally accepted limit for territorial waters as Gidel noted, during an era, moreover, which was more favourable to this rule than the present era. [16]

Furthermore this principle was only dominant with respect to territorial waters and did not prevent appropriation by means of special coastal zones in various matters (customs, fisheries, etc.).

(3) These tendencies towards the geographical extension of the rights of the coastal State have been particularly accentuated since the end of the Second World War with the essential motivation of preserving economic coastal property. "This in depth organisation" confirms the observation that, if "Juridically, the frontier is a line, geographically and politically, it is a zone, a band of adjacent territory, the regulation of which tends to be adapted to the physical characteristics of the coast and the human activities which take place there". [17] The contemporary claims of States thus illustrate perfectly the notion of "confinement" developed by Charles De Visscher and the functional orientation of appropriations. This latter characteristic, essential element of the new international law of the sea, underlies what it is possible to call the "dialectic" of appropriation.

C. *The dialectic of appropriations*

The history of appropriations gives a hint of a double dialectical movement involving different subjects of international law.

---

countries, to not rely entirely on a strict juridical interpretation: the nearly exclusive use of a freedom by a small number of States brings about the same result as an explicit appropriation.

16. Gilbert Gidel, *op. cit.*, Vol. 3, p. 123: "It is impossible to find, among States, a common will to conduct themselves reciprocally and obligatorily in a certain manner with respect to the determination of the extent of adjacent maritime surfaces submitted to their juridical competence as coastal States".

17. Charles De Visscher, *Théories et réalités en droit international public*, 1970, p. 238, citing J. Gottman, *La politique des Etats et leur géographie*, 1952, p. 122.

(1) *The dialectic between classical subjects of international law*

Already foreseen in previous developments, this situation opposes the coastal States and the great maritime powers. [18] The economic power of the latter having provoked the *de facto* appropriation of many of the uses of the sea, a reaction developed on the part of coastal States whose adjacent zones were threatened.

The abusive exploitation of offshore origin (maritime powers) led to an appropriation from the land as, in the 16th century, the claims of coastal States had led to the principle of freedom of the seas.

(2) *The dialectic between new subjects of international law*

This situation, extended over a greater period of time, opposes the individual, the State and the international community of "mankind". [19]

In Antiquity and at the beginning of the Middle Ages, the rights of private land holders along coasts were often recognized with respect to the underground of the seabed and exclusive fishing zones up to a certain distance. [20]

However, during the Middle Ages, this privatization led to "a securing of the jurisdiction over territorial waters (variable in form

18. It is evident that the great maritime powers also have interests of a coastal nature, but two considerations militate in favour of such an opposition: the maritime powers sometimes promote the consequences of their coastal situations (cf. for example the Truman Declaration of 1945) but their strategic and commercial interests on a large proportion of the oceans often come into competition with their interests as coastal States. Furthermore, the most extreme appropriations have been made by developing coastal States which accentuates the economic conflict with the industrialized maritime powers.

19. In the present state of international law, the introduction of the individual and mankind as subjects could lead to contestation particularly in the case of the latter. However, the Declaration of Principles of December 17, 1970 (Geneva, Assembly resolution 2749-XXV), voted 108-0 with 18 abstentions, has declared the seabed to be common heritage of mankind beyond national jurisdiction. It is then permissible to note a movement towards the implicit recognition of mankind as a subject of international law, for the interest of mankind is not simply that of the concertation of all States; it is a notion integrating the State, the collectivities and the individual.

20. For precise examples of the phenomenon, see the report prepared for the Senate on the proposed law concerning the delimitation of French territorial waters (December 14, 1971, No. 97) pp. 2 and 3.

and extent) by cities and States to the detriment of coastal landowners".[21]

This "general" dialectic then gave birth to a special dialectical situation, previously examined, between States, which in turn, led to a new phase very recently: the "appropriation-auction" between coastal States and maritime powers has led to the conferring on mankind of the seabed and the oceans beyond national jurisdiction (resolution 2749-XXV).

Although the limits of this property are not yet determined, this assignment represents a new type of appropriation, in the name of mankind, brought about by the ambitions of States.[22]

This progression, from the individual to the State, then to the international community, foreshadows perhaps a new hierarchy of subjects of international law, but constitutes definitely a framework for national appropriation which is still relatively flexible. The juridical value of this limit to the claims of States is still a subject of caution,[23] but it permits a better appreciation of appropriation from two essential directions:

– with respect to *the geographical extent of expropriation*, a physical dividing line between State zones and the international zone;

– with respect to *the juridical nature of appropriation*, a much more flexible dividing line, originating gradations in appropriation, with, most often, a "functional jurisdiction" as common denominator.

I. THE GEOGRAPHICAL EXTENT OF APPROPRIATION

"The delimitation of maritime areas always has an international aspect; it could not depend solely on the will of the coastal State

21. Report to the Senate, *op. cit.*, p. 5.

22. In this dialectical perspective, one can note the specificity of the interests of mankind with respect to the interests of the State: mankind is formed by the State (which creates it) but is equally against the State.

23. Concerning this question, it is interesting to note the statement of Mr. Jorge Castañeda (Mexico): the Declaration of Principles of December 17, 1970, "constitutes a juridical basis permitting the classification as illegal, hence forward, of every unilateral act of a State which wants to appropriate the resources of the seabed and the oceans or to claim any sovereignty whatever over this zone", 58th Session of the Committee on the Seabed, March 24, 1971, UN Doc. A/AC.138/SR.58, p. 197.

as expressed by its internal law. If it is true that the act of delimitation is necessarily a unilateral act, because the coastal State is the only party qualified to effect it, on the other hand, the validity of the delimitation relative to other States falls within the province of international law". [24]

This delicate coexistence between internal law and international law and their complementary character leads us, in order to understand the geographical extent of the different claims, to a distinction between unilateral appropriation by national legislation and multilateral appropriation by international negotiation.

The value of this distinction depends on the resolution of a preliminary question, the question of what status to attribute to an internal appropriation. What is the relationship between the national jurisdiction of the coastal State and the width of territorial waters? On this fundamental principle, there exists a sharp difference of opinion:

– For certain States (particularly the great maritime powers and the socialist States) "The question of the breadth of territorial waters and the exclusive fishing zone has never been governed solely by the national jurisdiction of a coastal State . . . In the opinion of the Court (*Fisheries* case) the validity of a delimitation in maritime areas with respect to other States is governed by international law; in other words, the limits fixed in conformity with the internal law of the coastal State cannot exceed the maximum limits authorized by international law". [25] The only divergence of opinion between these States is the maximum breadth recognized

24. *Fisheries* case (United Kingdom *v.* Norway), Judgment, *ICJ Reports 1951*, p. 132. This citation is often used by the opponents of the extension of national jurisdiction to 200 miles (cf. for example the declaration of Mr. Natorf (Poland) to the Seabed Committee, A/AC.138/SR.54, p. 125). Then, in its judgment on the *North Sea Continental Shelf* cases, the ICJ declared that "the delimitation is an operation which consists in determining the limits of a zone already in the jurisdiction of the coastal State and not to define this zone *de novo*". By using this vocabulary, these opponents strengthen the position of coastal States on the basis of their claims, while their other arguments are founded generally on the conception that waters beyond a maximum of 12 miles constitute high seas. As a result, one can only subscribe to the analysis of Charles De Visscher for whom the imprecise definition of the high seas in the Vienna Convention of 1958 evokes "not the clear notion of a precise, linear delimitation but the existence of imprecise zones of jurisdiction characteristic of the notion of 'confinement' ".

25. Declaration of Mr. Natorf (Poland), *op. cit.*

by customary international law, from 3 to 12 miles according to the various States.[26]

– For other States (certain medium powers and several developing countries) "in the absence of a rule of international law (that of 3 nautical miles being outdated for some time) each State has the prerogative to determine, in the exercise of its sovereignty, the external limits of its jurisdiction according to the requirements of national security and economic survival. This practice will remain legal and justifiable as long as the international community has not adopted a rule forbidding it".[27] For these States, the 12-mile rule with respect to territorial waters and the contiguous zone, being applied by less than 40 States parties to the Geneva convention, and national legislation on the limits of jurisdiction being varied, there exists no "international custom as proof of a general practice accepted as law" (Article 38 of the Statute of the ICJ).[28]

This examination of the various positions confirms the "anarchy" of demands and the lack of a common position.[29] Having adopted a pragmatic approach to the evolution of national appropriation, we will envisage what is, and not what should be, in the

26. Furthermore, one should note the attenuation of this divergence resulting from the articles proposed by the United States providing for, among other things, the possible extension of territorial waters to 12 miles (UN Doc. A/AC.138/SC.II/L.4 and Corr. I). Similarly, France, previously opposed to a unilateral extension beyond 3 miles (cf. concerning this, 1959 *Annuaire français de droit international*, p. 898; 1963 *A.F.D.I.*, p. 1077; 1963 *A.F.D.I.*, p. 1058; 1964 *A.F.D.I.*, p. 675) has extended its territorial waters to 12 miles by law No. 71.1060 of December 24, 1971 (*J.O.* of December 30, 1971).

27. Declaration of Mr. Tolentino (Philippines) at the 55th Session of the Seabed Committee, UN Doc. A/AC.138/SR.55, p. 132. To the same effect, and more bluntly, "In the opinion of the Algerian delegation, the delimitation of territorial water falls exclusively within the competence of the coastal State" (Mr. Allouane, A/AC.138/SR.54, p. 120).

28. Declaration to this effect by Mr. Alcivar (Ecuador) concluding that the absence of custom in this area "reduces to nothing the fallacious arguments of those who contend that the limit of 200 miles is arbitrary, for, if this reasoning were accepted, no matter what width fixed by a State, be it 3, 12, 50 or 100 miles would also be arbitrary", 56th Session of the Committee on the Seabed, UN Doc. A/AC.138/SR.56, p. 151.

29. A lack already noted by Gidel with respect to the 3-mile rule, but presently more accentuated with jurisdictions attaining 200 miles and by new politico-economic motivations with respect to the classical considerations of security.

best of juridical worlds.[30] Consequently, neither the national nor the international approach to appropriation can be asserted as dominant in the present uncertain state of the law of the sea.

Paragraph I. *Unilateral appropriation: national legislation*

The present state of national legislation presents a broad spectrum of solutions. The heterogeneity of these positions necessitates, for a complete and realistic approach to the problem, an account of the difficulties involved in a homogeneous solution.

A. *The difficulties facing a homogeneous solution*

The riparian State, envisaged as a single concept, does not portray the reality of the situation. There exists not a coastal State but rather coastal States representing profoundly diverse geographical, economic, political and strategic situations.

(*a*) *The diversity of geographical situations*[31]

Several examples, in no way exhaustive, can explain an important aspect of the motivations of States concerning appropriation while exemplifying the diversity of these motivations.

(1) *The difference between oceans and "Mediterraneans"*[32]

In the matter of appropriation it appears necessary to draw a

30. For more detail as to the juridical quarrel between States concerning the validity of unilateral acts in this area, cf. the declarations to the Committee on the seabed by Mr. Ogiso (Japan), A/AC.138/SR.53, p. 100, and by Mr. Castañeda (Mexico) to the Subcommittee II, A/AC.138/SC.II.SR.II, p. 7.

31. For the maximum emphasis of the geographical particularity of each situation, we won't deal with appropriation in geographical situations common to a large number of coastal States. Thus the Dutch law of December 3, 1964, "Refers only to the continental shelf, in order to explain, that from a geographical point of view, the planned maritime installations are those erected 'outside of territorial waters, on that part of the bed of the North Sea, the limits of which correspond to the part of the continental shelf which belongs to Holland' " (Ch. De Visscher, *Problèmes de conflits en droit international public*, p. 169).

32. The theory of the "Mediterraneans" was advanced in 1968 by Italy at the Seabed Committee, A/AC.135/I, Add. 9.

distinction whether the State is adjacent to a sea or an ocean. When certain Latin American States extended their sovereignty over a 200-mile zone they evoked the rough outline of a theory to this effect. In fact, in simple quantitative terms, such an appropriation appears trivial given the immensity of the ocean, whereas it appears extravagant in the partially closed seas such as the Baltic or the Mediterranean.

But especially, in qualitative terms, the difference in geographical situations creates the links of varying intensity between the coastal States [33] and between the maritime environment and the riparians. [34] The representative of Iran went so far as to define "marginal seas" as true microcosms, necessitating different régimes and justifying thus certain appropriations: " . . . the juridical divergence is accentuated between the régime applicable to oceanic areas and the régime applicable to marginal seas or seas of limited size, so that the first cannot be automatically applied instead of the second without harmfully affecting the interests of coastal States. Usually, the marginal seas are geologically part of the continental mass; biologically, they belong to the same ecosystem as the neighbouring land; economically, they are linked with the socio-economic framework of the coastal communities, which depend more and more on marine resources for their subsistence and their economic development". [35]

The logical outcome of such positions is a collective appropriation on the part of coastal States adjacent to this type of sea and would introduce a political and not a geographical conception of "closed seas". [36]

33. In this regard, one can consider that the "Declaration making the Indian Ocean a Peace Zone" (Resolution 2832-XXVI) has been facilitated or at least motivated by the close links which can exist between coastal States and this limited zone.

34. To this effect, see C. A. Colliard, *Le fond des mers*, A. Colin, 1971, p. 93.

35. Declaration of Mr. Massoud Ansari (Iran) at the 59th Session of the Seabed Committee, UN Doc. A/AC.138/SR.59, p. 229.

36. In this vein, Mr. Massoud Ansari, *op. cit.*, declared that "the intrusion into these seas by fishing fleets from distant countries creates an abnormal situation, which seriously disturbs the economy of coastal regions".

(2) *The geographic situations determining the drawing of base lines*

Different problems arise. In general, the coastal State can set new base lines, which are more advantageous, but always founded on geographical characteristics. Thus France, by the decree of October 19, 1967,[37] defined straight base lines and lines closing bays, to be used in determining the base lines from which to measure the width of the territorial waters. Whereas, "previously, this limit was determined by the low-water mark. With the setting of new base lines, the limit of territorial waters follows a more geometrical pattern which is, in some areas, up to 25 miles from the coast".[38]

The "island" situation can also lead to totally different results depending on the position. The most classic example in this area is furnished by the islands in the north of the Persian Gulf. Certain of them, by reason of their limited dimensions, provided a questionable geographical support for appropriation based on the systematic application of the criterion of median line.[39] The difficulty stems from the fact that the Geneva conventions do not distinguish between islands and continental coastal States with respect to the methods for delimiting the territorial waters and the continental shelf.

In order to avoid abusive appropriations, it has been proposed that "a distinction be created between archipelagos and islands which constitute or could constitute independent States on the one hand, and those which could never become independent

37. *J.O.* of November 1, 1967, p. 10755.

38. Ch. Rousseau, *Revue générale de droit international public*, No. 4, 1967, p. 1165. Another example of appropriation based on geographical particularities is given by the Protocol entitled "Rio de la Plata passed on January, 1964, between Uruguay and Argentina despite the opposition of other States contending that the coastal States had sovereign rights only on a fringe of territorial water parallel to the indentation of their coasts while the remainder of the vast stretches of water between the banks of the Rio were high seas" (Ch. De Visscher, *Problèmes de confins en droit international public*, *op. cit.*, p. 124). The protocol considers as internal waters the entire zone situated inside the straight line described by the declaration. For more detail, cf. Hector Gros Espiell "Le régime juridique du Rio de la Plata", *Annuaire français de droit international*, 1964, pp. 725-736.

39. Cf. S. Oda, "Boundary of the continental shelf", *Japanese Yearbook of International Law*, 1968, p. 264; J. A. C. Gutteridge, "The 1958 Geneva Convention on the Continental Shelf", *BYBIL*, 1959, p. 120.

States. It is also necessary to distinguish between islands geographically close to coasts and isolated islands and to decide whether rocks and sand banks constitute islands for the purposes of defining the limits of jurisdiction".[40]

The juridical formulation of these principles is dealt with in Article 37, sections 1 and 2, of the proposed treaty on maritime areas presented by Malta[41] which limits, in the absence of special agreements, the maritime jurisdiction around islands to island States or States formed by an archipelago. This latter geographic particularity has also been the object of demands which could lead to considerable appropriations.

(3) *The special geographic case of the archipelagic State*

What is the juridical nature of the waters lying between the islands forming the territory of these States? The Geneva Conference of 1958, being unable to set a régime relative to archipelagos, the question was raised again in 1960, during the second conference by the delegation from the Philippines[42] and that of Indonesia.[43] It was, however, impossible to arrive at an agreement and the question is now before the Seabed Committee.[44]

In fact, the national legislations of these States set their territorial waters on the basis of straight base lines joining the specified

40. Declaration of Mr. Pardo (Malta), 57th Session of the Seabed Committee, UN Doc. A/AC.138/SR.57, p. 177. International practice had already witnessed the extension of the coastal State's authority over a particular type of island, the artificial island. Thus, after the precedent of "Radio-Nordzee" in 1964 (Ch. Rousseau, *Revue générale de droit international public*, 1965, p. 517), the Italian Government has launched an action against the artificial island of "the free state of the Roses", situated, moreover, outside its territorial waters (Ch. Rousseau, *Revue générale de droit international public*, 1969, p. 189).

41. UN Doc. A/AC.138/53 and official G.A. Doc., 26th Session, A/8421, p. 109.

42. Cf. Declaration of Mr. Tolentino, 5th Session of the Plenary Commission, official docs., p. 55, and, particularly, the typewritten accounts, pp. 75 and following.

43. Cf. Declaration of Mr. Subardjo, 14th Session of the Plenary Commission, official docs., p. 100, and particularly, the typewritten accounts, pp. 268 and following.

44. "It is clear that no consensus has evolved for any particular system of delimiting the bound of authority over waters of archipelagic islands", McDougal and Burke, *Public Order of the Oceans*, pp. 418-419, Yale University Press, 1963.

points on the outer islands of the archipelago. Thus all waters separating the islands should be considered as interior waters according to a geographic principle founded on political and economic considerations. "According to this conception, the islands of the archipelago, the number of which exceeds 13,000, and the waters which separate them constitute a single unit; for the Indonesian people and the Government, this is a reality which need not be demonstrated. This conception of a unit is also an economic necessity since the inhabitants of the Indonesian islands have always used the sea for their subsistence. Finally, it has a political significance, for the integrality of its terrestrial, maritime and aerial territory is essential for the survival of Indonesia". [45]

(4) *The juridical régime for frozen waters*

Mr. Lester B. Pearson wrote in 1946 that a large part of the Arctic regions were Canadian and that this included "not only the northern territory of Canada, but also, the islands and the frozen sea to the north of the continent between the meridians of her east and west frontiers extended as far as the North Pole". [46]

Although official positions since then have been more restrained and the Prime Minister, Mr. P. E. Trudeau, stated that "the sector theory applied only to the continental shelf and the seabed, not to water and ice". [47] Canada always appears to claim the ice, but in an ambiguous manner. On April 29, 1970, the director of the juridical service of Foreign Affairs claimed that "the theory that ice is part of the territory has certainly not been abandoned nor forgotten". [48]

45. Declaration of Mr. Njotowijono (Indonesia) at the 55th Session of the Seabed Committee, UN Doc. A/AC.138/SR.55, p. 139. To the same effect, declaration of Mr. Tolentino (Philippines), p. 134.

46. Foreign Affairs, July, 1946, pp. 638-639, cited in *Revue générale de droit international public*, 1970, No. 1, p. 126.

47. *Revue générale de droit international public*, 1970, No. 1, p. 126.

48. Cited by Mr. J. Y. Morin, *Canadian Yearbook of International Law*, 1970, p. 234. It should also be remarked that, with respect to a crime committed on an "ice island" (off Ellesmere Island which is Canadian territory), Canada claimed jurisdiction over all matters.

(*b*) *The diversity of economic situations*

The representative of France at the Seabed Committee stressed [49] once more that "the new law of the sea will be of an essentially economic nature". Consequently, the diversity of economic situations should be taken into consideration with respect to the marine domain as well as with respect to States.

(1) *The global conception of the marine domain*

It is often considered that "the sea forms a physical and ecological unit" and that "all the divisions introduced by man, such as territorial waters, contiguous zone and the rights of coastal States and those without coasts, are secondary and ephemeral". [50] However, this perspective, though juridically attractive because of the universality which it permits, should be varied because of economic considerations.

Although it constitutes a homogeneous complex, the resources of the sea are not evenly distributed: *physical homogeneity is coupled with economic heterogeneity*. As a result, the appropriations effected by different national legislations will be accepted in different ways by third States and it will be prepared by coastal States according to the economic potential of the areas involved.

(2) *Weighing the particular situations of States*

A study by FAO concerning marine biological resources has recognized the intensive exploitation of numerous fish stocks, but it added that: "there remain, however, substantial resources which are under-utilized. The coastal waters of numerous developing countries offer the possibility of an increase in the production of their small local fisheries thus improving socio-economic conditions". [51]

Consequently certain coastal States disposing of such an economic potential are going to justify national appropriation by rais-

49. Declaration of Mr. Jeannel to the 54th Session, UN Doc. A/AC.138/SR.54, p. 108.

50. Declaration of Mr. Galindo Pohl (El Salvador) to the 63rd Session of the Seabed Committee, UN Doc. A/AC.138/SR.63, p. 30.

51. FAO Doc. C71/20, of October 8, 1971. Cf. to the same effect, the declaration to the 46th Session of the Seabed Committee by Mr. Zegers (Chile), UN Doc. A/AC.138/SR.48, p. 40.

ing the obligations that they have towards their people to struggle against underdevelopment.[52] But, already in this area, we must consider the attention being paid to political arguments.

(c) *The diversity of political situations*

"The greater a State's maritime power, the more that State tends to limit its territorial waters".[53] Despite the evolution of technology since the Second World War, the strategic interests of the maritime powers appear not to have changed and rest on territorial waters of 12 miles at the maximum because of their political ambitions.[53a] Other coastal States, for reasons of security, can only adopt a contrary attitude.

But the diversity of political situations does not apply solely to a cleavage between States according to their power; it can operate at the level of "blocs". Thus any sea in which the two current "hegemonies" are present, directly or by means of an intermediary

52. Another form of economic particularity has been advanced by certain developed countries, such as Iceland, which have an economy based on the fishing resources of the sea. For many developing countries, appropriation is only a just response to the effective appropriation of developed countries and constitutes a weapon in the anti-colonialist struggle: "there are still third world countries whose territorial waters and continental shelf are coveted just as their land was coveted in the past. In fact, they are alone today at the centre of the debate on the Mediterranean and the oceans whose waters touch the coasts of countries belonging almost exclusively to the third world; according to certain international agreements, *the seas located beyond the 40th parallel north have become the exclusive property of coastal States* . . . this division was made according to juridical norms and considerations of an economic nature, the application of which is refused today where developing countries are concerned". Declaration of Mr. Allouane (Algeria) to the 54th Session of the Seabed Committee, UN Doc. A/AC.138/SR.54, p. 119.

53. Cf. Gidel, *op. cit.* T. III, p. 141. To the same effect Ch. De Visscher, *Théories et réalités en droit international public*, p. 239. For an enumeration of the political and economic interests of the United States favouring a narrow national jurisdiction, cf. declaration of Mr. Arias Schreiber (Peru) to the 46th Session of the Seabed Committee, UN Doc. A/AC.138/SR.46, p. 20.

53a. It is however to be noted that the use of atomic arms provokes temporary appropriations for "security zones" which are often very broad. For example, in 1969, the USSR, for tests on the high seas (Pacific), established forbidden zones with a radius of 500 miles and then of 120 miles, *Revue général de droit international public*, 1969, p. 463.

State, can only become juridically a closed sea with difficulty (Baltic, Mediterranean).[54]

Being a coastal State on a sea can also lead indirectly to political preoccupations. For example, Article 9 of the declaration on the continental shelf of the Baltic Sea, signed at Moscow, October 23, 1968, by the Democratic Republic of Germany, Poland and the USSR, stipulates that, "the parts of the continental shelf of the Baltic Sea belonging to the respective coastal States cannot be ceded for research, exploitation or other exploration to third States who are not situated on the coast of the Baltic Sea or to physical or juridical nationals of third States", the other Baltic States, not being great economic powers, the objective of the USSR was perhaps to eliminate the temptation to coastal States to have their continental shelf exploited by western countries, in particular the United States.

Such a diversity of interests and situations could only lead to diversity in the legislation.

B. *The heterogeneous character of the legislation*

An account of the various particularities should provide a sufficiently broad survey of national laws. But this heterogeneous aspect has a second side which comes to light internally in a large number of States, in the new diversification of laws on the marine environment.[55]

As a result, the geographic extent of appropriation can no longer be fully appreciated by the sole reference to territorial waters but must also take account of adjacent zones and the continental shelf.[56]

54. The example of the Baltic is perhaps the most pertinent for the socialist coastal States themselves would, perhaps, have no interest in a "juridically closed sea" which could only increase the Soviet hegemony in the zone.

55. A former diversification existed often between the interests of security, customs, sanitary control, etc. But the extension of economic uses of the sea has resulted in a complete modification with the recent appropriations for adjacent zones and the continental shelf.

56. This first quantitative balance sheet can give a true appreciation of national demands only when considered in the light of their juridical nature (second part) which provides their foundation and justification.

(*a*) *The limited extension of territorial waters*

According to a United Nations document [57] enumerating the legislation on the territorial waters of 93 States, the following balance sheet, after being put up-to-date, [58] shows:

– 3 miles: 20 States
– 4 miles: 3 States
– 6 miles: 12 States
– 10 miles: 25 States
– 12 miles: 47 States
– More than 12 miles: 9 States.

Thus of 93 States enumerated, 84 have territorial waters of 3 to 12 miles while only 9 exceed this limit. Also, often, when an extension of the prerogatives of the coastal State is expounded, it should be noted that this is done only in a limited manner under the guise of territorial waters. [59]

The 12-mile rule has received the consent of half of the States concerned and the United States has just accepted it as a compromise. [60] Although it could be considered as an appropriation in comparison with the 3-mile limit, [61] the enlargement of territorial waters to 12 miles by numerous States *could constitute a limit to further extensions by other States* and lead them to a reasonable compromise: "the powers should admit that they must accept the possibility of an extension to 12 miles if they want to have any chance to lead the international community to consent to the fixation of a limit unilaterally on the high seas which have been multiplying recently". [62] This limit does not appear, however, to

57. UN Doc. A/AC.138/50 (August 6, 1971) and also the fishing circular of the FAO No. 127, FID/C/127.

58. Since the publication of this document, Costa Rica has adhered to the 12-mile limit (Decree No. 2203, February 10, 1972) as well as France (law of December 24, 1971) while Nigeria has opted for 30 miles (decree of August 26, 1971).

59. To this effect, see the declaration of Mr. Castañeda (Mexico) to the 58th Session of the Seabed Committee. UN Doc. A/AC.138/SR.58, p. 199.

60. The American document presented to the Seabed Committee, *op. cit.*, note 26.

61. Only an appropriation by comparison with 3 miles, since, for several States, the Convention of 1958 on territorial waters (Art. 24) permits an extension of sovereignty to a 12-mile maximum (cf. National Assembly, December 8, 1971, No. 2107, p. 6517).

62. Report of the Foreign Affairs Commission on Defense, on the armed forces, of the Senate, *op. cit.*, p. 16.

have slowed down the rate of unilateral appropriations for zones of special jurisdiction, distinct from territorial waters.

(*b*) *The growing extension of "adjacent" zones*[63]

The object of appropriation of these zones, in its economic or, sometimes preventive character, differs profoundly from that of territorial waters, which constitutes an equilibrium between the security of the coastal State and the freedom of navigation.[64]

The fishing riches near coasts is the most frequent motivation for appropriations by coastal States. This tendency affects a considerable number of States having territorial waters less than 12 miles as is shown by the UN statistics on this category of States.[65]

– *Exclusive fishing zone*
 12 miles: 27 States
 18 miles: 1 State.
200 miles: 4 States
– *Fisheries conservation zone*
 20 km : 1 State
100 miles: 3 States
200 miles: 1 State

This movement has perhaps not yet run its course, and the dialectic of appropriations could incite to ensure for themselves acquired rights and short term profits as opposed to the tendency towards appropriation, profitable only in the long term, to the profit of the international community. A resolution of the Council of Ministers of the OAU has, thus, pressed the governments of member States to take all the measures necessary to extend their

63. The term "contiguous zone" does not suit these new economic or "anti-pollution" zones since it evokes Article 24 of the Convention on territorial waters and the contiguous zone which mentions only customs, fiscal, sanitary and immigration objectives.

64. "France contends that the régime of territoriality of waters does not and cannot have an essentially economic object; territorial waters constitute a belt of protection, the extension of which is dictated beyond a doubt by the facts of modern life, but, which cannot be seen as conferring special economic rights". Senate report, *op. cit.*, p. 16.

65. According to the calculations made in UN Doc. A/AC.138/50, *op. cit.*

sovereignty over the resources of the high seas adjacent to their territorial waters.[66]

For its part, Canada has established new fishing zones adjacent to the coast on the original basis of "fisheries closing lines".[67] The appropriation realized is extensive in certain areas since the decree setting the limits[68] closes the Gulf of St. Lawrence by two series of straight lines as well as the Bay of Fundy and joins Queen Charlotte Basin, the Straits of Hecate and the Dixon Entrance by means of "closing lines" of 100 miles along the islands parallel to the Pacific coast.

The Canadian Government has also established in Arctic waters pollution prevention zones of 100 miles[69] from coasts thus establishing a new appropriation still geographically distinct.

The different legislation by its diversity and the economic or technical foundation particular to each State, appears to establish a standard near to that expressed in the Declaration of Lima to the effect that "the right of coastal States has been recognized to establish the limits of their maritime sovereignty or jurisdiction in conformity with reasonable criteria given the geographical, geological and biological realities as well as their socio-economic needs and responsibilities".[70]

66. OAU Resolution 250 (XVII), June 25, 1971.

67. 1970, 18-19 Eliz. II, Bill C. 203 entitled "Law amending the law on territorial waters and fishing zones". For the Canadian Government the arms of the sea transformed into adjacent fishing zones do not constitute part of territorial waters. J. Y. Morin considers that "fishing zones" are not "contiguous zones" within the meaning of the 1958 Convention, but rather, areas under the territorial authority of coastal States for the limited end of fishing. They are "forbidden zones" (*Canadian Yearbook of International Law*, 1970, p. 198).

68. Cf. J. Y. Morin, *op. cit.*, pp. 195-196, note 105. See also, J. A. Beesley, "Fisheries Diplomacy", *Western Fisheries*, June, 1971, pp. 33-38; July, 1971, pp. 23-29. "New closing lines important but only small step forward", *Western Fisheries*, January, 1971, pp. 48-50.

69. 1969-1970, 18-19 Eliz. II, Bill C. 202. From a geographic point of view, it has been noted that these zones "Are not entirely foreign to . . . the forbidden zones provided in the 'International Convention on the Prevention of Hydrocarbon Pollution of the Seas' of 1954. In fact, according to this convention, it is forbidden to all tankers to discharge hydrocarbons within these zones which, since 1962, include the maritime regions of the Canadian coast up to 100 miles from the nearest land. In the Atlantic, north of the 60th parallel, the international forbidden zone is confused with the national protection zone", J. Y. Morin, *op. cit.*, p. 228.

70. Declaration of the Latin American States on the law of the sea. Lima, August 8, 1970, UN Doc. A/AC.138/28.

This tendency would mark the end for universally fixed zones of appropriation to the profit of functional zones varying geographically in time as well as in space.

(*c*) *The quasi-undetermined extension of the continental shelf*

International law contributes to the indeterminate character of national appropriations of the continental shelf [71] through two elements:

– The geographic uncertainty introduced by the criterion of "exploitability" in the first Article of the Geneva Convention on the continental shelf, as opposed to a fixed limit.

– The present uncertainty as to the delimitation of the international zone on the seabed. [72]

As a result, national legislation gives effect to the lack of an international consensus in four ways: [73]

(*a*) certain States claim rights over the continental shelf but without defining the geographic extent of these rights; [74]

(*b*) other States include continental shelf zones in their national territory but always without defining the actual area covered; [75]

(*c*) several countries have incorporated, in their legislation, one of the criteria proposed by the Geneva Convention on the continental shelf; [76]

71. This uncertainty attains the level of the notion of the continental shelf which, by the criterion of exploitability, is not distinguishable from other geological zones on the seabed.

72. The existence of this international zone was affirmed by resolution 2574 A (XXIV) of the General Assembly, December 15, 1969.

73. The following examples are extracts from a study by the Secretariat of the UN, A/AC.135/19, pp. 27-31. For a complete study of the legislation on the limits and scope of national jurisdiction over the continental shelf, see UN Doc. A/AC.135/II and Add. 1.

74. Thus the presidential proclamation of the United States No. 2667 of September 28, 1945, posits that "the continental shelf can be considered a prolongation of the land mass of the coastal State and thus as part of it". To the same effect the royal declaration of Saudia Arabia, May 29, 1949, and the Iranian law of June 19, 1955.

75. Dominican law No. 3342 of July 13, 1952; Indian proclamation of August 30, 1955.

76. Israeli law No. 21 of February 10, 1953, Argentina (1966), Honduras (1965), have adopted the criterion of exploitability; the declaration of the Governor-General of Pakistan dated March 9, 1950, and law No. 2080 of Portugal (March 21, 1956), have opted for the criterion of 100 fathoms or 200 metres.

(*d*) several Latin American States have extended their sovereignty over the continental shelf up to a distance of 200 miles from the coast. [77]

The conventions between several States delimiting their continental shelves do not bring to bear any new elements since they employ one of the preceding criteria. However, they offer the negative advantage of effecting a division between two national sovereignties rather than between the sovereignty of the State and the international marine zone, a position often envisaged in the framework of international negotiation.

Paragraph II. *Multilateral appropriation: international negotiation*

Inter-State agreement is also used for the objective of national appropriation as much at the regional level as at the universal level.

A. *The pretensions of States within the regional framework*

The physical unity of the marine environment submitted to a broad spectrum of national demands has sometimes led regions to a consciousness of the interdependence between man, the land and the sea. [78]

This relationship being differently established depending on the case, it appears, as a result, easier to realize unanimity by accepting diversity than to realize unity by imposing an unjust uniformity. [79] The regional framework, however, can sometimes realize a

77. For example, the Chilean presidential declaration of June 23, 1957, and the Peruvian presidential decree No. 781 of August 1, 1947.

78. This necessity to break out of the national framework tends to create, in the Seabed Committee, hesitations between regionalism and universalism. For certain States, the regional level should be an integral part of any future international régime, which leads to a certain ambiguity: the division is no longer clearly defined between collective appropriation by a group of coastal States and management to the profit of the international community. To this effect, see the declaration of Mr. Legnani (Uruguay) to the 47th Session of the Seabed Committee, UN Doc. A/AC.138/47, p. 35.

79. Declaration of Mr. Tolentino (Philippines) to the 55th Session of the Seabed Committee, UN Doc. A/AC.138/55, p. 133. To the same effect, the declaration of Brazil. Official docs. of the Second Conference of the United Nations on the Law of the Sea, p. 71.

grouping of complementary and not antagonistic interests.

Pursuing this analysis to its end, the notion of regionalism in appropriation could even go beyond its geographic significance. For example, the demands founded on economic considerations of numerous developing coastal States could be discussed among these countries which would lead to a "categorical regionalism" (founded on under-development), no longer solely geographic.[80]

The possible existence of different bases for regionalism should not cause us to forget the diverse degrees which this concept can involve.

In the first place, when one confines the notion of a region to its particular geographic sense, this leads to a simple harmonization of the different national appropriations.

A second possibility has the States of a region participating in the fruits of a collective appropriation. In this case, regionalism is not only a framework for demands, but represents as well an area of inter-State participation. Some examples demonstrate that positive law has produced a multiplicity of solutions based on these theoretical underpinnings, as much in the industrialized countries as in the developing countries.

(*a*) *National appropriation and Latin American regionalism*

The approach of the Second World War brought to the fore again the notion of an "American maritime zone":[81] in 1939, at Panama, the American foreign ministers decided to set, implicitly, the breadth of the American continental sea at 300 miles for the purposes of security.[82] Since then the Inter-American Mutual Assistance Treaty (Rio de Janeiro, 1947) has recognized a "maritime continental area" even more extensive, but still considerably inferior to the zone of application of the treaty providing for the banning of nuclear arms in Latin America (Mexico, 1967).

80. Latin America provides an example of geographic regionalism and of "categorical" regionalism juxtaposed.

81. These different examples are cited by Mr. Legnani (Uruguay) to the 47th Session of the Seabed Committee, UN Doc. A/AC.138/47, p. 34/35.

82. This example affects the entire American hemisphere which demonstrates once again the greater harmony which exists between north and south with respect to security interests than that existing between economic interests which are often antagonistic.

At the economic level, Latin American regionalism is also long established involving most frequently the "demand" form defined above: declaration of Santiago of August 8, 1952, and the Lima agreement of December 4, 1954,[83] declarations of Montevideo (May 8, 1970), and of Lima (August 8, 1970), on the law of the sea.[84]

The "participation" regionalism in Latin America takes two forms, essentially. On the one hand, certain countries having fixed their territorial waters at 200 miles, have established, on the inside, an exclusively national fisheries zone and, beyond this, a zone where foreign fishermen can operate according to different conditions.[85] It is not specified that permits will be issued giving a preference to nationals of other Latin American countries but this possibility is not to be excluded in the future if the degree of economic solidarity is accentuated.[86]

Moreover, by different agreements, several Latin American countries have granted each other reciprocal fishing rights[87] which represent, perhaps, the embryo of a regional agreement on this problem, although other agreements have been signed with States outside the region.[88]

83. *Legislative Series* of the United Nations, Laws and regulations on the régime of the territorial sea, ST/LEG/SER/B/6, pp. 723 and 729.

84. Office of public information, UN/NV/185 and UN Doc. A/AC.138/28.

85. For example, the Argentine law on fisheries No. 17500 of October 25, 1967, reserving for nationals the exploitation of the resources of the sea in a 12-mile area. Beyond this, authorizations to fish can be granted to foreign ships under the conditions stipulated in decree No. 8802 of November 22, 1967, and the regulations passed since then. In the same spirit, cf. the Brazilian decree No. 68458 of April 1, 1971.

86. To this effect Mr. Aguilar (Venezuela) proposed that "States could conclude regional agreements by virtue of which zones situated within the 200-mile limit to which they have a right will be exploited, communally; they could also conclude bilateral or multilateral agreements which would give them reciprocal rights on the respective portions of the zones belonging to them", 64th Session of the Seabed Committee, UN Doc. A/AC.138/SR.64, p. 49.

87. A fishing agreement signed by Argentina and Brazil, December 1967, stipulates that nationals of each contracting party can fish in the territorial waters of the other beyond a 6-mile limit measured from the base line of the said zone.

88. For example the fishing agreement between Japan and Mexico.

(b) *National appropriation and European regionalism*

(1) *The Baltic*

The regional character of appropriation in the Baltic does not arise with respect to the delimitation of territorial waters or a reserved fisheries zone [89] but rather with respect to the continental shelf.

Now that it is possible to survey a maximum depth of 470 metres, it should be stressed that 95 per cent. of the Baltic has a depth less than 200 metres, which permits the appropriation of the entire continental shelf by the coastal States and its delimitation by bilateral agreements. [90]

The regional nature of the total appropriation is perfectly explicit in the first Article on the declaration on the continental shelf of the Baltic Sea: [91] "In conformity with the dispositions of the Geneva Convention of 1958 on the continental shelf, the surface and the underground of the Baltic seabed form a continuous shelf, subject to delimitation by the respective Baltic States".

(2) *Western Europe*

Many of the countries of Western Europe, not having extended their territorial waters to 12 miles, faced mounting competition in

89. In fact, with respect to territorial waters, Finland and Sweden practise 4 miles, Denmark, West Germany, Poland and East Germany, 3 miles. Only the USSR has declared itself in favour of 12 miles. The Nordic States and the USSR have no fishing zone beyond their territorial waters. In fact, although Denmark and Sweden have established a fishing zone of 12 miles (1965 and 1968 respectively), this zone exists only in the Skagerrak and the Kattegat. On the other hand, West Germany and Poland (1970) have established a 12-mile fishing zone.

90. Agreement between Finland and the USSR concerning the limits of maritime zones and the continental shelf of the Gulf of Finland, May 20, 1965 (United Nations, *Treaty Series*, Vol. 566, pp. 32 to 37). Agreement between Finland and the USSR on the limit of the continental shelf in the north-eastern part of the Baltic, May 5, 1967 (Vol. 640, pp. 112 to 115). Treaty between Poland and the USSR on the delimitation of the continental shelf in the Gulf of Gdansk and the South-Eastern Baltic, August 29, 1969 (*Revue générale de droit international public*, 1971, No. 2, pp. 603-604).

91. Signed at Moscow, October 23, 1968, by the USSR, Poland and East Germany, but open to adhesion by all Baltic States (Art. 11). Recall Article 9, *op. cit.*, accentuates the regional character of the appropriation by excluding States not on the Baltic coast and their nationals from the exploration and exploitation of the continental shelf of the Baltic. Text of the

their adjacent waters (the North Sea and the English Channel essentially).

The London Convention on Fisheries (March 9, 1964) signed by 13 European countries[92] sanctions national appropriations, but also, in an indirect way, regional appropriation:

– *Article 2.* The coastal State has the exclusive right to fish and the exclusive jurisdiction with respect to fisheries in a six-mile zone measured from the base line of the territorial waters;

– *Article 3.* In the zone between six and twelve miles measured from the base line of the territorial waters, the right to fish is exercised only by the coastal State and the other contracting parties whose fishing ships have habitually fished in this zone between January 1, 1953 and December 31, 1962.[93]

This geographic regionalism also has its political side which is accentuated by the fact that the members of the arbitral tribunal provided for in Annex II must have the nationality of an OECD member State (Art. 4, Annex 2).

A final example of national appropriation and regional delimitation is provided by the continental shelf of the North Sea, generally at a depth of less than 200 metres (except the Norwegian trough which is between 200 and 650 metres deep) which permits the use of the uncontested depth criterion of the Geneva convention except for the Norwegian continental shelf.[94]

---

declaration, J. P. Queneudec, *Droit maritime international*, Pédone, 1971, pp. 30-32.

92. West Germany, Austria, Belgium, Denmark, Spain, France, Ireland, Italy, Luxembourg, Holland, Portugal, the United Kingdom, Sweden.

93. With respect to the issue of appropriation the effect of the regulations of the Common Market poses certain problems. Regulation No. 2141/70 of the Council of October 20, 1970 (*J.O.C.E.*, L236 of October, 1970) provides in Article 2, section 1, the principle of freedom of access of fishing ships bearing the flag of one of the member States in the maritime waters under the sovereignty or the jurisdiction of other member States. This principle could be interpreted as a limit to national appropriation. But, from the point of view of third States with respect to the Six, it could support national appropriation since these do not prejudice the interests of member States of the EEC. Thus, regional appropriation emerges, subordinated and closely linked to national appropriation. The ambiguity remains, however, since while from the point of view of third States, this resembles the first type of appropriation, from the point of view of the Six, this measure could appear to be an appropriation of the "management" type.

94. Agreement delimiting the respective continental shelves of Great Britain and Norway (March 10, 1965), Great Britain and Holland (October 6,

However, with respect to this problem, the terminology requires some explanation: according to several developing countries the European North Sea States have appropriated the entire continental shelf of this sea,[95] so they must not oppose maritime claims of developing countries.

It would appear, however, that this interpretation confuses the degree and the nature of the appropriation. The International Court of Justice in the *North Sea Continental Shelf* cases affirmed that "the rights of the coastal State concerning the continental shelf zone which constitutes a natural prolongation of its territory under the sea *exist ipso facto and ab initio* by virtue of the sovereignty of the State over its territory and by an extension of this sovereignty in an exercise of sovereign rights for the purpose of exploration of the seabed and exploitation of its natural resources".

"From the geological point of view, the underground of the North Sea is part of the continental platform on which the European Continent and the British Isles rest. A large part of the North Sea covers land which has only recently been submerged".[96] Consequently, the continental shelf of the North Sea is truly the natural prolongation of the territory of coastal States: *thus there is not appropriation but only occupation* of a territory previously neglected, but which was always under the sovereignty of the coastal power, which is not true of the adjacent waters in the case of the "extensive" demands.[97]

The necessary harmonization of the different interpretations

1965), Great Britain and Denmark (March 3, 1966), treaties between Holland and West Germany concerning the lateral delimitation of the continental shelf near the coast (December 1, 1964), and Denmark and West Germany (June 9, 1965); agreements delimiting the continental shelf between two countries: Denmark-Norway (December 8, 1965) and Denmark-Holland (March 31, 1966). Texts reproduced in UN Doc. A/AC.135/10/Rev. 1.

95. Cf. the declarations to the Committee on the Seabed of Mr. Arias Schreiber (Peru) and of Mr. Allouane (Algeria) to the 46th and 54th Sessions, UN Doc. A/AC.138/SR.46, p. 17 and A/AC.138/SR.54, p. 19.

96. Ch. Vallée, *Le plateau continental dans le droit positif actuel*, Pédone 1971, p. 255.

See also J. Lang, "The Continental Shelf of the North Sea", *LGDJP* 1970, p. 163.

97. This interpretation illustrates the difficulty in establishing a precise dividing line between law and geography which are often closely linked. The same applies with respect to law and the economic justifications of the demands of numerous States.

thus lends importance to the works undertaken under the auspices of the United Nations.

B. *The claims of States within the framework of the United Nations*

The "Committee on Peaceful Uses of the Seabed and the Oceans Beyond the Limits of National Jurisdiction"[98] has seen the presentation of different State proposals on the future international régime for the seabed. For our purposes, these propositions have a double interest:

–Certain proposals delimit clearly national and international zones attributing to an international organism the responsibility for the management of the common heritage of mankind.

–Other propositions also effect this geographical division between the coastal State and the international community. However, given the limited role which they attribute to the international organ, the management for the good of mankind is in danger of masking implicit national appropriations, changeable in time as well as in space.

(*a*) *Geographically explicit national appropriation*

The diversity of national interests comes to bear directly on the submarine limits of national jurisdiction which should define the future international régime for the seabed. The position adopted in the Seabed Committee by the delegate from Singapore illustrates, significantly, the difficulties encountered with the different criteria for delimitation: "logically, it is impossible to divide the world into less than nine interest groups. First there are the coastal States whose continental shelf is extensive; secondly, there are coastal States which have a limited continental shelf or none at all but which face the high seas; third, landlocked States; fourth, States whose coastline is only prolonged by a continental shelf; fifth, coastal States whose economy depends on fishing in zones contiguous to their coasts; sixth, States whose economy is linked to liquid or mineral resources; seventh, archipelagal States for whom the definition of territorial waters has a special significance;

98. Cited in this report under the title "Seabed Committee".

eighth, the group of developed maritime States; and, finally a group of maritime States disposing of underwater technology". [99]

However, three criteria have been proposed most frequently in the course of discussions and proposed treaties, the third being a simple juxtaposition of the first two.

(1) *The criterion of distance*

The national appropriation of a maritime zone of 200 miles, already realized by several Latin American States in their respective legislation, has also been proposed by Malta in a proposed treaty on maritime areas. [100]

The French document presented to the Committee in 1970 [101] provided no delimitation of national jurisdiction, but the representative of France made a declaration in favour of a zone defined by the simple criterion of distance calculated from the coast, [102] a position shared by Brazil. [103]

(2) *The criterion of depth*

Among the different texts, only the proposed convention of the United Nations on the international seabed zone presented by the United States adopted the 200-metre criterion as a limit to the national seabed. [104]

(3) *The "mixed" criterion*

With its combination of the two preceding criteria, the mixed criterion is the most frequently invoked since the possible choice

99. Declaration of Mr. Koh to the 50th Session, March 17, 1971, UN Doc. A/AC.138/SR.50, p. 59. It is also necessary to note that recognition by the UN of an international zone beyond national jurisdiction excludes any régime which would extend the sovereignty of States over the entire seabed. On this problem, cf. UN Doc. A/AC.135/19 Add. 2.

100. UN Doc. A/AC.138/53, title 2, Chapter IX, Art. 36. As we have already remarked, the Maltese proposal does not recognize this jurisdiction in the case of islands which are not States in themselves, except under special agreements (Art. 37, sec. 2).

101. UN Doc. A/AC.138/27.

102. Declaration of Mr. Jeannel to the 54th Session of the Committee, March 22, 1971, UN Doc. 138/SR.54, p. 109.

103. Declaration of Mr. Saraiva Guerreiro, UN Doc. A/AC.138/SR.54, p. 112.

104. UN Doc. A/AC.138/25, Art. 1, sec. 2. It must be noted that this document establishes a zone under international mandate reserving certain rights to the coastal State and being based on a geological criterion (Art. 26).

between distance and depth permits the satisfaction of the maximum number of coastal States. Furthermore, the origin of the proposals employing this notion testifies to the relatively generalized interest it arouses. [105] However, this beginning of unanimity is rendered more uncertain by the fact that the numerous texts mention distance without specifying it in quantitative terms in most cases.

(*b*) *National appropriation politically and economically implicit*

A State, by its economic supremacy or its political importance, could exercise, in the future international zone, an activity equivalent in practice to national appropriation. In this light appropriation would be a quasi-automatic consequence of the application of a type of international régime proposed by certain powers and the existence of a gradation in development.

To this effect, the French proposal [106] foresees as organs of the mechanism in the international zone, a conference of plenipotentiaries and a technical committee backing it up, which would be only "organisms for meeting, exchange of views, negotiation and, eventually arbitration". For the exploitation of mineral resources not requiring fixed installations, a simple non-exclusive registration is provided for while for mineral substances requiring fixed equipment, the States would be granted zones. Even in this latter case and despite the provision for quotas, technological inequalities could transform into appropriation what is presented as a framework for international management. [107]

105. The United Republic of Tanzania (A/AC.138/33, Art. 3), Poland (A/AC.138/44, Art. 3, sec. 15), proposal submitted by Afghanistan, Austria, Belgium, Hungary, Nepal, Holland and Singapore (A/AC.138/55, I.A.: choice between 200 metres or 40 miles). The proposition of the USSR (A/AC.138/43, Arts. 2 and 3) would have the international zone begin beyond the continental shelf. But, when there is no continental shelf, another criterion is foreseen (undefined) which would logically be based on distance.

106. UN Doc. A/AC.138/27 II B (*b*) 3.

107. All the more since "the grant of a zone to a State is dependent on the presentation of a candidate company for a claim in this zone" (B, a, 2), a company which would have to provide sufficient financial and technical guarantees.

The British proposal (A/AC.138/26) and that of Japan (A/AC.138/63) could lead to the same "deviations" because of the emphasis placed more on

To a certain extent, the management could be analyzed from a different perspective: it would amount to organizing the co-ordination of appropriations by the most developed States in order to avoid conflicts of sovereignty, the management for the profit of mankind representing only the constantly invoked "by-product" of a situation of force typical of relational society.

Thus, in this latter hypothesis, national appropriation can develop to the benefit of powerful States without the classical support of territorial sovereignty. Once again, the interests of a category of States provoke a certain form of appropriation. Consequently, these situations of fact have led to a renovation of the juridical nature of appropriation and of its different expressions.

II. THE JURIDICAL NATURE OF APPROPRIATION

Oceanography uses certain technology amongst the most advanced of contemporary science. Whether it is a simple coincidence or the expression of a logical parallelism, the law of the sea tends to be an advanced element among the other branches of law.

Particularly, sovereignty tends to lose its mythical aura and take on a more concrete significance. Traditionally, sovereignty represented the essential attribute of a State in the international society resting on the very concept of the State. This completely abstract conception leads to juridical equality between States.

However, recent aspects of international law tend to view the State from the point of view of economic reality and no longer from the point of view of a conceptual abstraction. International society since decolonization [108] compared to the former régime, is characterized by the same differences as those which existed between the English nobility and the French nobility of the former régime: the developing State does not consider it a derogation from international practice to project on the international level its internal economic difficulties. This consciousness of the necessity

---

inter-State co-ordination than on management for profit of the entire international community.

108. Decolonization of the 1960s, but also Latin American juridical regionalism, must be taken into consideration for this represents the first contestation of the European juridical and political order.

for a global strategy has led the developed States to adopt the same approach, particularly with respect to the protection of the environment.

This global strategy, dictated more and more by the international nature of problems, should provoke the international approach which led to the recognition of the existence of a "common heritage of mankind".

The juridical nature of appropriation should thus be analyzed stressing two elements:

– the updating of the basis of States' claims which give effect not simply to the political presence of the State, but also to the consequences of the economic use of the oceans;

– the extension of the rights of States as opposed to the concept of the common heritage of mankind, that is to say, the difficult equilibrium between these two types of appropriation and the transgression of sovereignty in the new formulas.

Paragraph I. *The updating of the basis of States' claims*

On April 7, 1970, Canada amended the clause dealing with its acceptance of the jurisdiction of the International Court of Justice [109] removing disputes relating to conservation, the exploitation of the living resources of the sea and the prevention of pollution in adjacent zones.

Canada's reasoning is particularly interesting since Canada justifies this unilateral action along its coasts as a positive contribution to international law, "a current initiative of striking importance and relevance in the context of the dynamic creative development of international law". [110] In this new perspective,

109. According to the procedure in Article 36, section 2, of the Statute of the Court.

110. Cited by Richard B. Bilder, "The Canadian Arctic Waters Pollution Prevention Act", *Proceedings of the Fifth Annual Conference of the Law of the Sea Institute*, Rhode Island, 1970, p. 218. To the same effect, External Affairs Minister Sharp affirmed that "the Bill we have introduced should be regarded as a stepping-stone towards the elaboration of an international legal order which will protect and preserve this planet . . . We are determined to act as pioneers pushing back the frontiers of international law", p. 218.

the Court, by applying traditional principles would run the risk of hindering the development of law. [111]

This Canadian position portrays in a significant manner the character of the basis of States' claims compared to classic international law and the symbolic relationship of these claims with the economy, strategy and the environment.

A. *National appropriation, product of the economic exploitability of the oceans*

Certain aspects of international law since the Second World War provide several examples emphasizing the "subordination of certain spatial relations to human ends". [112] Thus, in the *Fisheries* case, the International Court of Justice admitted that "fishing rights founded on vital needs of the population and attested to by practice established peacefully over a long period of time can be legitimately taken into consideration . . .". [113] To the same effect, Article 4, section 4, of the Geneva Convention on territorial waters admits that, "for the determination of certain base lines, economic interests particular to the region in question whose reality and importance are clearly attested to by long practice" can be taken into consideration.

In spite of everything, these principles are based on the exceptional character of certain situations. Now, several delegations to the Seabed Committee appear to consider more and more that the delimitation of maritime boundaries is more an economic than a political problem: "to negotiate the limits is essentially to negotiate resources and, for the coastal State, that is to negotiate its marine property, that is to say, the resources existing in proximity to its coasts, property indissolubly linked to its territory". [114]

As a result, economic development is going to determine the sovereignty of the coastal State over its resources while the prin-

111. Declaration to this effect of Canadian Prime Minister, P. E. Trudeau, cf. Bilder, *op. cit.*, p. 211.

112. Ch. De Visscher, *Problèmes de confins en droit international public, op. cit.*, p. 112.

113. Ch. De Visscher, *loc. cit.*, p. 111.

114. Declaration of Mr. Zegers (Chile) to the 48th Session of the Seabed Committee, UN Doc. A/AC.138/SR.48, p. 43.

ciples of rational economic management lead to a necessary conservation of the latter.

(*a*) *Sovereignty, the consequence of economic development*

Since their accession to independence, the developing coastal States have become conscious, not only of their proverty, but also of the immense potential of the adjacent marine resources. This double awareness should be rapidly synthesized in what certain authors qualify as "bioma" or "ecosystem theories": [115] "there is an indissoluble link between the land, man and the sea, between economic development and the vast resources of the ocean". [116] The sea and man constitute a biological unity, the population of the coastal State represents only a link in this biological chain stretching from microscopic plants to the large marine mammals.

The conservation of the biological unity permits, in a first stage, the maintenance of a nutritional equilibrium for the coastal States and, later, contributes to economic development. [117] This first theory is then refined and extended: "the possibilities of exploitation of the seabed have enlarged the scope for demands. *There has been an extension of 'biological rights' to 'mineral rights' of the coastal State in a global strategy for development".* [118]

115. See Cisneros: "The 200-mile limit in the South Pacific: a new position in international law with a human and juridical content", ABA Section of international law and comparative law, 1964, *Proceedings* 56 (1965), pp. 58-60.

116. Declaration of Mr. Zegers (Chile) to the 48th Session of the Seabed Committee, UN Doc. A/AC.138/SR.48, p. 40.

117. See, to this effect, the declarations of the representative of Peru to the 486th Meeting of the 6th Commission of the General Assembly and the 46th Session of the Seabed Committee (UN Doc. A/AC.138/SR.48, p. 16) and of Mr. Perez-Hernandez (Spain) to the 48th Session (UN Doc. A/AC.138/SR.48, pp. 46-47). Similarly, at the conference of 1958 on the law of the sea, the delegate from Chile insisted on the fact that the "Declaration of Santiago" was of a defensive nature and that "its sole object was the conservation of the living resources of the sea for the benefit of the inhabitants of the region", UN Conf. Rec. 7, UN Doc. A/Conf.13/39 (1958).

118. Alain Piquemal, *Le Fond des mers, patrimoine commun de l'humanité*, Masters Thesis, 226 p., Nice, 1971, p. 69. "The United States contest the principle of biological unity, preferring to it that of 'economic relationship' ": "the relationship of coastal communities to the sea is . . . *one of an economic rather than a biological character*" (United States, Comments on the proposals of Ecuador, Chile and Peru in Santiago negotiations, 37). This

The action undertaken by the UN in the framework of the protection of natural riches can be invoked to this effect. Thus General Assembly resolution No. 1803 (XVII) of December 14, 1962, declares: "the right to permanent sovereignty of peoples and of nations over their riches and their natural resources should be exercised in the interests of national development and the well-being of the affected population". [119]

As a result, the Latin American developing countries have only had to enlarge the national base covered by the UN resolutions with, however, a difference in the reasoning: "in resolution 1803 (XVII) of December 14, 1962, the right of sovereignty should have as a *consequence*, national development. To the contrary, in the Latin American declarations, there is an inversion and the necessity for economic development has as a consequence the extension of the principle of sovereignty up to a distance of 200 miles from coasts". [120]

(b) The conservation of resources, an element of rational economic management

Contrary to what was formerly advanced, the marine biological resources are not inexhaustible and regulation is indispensable in order to ensure their protection. In the absence of such regulation at the international level, numerous countries have had to restrict the freedom of fishing on the high seas and establish special maritime jurisdictions.

This extension of national appropriation towards the high seas is interesting since it rejuvenates the classic concept of "State security": the "economic security" of the State and its population, that is to say the guarantee of optimum economic development, has been added to security of a military, customs or other nature . . . as a motivating force with respect to territorial waters and the contiguous zone. This evolution is, beyond a doubt, not

---

principle is interesting for the economic relationship better explains the demands for mineral resources, *loc. cit.*, p. 69, note 123.

119. Principle confirmed by resolution 2158 (XXI) of November 25, 1966. It is to be noted that resolution 250 (XVII) of the OAU proclaiming permanent sovereignty of African countries over fishing resources off African coasts brings to mind in its whereas clauses resolution 2158 (XXI) A.G.

120. Alain Piquemal, *op. cit.*, p. 16.

surprising since it gives effect to economic "interventionism" by the State in more and more varied areas.

To a certain extent, concerning the question of the limits of national jurisdiction in the law of the sea, the "consumer" has replaced the military. Already, the criterion of exploitability of the convention on the continental shelf has opened the way, but the occupation of fishing zones is still more important for countries living principally from the resources of the sea. The difference existing between *the indispensable* and *the superfluous* could symbolize the degree of interest between biological resources for the developing countries and the mineral perspectives of the continental shelf for industrialized countries.

However, certain countries, principally the USSR have contested the economic rationality of the extensive fishing zones practised by different developing countries [121] and denounced the unfortunate effects of such a policy: "the extension of territorial waters and the exclusive fishing zone will benefit neither all the developing countries nor only developing countries, but only countries, be they developed or developing, who possess rich fishing stocks off their coasts. The extension of the exclusive fishing zone does not necessarily signify either conservation of the biological resources of the sea or their rational exploitation. It could even be that it would have the effect, on important fishing stocks, of smaller catches if foreign ships are forbidden to fish where the coastal States, lacking a sufficiently developed fishing industry, could not realize the optimal catch. Besides, the excessive unilateral demands of certain States risk creating international tensions and provoking conflicts".[122]

121. Soviet experts have calculated that, if the majority of countries imposed a 200-mile limit, more than 144 million square kilometres of the 361 million square kilometre total surface area of the ocean–that is 40 per cent. of this area–would become territorial waters. Thus 44 per cent. of the Pacific Ocean would become territorial waters and only countries possessing a long coastline would benefit from such a situation. The United States would dispose of more than 8 million square kilometres of territorial waters, Canada, more than 5.5 million and the USSR more than 9 million. Declaration of Mr. Khlestov (USSR) to the 6th Session of Sub-Committee II of the Seabed Committee, July 30, 1971, UN Doc. A/AC.138/SCII/SR.6, p. 11.

122. Declaration of Mr. Natorf (Poland) to the 54th Session of the Seabed Committee (UN Doc. A/AC.138/SR.54, p. 125). To the same effect, declarations of Mr. Khlestov (USSR) to the 56th Session (UN Doc. A/AC.

National appropriation towards the high seas, linked with a more and more intensive economic use of the oceans by coastal States, thus conflicts once again with the de facto appropriation towards shorelines by the great maritime powers on the high seas. The latter also have a large role to play in the new strategic perspectives.

B. *National appropriation and strategic perspectives*

The different national demands could impair directly the strategic interests of the great powers through the problem of straits. [123]

Article 16, section 4, of the Convention on Territorial Waters and the Contiguous Zone stipulates that "innocent passage by foreign ships cannot be suspended in straits which, placing in communication one part of the high seas with another part of the high seas or with the territorial waters of a foreign State, serve international navigation".

Consequently, several States have feared that extension of territorial waters might jeopardize this principle: without evoking appropriation of 200 miles, "the fixation of territorial waters at a distance of 12 miles is directly linked to the question of free pas-

---

138/SR.56, pp. 158-159); of Mr. Ogiso (Japan) to the 53rd Session (UN Doc. A/AC.138/SR.53, p. 101) and of Mr. Graham (United Kingdom) (UN Doc. A/AC.138/SC.II/SR.14, p. 5). Moreover, it appears, according to Mr. Khlestov, that *fishing does little harm to the biological riches of the developing countries since only these countries fish in their waters: the statistics of the FAO show that of a total* of 56.6 million tons fished on the high seas in 1968, 23.1 million tons came from the Atlantic—of which about 17 million were from the North Atlantic region far removed from the developing countries of Asia, Africa and Latin America. The total catch in the Pacific was up to 31.3 million tons of which about 16 million tons were from the North Pacific. About 12 million tons came from the South-Eastern Pacific, in particular from the zone situated off the coast of Peru, Chile and Ecuador. In this region, fishing is done mainly by coastal States. Only 3 per cent. of world catches come from the Indian Ocean which bathes the coasts of developing countries in Asia and Africa.

123. The regulation of passage through straits extends outside even this framework and affects the freedom of navigation in its entirety. But the example of the Strait of Tiran demonstrates sufficiently that the freedom of passage in general can have strategic repercussions directly endangering the political and economic security of the State. Moreover, innocent passage through straits is more likely to be limited when warships are involved.

sage in straits used for international navigation and of freedom of overflight of these straits". [124] To this effect, Soviet experts have calculated that if territorial waters were fixed uniformly at 12 miles, more than 100 straits would become territorial waters of coastal States.

However, it is clear from different declarations that countries having extended their territorial waters still guarantee freedom of passage in the straits.

Thus Mr. Yvon Bourges, during the discussion in the National Assembly of the proposed law relative to the delimitation of French territorial waters, declared: "in conformity with our general doctrine of freedom of navigation and while waiting for an international convention to determine a conventional régime for passage in straits covered by the territorial waters of coastal States, we must set the example by allowing in these straits a zone for passage submitted to a less restrictive régime than innocent passage". [125]

Similarly, a Malaysian law of 1969 has set the breadth of territorial waters at 12 miles. Indonesia, immediate neighbour of Malaysia in the Strait of Malacca, having done the same, the two Governments have concluded an agreement fixing the demarcation line between their territorial waters in this strait and have guaranteed the right of innocent passage of foreign ships. [126]

124. Declaration of Mr. Khlestov (USSR) to the 56th Session of the Seabed Committee, UN Doc. A/AC.138/SR.56, p. 161.

125. *J.O.*, Debates, National Assembly, 1st session, December 8, 1971, p. 6517. To the same effect, Senate report, *op. cit.*, pp. 16 and 18. The straits in issue are the Straits of Dover (if Great Britain adopted 12 miles), the Strait of Bab-el-Mandeb facing the territory of Afars and Issas and the Strait of Bonifacio between Corsica and Sardina.

Article 3 of the law of December 24, 1971 on the delimitation of territorial waters gives juridical effect to these positions: "when the difference between the base lines along French coasts and those along the coasts of a foreign State facing them is equal to or less than 24 miles or no longer permits the existence of a high seas zone sufficient for navigation, dispositions can be taken into account to assure free maritime and aerial navigation, respecting international conventions and, if applicable, after agreement with the affected States".

126. See the declaration of Mr. Vohrah (Malaysia) to the 58th Session of the Seabed Committee, UN Doc. A/AC.138/SR.58, p. 195. Joint declaration to the same effect of Chile and Argentina with respect to the "Beagle" channel (*Revue générale de droit international public*, 1971, No. 4, pp. 1231 to 1237).

It would however be necessary to establish precisely the scope of national appropriations. In fact, submitting straits to the régime of territorial waters and even guaranteeing the right of innocent passage, would not give the freedom of overflight of these territorial waters. Otherwise, two different régimes inside territorial waters would be created which would appear unacceptable to certain delegations. [127] To this effect, Article II, section 1, of the proposed articles on the breadth of territorial waters, the straits and fisheries, presented to Sub-Committee II by the United States, attempts to harmonize appropriations with an extended freedom of passage: "in the straits used for international navigation between one part of the high seas and another part of the high seas or the territorial waters of a foreign State, all ships and all aircraft in transit have the right, for the purpose of passage through the straits and over them, to the same freedom of navigation and overflight as on the high seas". [128]

This problem of freedom of passage has also arisen in the context of the struggle against pollution.

C. *National appropriation and the protection of the environment*

The prevention and control of pollution of the seas can raise direct conflicts of interest between coastal States and maritime States, conflicts insufficiently regulated by existing agreements. Canada has thus remarked that "conventional law elaborated under the auspices of IMCO has naturally had as its goal the protection of the interests of navigation on the basis of traditional principles of international law; *the protection of the interests of coastal States has not been a major preoccupation*". [129]

127. See the declaration of Mr. Kaniaru (Kenya) to the 8th Session of Sub-Committee II of the Seabed Committee, UN Doc. A/AC.138/SC.II/SR.8, p. 11.

128. UN Doc. A/AC.138/SC.II/L.4 and Corr. 1, *op. cit.* See also the declaration of Mr. Pardo (Malta) to the 57th Session of the Seabed Committee establishing a distinction between the straits and a regulation, UN Doc. A/AC.138/SR.57, pp. 180-181.

129. Declaration of Mr. Beesley (Canada) to the 58th Session of the Seabed Committee, UN Doc. A/AC.138/SR.58, p. 209, which furnishes, as an example, the international convention on intervention on the high seas in case of an accident leading to, or which could lead to, hydrocarbon pollution

The defence of the marine environment by the coastal State thus broadens the considerations to be taken into account with respect to innocent passage. The Canadian Government has made it known that it "cannot accept a right of innocent passage if this right is defined in such a way that it prevents coastal States from exercising control over water pollution. *The passage of a ship which could create a pollution hazard is not inoffensive* since it constitutes a menace to the security of the coastal State contrary to Article 14 of the Convention on Territorial Waters". [130]

The Canadian legislation, already cited in the first part, poses all the more problems since the extension of territorial waters to 12 miles places the North-West Arctic passage under the territorial competence of Canada. As a result, Canada, by its regulation of passage in this strait, diminishes the freedom of navigation in order to protect the marine environment. [131] The old principle of freedom gives ground to ecological necessity.

The "law on the prevention of pollution in arctic water zones contiguous to the continent and the Canadian arctic islands"[132] completes these dispositions permitting the Government to establish, by decree, the "zones of control of navigational security" in which it can forbid access to any ship not respecting the regulatory norms established.

The opposition is still manifest between the interests of coastal States and those of maritime States and always portrays a dialectical evolution: Canada has perhaps realized a new form of na-

---

adopted by IMCO in 1969: "that gives to the contracting parties the right to sink a damaged ship belonging to another contracting party when the action created a risk of pollution, but does not grant to coastal States the right to regulate the passage of ships presenting such a danger before the accident occurs".

130. Cited by J. Y. Morin, *op. cit.*, p. 217.

131. With respect to the nature of this strait, Canada, in a note of April 16, 1970, rejected "any proposition according to which the north-west passage is an international strait . . . The passage . . . has not achieved the status of an international strait by virtue of customary use, and it has not been defined as such by conventional international law. The Canadian Government reiterated its determination to open the passage . . . to safe navigation for merchant vessels of all States, *provided, however, that the necessary conditions are met for the protection of the fragile ecological equilibrium in the Canadian Arctic*". Cited by J. Y. Morin, *op. cit.,* p. 219, note 163.

132. Bill C. 202, 18-19 Elizabeth II, 1969-1970, *op. cit.*

tional appropriation but only as a reaction to the abusive practices of the maritime powers. These practices also constitute a form of appropriation since they destroy by their pollution parcels of the marine domain.[133] In this context, it was necessary to recognize a common heritage of mankind in order to limit the "escalation" of national demands.

Paragraph II. *The extension of States' rights as opposed to "The Common Heritage of Mankind"*

Although affirmed by different resolutions of the UN General Assembly, the international zone called "the Common Heritage of Mankind" has not yet been delimited. However, its existence can serve as an indication of the range of different national appropriations realized. Consequently, the latter are differentiated according to whether they appear as a *substitute for international action* or, on the contrary, as *a complement to international action*. The latter form reveals in this manner an attempt to move from the State to the international community according to a mixed formula associating the two entities.

A. *National appropriation, substitute for international action*

Certain countries do not express their fundamental hostility to a future international régime, but prefer to ensure their "economic well-being" in a unilateral way, even if they later modify their positions.

133. Related to this problem, the United States having had to dump containers of nerve gas in the Atlantic, the Seabed Committee discussed at the 37th Session a proposed declaration on the immersion of toxic substances on the seabed and in the oceans, UN Doc. A/AC.138/SR.37 and 38.

Implicit national appropriation by the great maritime powers has also been denounced by Mr. Beesley as an abusive use of freedom: "... the notion of freedom of the seas, such as it has evolved over the centuries, has been transformed into the equivalent of a mobile jurisdiction–sovereignty being exercised where the flag flies, for those countries powerful enough to impose their will", 63rd Session of the Committee on the Seabed, UN Doc. A/AC. 138/SR.63, p. 35.

However, in this framework limited to the State, the juridical solutions can differ according to the role played by the sovereignty. As it was noted by the representative of Australia to Sub-Committee II of the Seabed Committee, "it would be better now to recognize that the fixation of the limit of territorial waters is a *distinct question* from that of establishing the limits of zones where the coastal State exercises other, less important, forms of jurisdiction such as the control of fisheries. It is essential that this distinction be made and that the fear be suppressed, that the extension of a partial jurisdiction will lead to what is called 'creeping jurisdiction' through the progressive enlargement of territorial waters". [134]

It follows from this that appropriation in full sovereignty is applied in the traditional way to the concept of territorial waters, while appropriation limited to the exclusive use of marine resources gives effect to the new necessity for adjacent economic zones.

Under the circumstances, territorial waters are "a belonging of the State whose coasts they bathe. They are an inseparable part, because international law envisages them as the continuation of terrestrial domain into the sea. *The exact nature of this relationship is not one of simple proximity or contiguity, but one of 'continuity' in the precise sense of the term*". [135]

Thus, sovereignty can be analyzed as the juridical expression of the geographic notion of "continuity". On the other hand, the exclusive use in a functional way gives effect only to simple contiguity, to which recent national appropriations have given a different significance from that underlying the Convention on territorial waters and the contiguous zone.

(*a*) *The hypothesis of sovereignty, expression of "continuity"* [136]

Charles De Visscher noted several years ago that "tension continues between the traditional and essentially political notion of a

134. Declaration of Mr. Setter (Australia) to the 6th Session, UN Doc. A/AC.138/SC.II/SR.6, p. 5. See, to the same effect, the declaration of Mr. Small (New Zealand) to the 62nd Session of the plenary Committee, UN Doc. A/AC.138/SR.62, p. 22.

135. Ch. De Visscher, *Problèmes de confins en droit international public*, *op. cit.*, p. 43.

136. To better situate the notion of sovereignty over maritime areas, it is

homogeneous zone of full sovereignty and the modern vision of a diversified and competitive international *exploitation* of the riches of the sea". [137]

This analysis, still valid, should however be rounded out by the addition of a third possibility: national exploitation by the coastal State in an exclusive or preferential way, of a zone of "functional jurisdiction".

The political character of the sovereignty zone is illustrated in a highly significant way by the traditional justifications of territorial waters (military security, customs, etc.). For certain States, the consequences of this link to sovereignty are reflected directly in the delimitation of territorial waters: "the coastal State exercises all the attributes of sovereignty over territorial waters. With the exception of the right of innocent passage, it is legitimately entitled to restrict, if not to forbid totally, the exercise of the different freedoms of the sea, in the interior of this zone. The fact that a State decides not to make full use of this faculty *is absolutely irrelevant from a juridical point of view and does not result in the loss of its discretionary powers*. Under these conditions, it is juridically unthinkable that the coastal State has the absolute freedom to unilaterally define the true limits of its territorial waters".[138]

Sovereignty, permitting such a restriction of the freedom of the seas, should not then be extended over zones with uniquely economic purposes. To this effect, numerous experts have declared before the Foreign Affairs Commission of the National Assembly that the notion of territorial waters is distinct as much from the notion of a reserved fishing zone as from that of exploitation of the seabed and that any decision concerning territorial waters was not binding in the future with respect to particular problems. [139]

---

to be noted that the Convention on territorial waters affirms the sovereignty of the State over territorial waters (Art. 1, sec. 1), but it regulates the exercise of sovereignty under the conditions specified by the different articles and international law (Art. 1, sec. 2). Similarly, for the continental shelf, sovereign rights are involved, but they are limited to certain activities.

137. *Les effectivités du droit international public*, Pédone, 1967, p. 49.

138. Declaration of Mr. Castañeda (Mexico) to the 58th Session of the Seabed Committee, UN Doc. A/AC.138/SR.58, p. 199.

139. Report on the proposed law relating to the delimitation of French territorial waters, National Assembly, No. 2107, appendix to the oral pro-

Thus, it has been noted that in the majority of national appropriations it is a question "not of an extension of territorial waters strictly speaking, but rather of the exercise of a special jurisdiction for certain specific ends". [140]

The affirmation that territorial waters constitute a zone subject to the sovereignty of the coastal State can thus dissuade the coastal State from using this juridical form for purely economic motives. [141]

Similarly, the extension of national appropriation has been compared with the notion of contiguous zone in order to diminish its effect as Paul Reuter stressed: "the contiguous zone appears as an instrument of negotiation and understanding; everything granted with respect to the contiguous zone permits the extension of territorial waters to be contained". [142] Contiguity retains all of its topicality, but the new economic perspectives in the marine domain have bereft it of its traditional substance.

(*b*) *The hypothesis of exclusive use, expression of contiguity*

Article 24 of the Convention on territorial waters sanctions the existence of a zone contiguous to territorial waters on which the coastal State exercises different non-economic controls. Article 6 of the Convention on fishing affirms the interest of the coastal State with respect to the conservation of biological resources on the high seas adjacent to its territorial waters.

These dispositions thus give effect to national goals which no longer correspond with the present reality. Mr. André Gros pointed out that, for many States, the Convention on fishing had missed the real problem, "which stemmed less from the very

---

ceedings of the session of December 8, 1971, p. 10. These declarations were made after Mr. Sanford, the representative from Polynesia, proposed his amendment to set the limit of territorial waters at 250 miles for the French territories in the Pacific.

140. Jorge Castañeda, *op. cit.*, p. 199.

141. This objective could however be attained through the rigid position of certain countries who are partisans of a fishing jurisdiction limited, in general, to territorial waters (FAO Doc. COFI/72/7, Supp. 1 of November 16, 1971, pp. 2 to 4). As a result, the maximum limit of territorial waters not being set, the coastal States could have a tendency to extend to the maximum their territorial waters in order to exploit the fishing resources.

142. *Droit international public*, 1968, p. 206.

general issue of conservation of the riches of the sea threatened by over-exploitation or irrational exploitation than from *the concern of each State to reserve for itself the exploitation of fisheries*". [143]

Thus the interventionist role of the State takes on a new dimension in the international context: the State must act, with respect to other States, not only to guarantee its political security but also to promote the "economic security" of its people. International reality reproduces to a certain degree the internal evolution: the "police" State has become the "welfare" State through the expedient of "functional jurisdictions".

In this framework, a greater and greater number of States have declared themselves in favour of preferential or exclusive fishing rights for coastal States beyond their territorial waters. [144] A synthesis of these demands as a whole, not based on sovereignty but on a functional jurisdiction, has led several delegations to recognize, beyond territorial waters set at 12 miles, an economic zone called the "patrimonial sea" with a maximum breadth of 200 miles. [145] This zone would give effect to the necessary equilibrium between the fishing rights of the coastal State and freedom of the high seas.

143. *Recueil ADI*, Vol. 97, p. 50. Cited by Charles De Visscher, *Problèmes de confins en droit international public*, *op. cit.*, p. 159. Mr. Castañeda (Mexico) also moves in this direction, regretting that, though at the moment effect is given to the special interest of the coast State in a right of unilateral intervention on the high seas, "this right has been submitted to such restrictions and safeguards that it has been practically deprived of any real scope . . . The dispositions of 1958 inspiring no confidence, the claims for exclusive fishing zones extending considerable distances from the coast have multiplied", 58th Session of the Seabed Committee, UN Doc. A/AC.138/SR.58, p. 200.

144. On the present state of national positions, see FAO Doc. COFI/72/7, Suppl. 1, pp. 5 to 12.

145. See the declaration of Mr. Aguilar (Venezuela) to the 64th Session of the Seabed Committee, UN Doc. A/AC.138/SR.64, p. 47. An original signification for contiguity has also been proposed by Mr. Stevenson (United States) in recognizing that "neither fish nor fishermen can be separated by artificial lines, and that the rights of a coastal State beyond the limit of its territorial waters should be defined *as a function of its economic interest* which represents for its fishermen a stock of fish moving in its adjacent coastal waters rather than as a function of the distance which separates this stock from the coast", 51st Session, UN Doc. A/AC.138/SR.51, p. 80. In this sense, contiguity would no longer be geographic, which confirms the theory of biological unity between the sea and man. Similarly, Mr. Castañeda (Mexico) considers, with respect to the criteria applicable to the definition of

The classical notion of the contiguous zone is thus abandoned as no longer corresponding to the needs of coastal States. [146] A new "functional" zone has been born with a juridical status as yet uncertain although it can be analyzed in contrast to territorial waters: "it involves isolating all jurisdictions, *sovereignty included*, which are lumped together in the notion of territorial waters for particular areas of competence such as exclusive rights, with respect to fishing for example, to take measures of control and conservation" [147] and measures of exclusive or preferential use.

But the marine domain appears more and more a whole, new forms of national appropriation have been proposed in order to harmonize the interests of the coastal State and those of humanity over its property.

B. *National appropriation, complement to unilateral action*

The theory of functional duplication of Georges Scelle is adapted perfectly to this new form of appropriation: the coastal State will act simultaneously to defend its own interests and those of the

---

the limits of these jurisdictions, that "the proportion of fishing resources of zones adjacent to the coastal State which should be reserved for it should be a function of its capacity to catch which, when the developing countries are involved, is destined to increase", UN Doc. A/AC.138/SR.58, p. 201. In this last hypothesis, the coastal State would effect an appropriation proportional to its capacities. However, this direction would not be suitable for developing countries who make their demands not on the basis of their technical capacity to catch, but on their fundamental economic needs. Here again we see the sometimes blurred dividing line between management and appropriation.

146. On the inadaptation of the classical contiguous zone to modern needs, see André Gros, "Entre deux Conférences sur le droit de la mer" in *Mélanges Basdevant*, 1960, p. 245.

147. Declaration of Mr. Beesley (Canada) to the 58th Session of the Seabed Committee (UN Doc. A/AC.138/SR.58, p. 207). This zone, being of a fundamentally economic character, its limits should not be universal, but should be calculated according to local conditions proper to a coastal State or a determined region. See to this effect the declaration of Mr. Andersen (Iceland) to the 9th Session of Sub-Committee II, UN Doc. A/AC.138/SC.II/SR.9, p. 5.

For a juridical definition of the economic zone, giving effect also not to the sovereignty of the State, but to its partial jurisdiction, cf. Declaration of Mr. Castañeda (Mexico) to the 11th Session of Sub-Committee II, UN Doc. A/AC.138/SC.II/SR.11, p. 10.

international community, appearing as a State and as a delegate of "mankind". [148]

There would also be a coincidence of the interests involved; the State would not effect a national appropriation except in pursuit of the general international interest. The temptation would be great to present certain propositions of this sort as measures of international management. However, the perspectives of application brought to light by the numerous delegations tend to restrict these dispositions to the category of appropriations founded essentially on economic and ecological bases.

(*a*) *The hypothesis of the "international economic mandate"*

The proposed international economic mandate finds its origin in the American proposal for a United Nations Convention on the international seabed zone. [149] This proposal provides for the existence of a zone under international mandate [150] where, at first sight, the coastal State has essentially the role of international manager: "except for express provisions set out in the present chapter, the rights of the coastal State in the zone under mandate off its coasts, are no more extensive than those of any other contracting party" (Art. 27).

But, Chapter III specifically reserves several important rights to

148. The juridical régime for piracy and the slave trade is also part of this functional duplication.

149. Official documents of the General Assembly, 25th Session, Supp. No. 21 (A/8021), Appendix 5. It is also interesting to note that the preamble of the Declaration of Montevideo on the law of the sea, *op. cit.*, affirms that "in applying measures to conserve the resources of the sea, the seabed and its underlying strata in maritime territorial zones adjacent to their coasts, *the coastal States act in the final analysis for the good of mankind* for whom the oceans are a primordial source of useful means for its subsistence and development". The implicit beginnings of an international mandate emerges from this text.

150. Art. 26: "the zone under international mandate is the part of the international seabed zone embodying the continental or insular margin between the demarcation line defined in Article 1 and a line situated either beyond the base of the continental slope or beyond the base of the slope of an island situated beyond the continental slope, at the point where the incline of the surface of the seabed no longer has a gradient of ( ) %". (The figure has been left blank by the project to be fixed during the possible negotiations.)

the mandatory coastal States: granting, suspension and annulment of permits, determination of minimum working conditions, etc. Moreover, the mandatory State collects and retains supplementary rents (Art. 28).

Thus, in the American proposal, the State-mankind equilibrium appears warped to the benefit of a camouflaged appropriation by the coastal State (mandatory). [151] According to the calculations of Mr. Espinosa (Colombia), the United States would collect about half the rights and rents furnished by the exploitation of the zone under mandate. [152]

However, only application of the American proposal would allow us to determine whether appropriation would prevail over management. The international economic mandate arises thus from a form of juridical existentialism: existence comes before essence, the manner in which the coastal State plays its mandatory role determines the judgment we make concerning the very concept of a mandate. In this sense, the role of a future international mechanism would not be to pass judgment on the *rights* of the mandatory State but to control *the exercise of these rights*, [153] which is equally valid with respect to the protection of the environment.

(*b*) *The hypothesis of the "international ecological mandate"*

The struggle against the pollution of the oceans necessitates, beyond a doubt, global solutions, but the action of the coastal State is not to be scorned. Here again and perhaps more clearly than in the economic domain, the State can act within the framework of a functional duplication.

151. It is further to be noted that this zone under mandate, by the geological criterion chosen to delimit it (cf. note 150), results in discrimination among coastal States to the disadvantage of countries having no continental shelf. Appropriation is then reserved for a precise category of coastal States.

152. 59th Session of the Seabed Committee, UN Doc. A/AC.138/SR.59, p. 22.

153. See to this effect the declaration of Mr. Tarcici (Arab Republic of Yemen) to the 65th Session of the Seabed Committee, UN Doc. A/AC.138/SR.65, p. 73.

The notion of appropriation has shown itself to be, first of all, delicate to grasp since it has often been affirmed that the authority conferred on the coastal States for the accomplishment of their "international ecological mandate" does not represent so much an exercise of sovereignty as an obligation to fulfil an international duty.

With this new hypothesis, appropriation can thus only result from an abuse of the *use* of the mandate to serve the international community and not from the mandate itself. The example of the Canadian legislation[154] on the prevention of pollution in the Arctic studied earlier is highly significant in this regard: if the Canadian administration applied a strict conception of the right of innocent passage, the north-west passage, which is a maritime route for supertankers from Alaska, could be closed to this type of ship. In this perspective, the United States have felt that these Canadian measures were an encroachment on the principle of freedom of the seas and thus, as a unilateral appropriation.[155]

These two examples of mandates which can be exercised by the coastal State are thus characterized by an oscillation between appropriation and management according to their use: management by the mandatory State can avoid national appropriation, but national appropriation can also be achieved under the guise of management. This latter interpretation is perhaps pessimistic, but it is often part of the vast dialectical movement governing the different phases of the law of the sea. The future juridical régime for the oceans will result from a dialectic between the global and the national approaches. In this respect, the United Nations provides a framework which, in its dimensions, if not universal then at least open to the world, permits this combined play of national preoccupations and imperatives of a general nature.[156]

154. Although the Canadian legislation is completely original in its establishment of controls up to 100 miles from the coast, several countries have also declared themselves in favour of such controls by the coastal State: cf. the declarations to the Seabed Committee by Mr. Small (New Zealand), 62nd Session, UN Doc. A/AC.138/SR.62, p. 20; of Mr. Beesley (Canada), 63rd Session, UN Doc. A/AC.138/SR.63, p. 37; and of Mr. Aguilar (Venezuela), 64th Session, UN Doc. A/AC.138/SR.64, p. 48.

155. For the details of the American protests, see J. Y. Morin, *op. cit.*, pp. 228 and following.

156. Cf. René-Jean Dupuy, *Le fond des mers*, A. Colin, 1971, pp. 9-10.

CONCLUSION

Any international attempt to regulate the law of the sea without taking account of the present state of national appropriations is condemned to failure. Reality should not be sacrificed for the idea of a potential renaissance still latent. The equilibrium among the different interests involved, though difficult to obtain, represents a surer guarantee of a durable solution than their subordination.

Consequently, a durable solution should not only sanction the present reality but also attempt to project it into the future. *The law, in order to completely fulfil its function of adaption should sometimes do revolutionary works.* The calculation of the possible limits of appropriation allows us to draw up a maximum framework for the future. In comparing it with the present balance sheet of tendencies towards appropriation, the range of possible solutions begins to appear.

A. *The possible limits of appropriation*

In the hypothesis with which we are preoccupied, appropriation is all the more difficult to limit because there is disagreement concerning the principles to apply. The law of the sea is presently experiencing a great schism in which each country feels itself entrusted with the mission of stating the law. For certain of them, the law disclosed is honoured, but in an entirely new perspective: being based on the economy and development, the State intends to make known the law through its unilateral affirmation, often confirmed by those of States in analogous economic situations. However, the State is also the first tangible limitation to national appropriation. In effect, the demanding State must take account of the possible reactions of other States. Not only is it under pressure from other users of the sea, but also it can fear measures of reciprocal extension which would work to its disadvantage in the final analysis. In this sense, each country must resort to an evaluation of the possible reactions of other States, and make a choice balanced by its various interests. Like an individual, the State must maximize its profit in determining at what level of appropriation the application of the principle of reciprocity by other countries would outweigh the advantages of its demand.[157]

Beyond this frequent research in the general course of international relations, three main limits appear in the law of the sea.

(1) *Land-locked States, a physical limit to appropriation*[158]

Studies done by UNCTAD show that land-locked developing countries generally figure among the least advanced of the developing countries.[159] Recognition of their interests has been realized by resolution 2750 B (XXV) of the General Assembly affirming that the exploration of the international zone and the exploitation of its resources should be for the benefit of humanity in its entirety, the particular interests and needs of the developing countries *including those which are land-locked* being taken into account.

However, the ambiguity of the different resolutions concerning the "common heritage of mankind" is manifested here more clearly: no limits have yet been set. Consequently, being unable to take the unilateral measures available to coastal States, the land-locked States have formed a pressure group in the Seabed Committee, protesting against any extension of national jurisdiction judged excessive.[160]

157. On the principle of reciprocity, cf. Michel Viraly, "Le principe de réciprocité dans le droit international contemporain", *Recueil des Cours de l'Académie de Droit International*, 1967, III, particularly p. 50; also W. Burke and McDougall, *The Public Order of the Oceans*, Yale, 1962, Introduction, p. IX: ". . . the interdependence of all peoples in the enjoyment of the oceans places the practices of reciprocity and retaliation at the disposal of even the smallest State".

158. For more details on the situation of these countries, cf. Report of the Secretary-General, "Study on the question of free access to the sea by land-locked countries and the special problems which these countries pose with respect to the exploitation and exploration of the resources of the seabed and the oceans beyond the limits of national jurisdiction", UN Doc. A/AC.138/37.

159. Report established by the group of experts of UNCTAD entitled "Special measures in favour of the least advanced developing countries", Doc. TD/B/288.

160. See for example, the declarations of Mr. Koh (Singapore), 50th Session, UN Doc. A/AC.138/SR.50, p. 60 and of Mr. Fekete (Hungary), 56th Session, UN Doc. A/AC.138/SR.56, p. 153.

Very often, States without continental shelves or shelf-locked States join forces with the land-locked States.

(2) *The notion of "common heritage of mankind", a moral limit to appropriation*

The Declaration of Principle of December 17, 1970, affirming the existence of a "common heritage of mankind" was considered by the representative of Mexico in the Seabed Committee as permitting "the characterization as illicit of any unilateral act of a State desirous of appropriating for itself the resources of the seabed and the oceans or claiming any sovereignty whatever over this zone".[161]

The juridical value of UN resolutions has long been discussed.[162] Without involving ourselves in this issue, the Declaration of Principle having been voted 108 to 0, with 18 abstentions, it could constitute a moral limit to appropriations. This aspect is not to be neglected since with the juridical limit of the international zone remaining uncertain, the coastal State has a rather wide latitude of choice in its demands. The law thus being powerless in the present circumstances, the hope placed by the developing countries in the exploitation of the common heritage of mankind could constitute a moral barrier to excessive appropriations.[163] However, is it still necessary to "moralize" the practice of freedom of the seas.[164]

161. Declaration of Mr. Castañeda to the 58th Session, UN Doc. A/AC. 138/SR.58, p. 197.

162. See for example Jorge Castañeda, "The Juridical Value of U.N. Resolutions", *Recueil des Cours de l'Académie de Droit International*, The Hague, 1970, I, p. 212 in particular. Also, Report of the Secretary-General, UN Doc. A/AC.138/12 + Add. I, 4th part, section 1, Dutch Memorandum of Aug. 18, 1950, considering that resolutions of the General Assembly constitute to a certain degree a source of law. Doc. of the 6th Ordinary Session of the General Assembly, Appendices, Ques. 48 of the order of the day, p. 9.

163. The dialectical movement is also present in this perspective. In the short run, the developing countries have a tendency to practise extensive appropriations. However, the establishment in the long term of an international juridical régime for the common heritage of mankind from which they would have everything to gain could halt the demands for extensive zones.

164. One could ask oneself if the principle of freedom of the seas breaks down to freedom of navigation, excluding in return, in zones adjacent to coasts, any reference to freedom of fishing, as a justification for the installation of fleets exploiting the fishing resources. Thus, the freedom of fishing is separated from the freedom of navigation in the zones of economic jurisdiction; moreover, the freedom of navigation would only be restricted by the principle that a competence of the coastal States would develop to regulate its exercise in ecological security zones.

(3) *The freedom of the seas regulated, a juridical limit to appropriation*

Freedom of the seas as it has been practised resembles Athenian democracy. Like the latter, there is only a restricted circle of privileged participants, the maritime powers of the time.

The developing countries thus denounce this formal freedom as having led to an abuse of the law. [165] The appropriations would thus, in part, be motivated by this abusive use.

The aspirations of the members of the international community lead one to believe that *equal opportunities at the juridical level is no longer sufficient*. It is necessary to attempt to proceed in such a way that all States have the possibility to make use of the rights granted to it, as Georges Scelle has so aptly put it: "the progress of juridical systems consists not only in proclaiming the theoretical equality of the law, but also to compensate to the extent possible, for inequalities of fact". [166]

The renovation to this effect of the principle of freedom by the Conference on the law of the sea planned for 1973 would develop a new obstacle to appropriation since it would eliminate one of the causes.

B. *The present balance sheet of tendencies towards appropriation*

The review in the introduction of the technical progress realized in the exploitation of the resources of the sea made us conscious of the importance of economic circumstances on the formulation of law. The present tendencies towards appropriation also require an appreciation of political realities in three essential areas.

(1) *The growing success of extensive appropriations*

The representative of Peru at the Seabed Committee brushed, on March 15, 1971, a rather complete fresco of the different appropriations realized by the coastal States and drew several conclu-

165. Cf. the declaration of Mr. Galindo Pohl (El Salvador) to the 63rd Session of the Seabed Committee, UN Doc. A/AC.138/SR.63, p. 31.

166. "Plateau continental en droit international", *Revue générale de droit international public*, 1955, Vol. LVIII, p. 11.

sions: "firstly, a clear and irreversible tendency towards the extension of national jurisdiction is to be noted; secondly, this tendency is not restricted to Latin America; thirdly, the narrow limits previously set are not sacrosanct as it was claimed in 1958. More than 40 States have extended the limits of their territorial waters or their fishing zones to 12 miles while 22 exercise their jurisdiction beyond 12 miles and the evolution continues to pursue its course". [167]

But two observations should be made: on the one hand, legislation lags far behind claims made in the Committee on the Seabed and on the other hand the resulting uncertainty leads to new contestations.

Thus, on April 14, 1972, the Government of the United Kingdom deposed with the Registrar of the International Court of Justice an introductory petition against the Icelandic decision mentioned previously. [168] Another limit to appropriation is thus perhaps in its formative stages, but it should be recalled that Canada has modified its clause accepting the jurisdiction of the International Court with respect to litigation relating to the extension of its territorial waters and security zones. Once again the International Court of Justice is confronted with a problem the solution of which could anticipate the regulations expected from the next conference on the law of the sea.

(2) *The disproportion of interests between maritime powers and coastal States*

The relationship which is established in an international conflict between the positions of protagonists cannot be analyzed solely

167. Declaration of Mr. Arias Schreiber to the 46th Session, UN Doc. A/AC.138/46, p. 15.

168. Communication of the International Court of Justice, No. 72/2, April 14, 1972. The Government of the United Kingdom stated in its petition that according to international law:
(*a*) the challenged decision of Iceland should be considered as unfounded and invalid. Iceland cannot unilaterally exclude the fishing boats of other countries from a new zone defined by it:
(*b*) the questions relating to the conservation of fishing reserves in the waters surrounding Iceland cannot be dealt with by means of a unilateral extension of the zone of exclusive fishing jurisdiction, but can be settled by agreement between Iceland and the United Kingdom.

by quantifying the forces involved. This objective element is insufficient, recourse must be had to the subjective notion, for each State, of the value of the stakes.

The test of wills is then a mark of international relations, particularly significant in the case of the law of the sea. Thus "the will of an actor is the result of the relationship which exists for him between the value he attaches to the goal he is seeking and the costs which he must accept in order to obtain it . . . A weaker country can prevail in a conflict if the goal is sufficiently more important for him than for his adversary". [169]

Consequently, it would appear that the power of a State is not of an absolute grandeur: a coastal State of medium importance can impose its demands on maritime powers if they are vital to it. However, such unilateral acts should not encroach too much on the freedom of navigation. For a maritime power, fishing on the high seas or exploiting mineral riches do not always represent vital stakes as is the case for certain coastal States, but the right of passage constitutes a commercial and military objective of the first order. In this case, the functional jurisdictions sketch perhaps the rough outline of a solution, freedom of navigation not being placed in jeopardy.[170]

(3) *The correction provided by the functional jurisdictions*

It has been noted that national appropriations beyond 12 miles concerned for the most part not territorial waters but reserved economic zones. A synthesis of the interests involved therein should not link the delimitation of territorial waters and "patrimonial waters". A relatively narrow zone of sovereignty would thus satisfy the maritime powers, guardians of freedom of navigation, while an adjacent functional zone of an economic nature would satisfy the desires of the threatened coastal States. This is the direction in which the work of the United Nations appears to be leading.

169. Jean-Pierre Derriennic, "Relations interétatiques inégales et conflits", *Revue française de sociologie politique*, 1968, pp. 848-861.

170. On this compatibility of interests, see the declaration of Mr. Galindo Pohl (El Salvador) to the 63rd Session of the Seabed Committee, UN Doc. A/AC.138/SR.63, p. 32.

Second Part

Seabed problems

Chapter I

THE EXCLUSIVE USE OF THE SEABED FOR PEACEFUL PURPOSES

The military aspect of problems relating to the seabed together with the question of the exploitation of mineral resources is the most important of the problems to which the United Nations has been directing its attention over the past two years. In any case, it is the most urgent if we wish to avoid a situation where certain of the great powers take advantage of technological progress in order to be the first to place military installations on the seabed. Experts are in agreement that missile launchers on the seabed would be less vulnerable in case of atomic attack and harder to detect. As well, it has been noted that the establishment of military bases on the seabed would considerably reduce the distances to enemy territory, thereby affecting the existing strategic equilibrium which is dependent on the equal ability of each of the great powers to be immediately aware of possible nuclear aggression unleashed against it.

It is known that the great powers have already devoted considerable research to the question of military installations on the seabed; the United States, in particular, spends 516 million dollars for its oceanographic programme, of which 300 million is used by the Navy.

The examination of the conditions governing an exclusively peaceful use of the seabed raises a certain number of theoretical options which should be articulated before deciding the manner in which they should be dealt with in the treaty to be prepared.

The present régime governing the seabed, as it relates to military use, can give rise to two contrary theoretical lines of reasoning.

In the first place, one can adhere to the traditional conception according to which the seabed is subject to the same régime as the high seas; this was the opinion of Gilbert Gidel and Sir Hersch

Lauterpacht.[1] Taking this approach, all the consequences flowing from the principle of freedom are brought to bear on the bed of the high seas, and the military use thereof is equally free in peace as in war, barring special rules, within the framework of international conventions which prohibit certain practices, for example, the one forbidding nuclear tests.

Even if it is considered that the use of nuclear arms is contrary to international law,[2] this problem takes on no particular significance when posed at the level of the seabed with respect to the installation of bases for the launching of projectiles. Furthermore, there would definitely appear to be no rule limiting the freedom of the nuclear powers in one important area.[3] *A fortiori*, no basis can be seen for proscribing the installation of conventional arms on the seabed.

However, another doctrinal approach would tend to prevent the automatic descent of the régime for the high seas to the seabed, leaving instead a gap in the law or a juridical void. To take the first approach would be as ridiculous as it would be to bring to bear on outer space an indefinite projection of territorial sovereignty in conformity with principles inherited from Roman Law. In reality, the rule of freedom of the high seas is of a customary origin; no international practice has as yet developed for the bed which until recently was inaccessible. With the exception of the régimes relating to slipways, pipelines or certain installations used in exploiting the live sedentary resources which are the only cases involving appropriations of the seabed, there are practically no precedents on which to base a customary law.

At this point, an observation with some value should be made: freedom of the seas is a law of *jus communicationis*, it concerns navigation and fishing which is simply accessory to navigation; thus it is a law of the surface or, at most, a law of moderate depths; it is not a law applicable to the bed. Moreover, the law relating to the continental shelf developed in a customary fashion

1. G. Gidel, *Le droit international de la mer*, Vol. 1, pp. 499-500; Oppenheim's *International Law*, Edited by Lauterpacht, 7th ed. Vol. 1, p. 556.

2. Charlier, "Questions juridiques soulevées par l'evolution de la science atomique", *RCADI* 1957.

3. W. T. Burke, *Law and the New Technologies of the Law of the Sea*, 1966, p. 224.

as technological progress permitted its utilization and these rules proved to be as different from those applying to territorial waters as they were from those governing the high seas under which the shelf extends.

In truth, the problem raises three options: a régime of freedom, a régime of occupation since the juridical void makes it possible for any State to appropriate militarily the seabed under the high seas, or the prolongation of the régime relating to the continental shelf by operation of the criterion of exploitability.

It is to be noted that all three solutions are alike in permitting the military use of the seabed. The last, like the first two, since there is no obligation on coastal States to restrict themselves to peaceful uses of their continental shelves. Consequently, two approaches give the same result; either the extent of the continental shelf is defined by means of a revision of the convention of 1958 and an international rule of non-militarization of the seabed is developed or without taking this preliminary step and without any other provision being adopted the principle of exclusively peaceful use is adopted. No matter which approach is taken, the continental shelf remains open to military use. The legality of placing military installations on the continental shelf was examined at the Geneva Conference in 1958, the Socialist countries demanding the insertion of a prohibitive provision in the Convention. The debates made it clear that the general opinion is that such installations are contrary to international law. It is argued that Article 5 of the Convention which authorizes only installations for the exploration and exploitation of natural resources by implication excludes military uses. Nevertheless, it is known that numerous such installations already exist and that perhaps they do not all consist of simple instruments for underwater detection. It is clear, by the same token, that it would be preferable to forbid certain arms than to attempt to delimit the underwater areas affected by the prohibition. In other words, the tendency is toward a functional rule rather than a territorial system.

Thus, the problems relating to prohibitions with respect to States and with respect to regions are, if not resolved at least simplified; only the definition of the notion of military use would be in issue.

(1) As to States, the declaration should involve the largest number possible; that the small ones should share the same status as the

large ones would only be a recognition of the importance of localized conflicts in the present-day world. Certainly, the Chinese problem would remain one of the most preoccupying, but it has not, up to now, prevented the conclusion of agreements such as that on outer space; the treaty providing for the prohibition of nuclear arms in Latin America had to forego the agreement of Cuba.

(2) With respect to the underwater domain, it would inevitably be subject to numerous ambiguities. It should be taken into account at this point that the solution posed is scarcely as easy as it appears since military installations have already been placed on the continental shelf and it is difficult to imagine that the States who have placed them there, with their strong sense of sovereign rights, would be disposed to remove them. This is, moreover, one of the main reasons why the time factor in this matter is so decisive; the longer we wait to adopt a régime of non-militarization, the more we run the risk of seeing the military powers establish military devices further and further out on to the seabed. Indeed, in spite of the ambiguities inherent in this formula, a declaration of peaceful use of the seabed without any other provision concerning its delimitation, together with a renunciation of the use of certain specified military material, would be of considerable interest. However, there is no question that a prohibition of certain types of installations affecting the entire marine domain including those parts falling under national sovereignty would be preferable.

(3) The notion of military use will not fail to cause difficulty. It does not seem, taking into account considerations of work ability, that it is possible to retain a distinction between offensive and defensive armaments as some have proposed in spite of the unsurmountable ambiguity.

There is another side to the problem; certain parties considering that peaceful use would be reconcilable with that satisfying international law and the principles of the Charter of the United Nations. This modest formulation brings us to the notion of legitimate defence with all the gaps it creates in a system of security; to adopt this system would permit the placing of armaments on the seabed; such action could only be authorized by a decision of the Security Council, except that, on the basis of Article 51, this consent can be dispensed with in cases of individual or collective legitimate defence. This would leave worrisome possibilities open to great powers or military pacts.

A more serious problem is that raised with respect to the permanent or temporary character of installations. In the latter case, we confront the problem of submarines which can remain for long periods of time on the seabed and which, by themselves, are warships and thus would be forbidden. Even if the non-militarization were limited to nuclear arms, the submarine would pose a particularly delicate problem. Here again we see the fundamental ambivalence of the marine domain: a path for navigation and an underwater territory susceptible to occupation or parking, the submarine profiting from this double vocation. We still hear advocated the conception of a prohibition of nuclear arms within the framework of a general agreement on disarmament and the specificity of the seabed is questioned in this regard.

In any case, a declaration of peaceful use of the seabed, in order to avoid suspicion, would require a system of control. It is useless to picture the creation of a perfectly supranational model provided with powerful means of detection and an independent personnel functioning in the general interest of humanity. Moreover, this dream has not been achieved elsewhere; it is questionable whether States would accept a highly integrated agency to deal with the exploitation of mineral resources. Such an approach, it can be expected, would be dismissed out of hand in the case of the enforcement of peaceful uses of the seabed. It should be recalled that the Treaty of Moscow on the prohibition of nuclear tests provides for no form of organized control. We should remain in the realm of the possible given the present state of international relations, take our inspiration, instead, from what already exists in other areas.

There obviously comes to mind the Treaty of Washington on the Antarctic which authorizes each of the contracting parties to designate observers from amongst its nationals to carry out the inspection, the other parties being fully notified. Here, a lateral control is involved which is relatively acceptable given the regional nature of the agreement which affects a specific continent and at present involves only 12 signatories.

It would be difficult to set up a mechanism to control the entire seabed except on a regional basis but this would run the risk of being insufficient.

It is conceivable that the assistance of existing institutions could be requested, in particular that of the IAEA. The Agency has at its disposal a system of "guarantees". This discreet word is used to describe a means of control which, according to Article III B of its constitution, forms part of a greater design, that of universal disarmament. However, the limits of this control of an essentially contractual nature are obvious when transposed purely and simply into the area with which we are concerned. These guarantees were created within the very particular framework of the Agency, where aid is furnished by the Agency, at its request, under its direction or under its control in order to permit it to be certain that this aid is not being used for military purposes (Article II). In order that the system of guarantees comes into force in a country, it is necessary that the country in question conclude an agreement with the Agency which can moreover be multilateral. Thus the Agency cannot take the initiative in exercising the control; it is a question rather of a solicited control. The State or States party to a co-operation agreement in the area of atomic energy accept the Agency, after a fashion, as witness to the peaceful nature of their uses.[4]

It is evident that such a mechanism does not provide the policing power required in the case of the seabed which would necessitate the discretionary right to bring the control to bear in a situation. Similarly, the Treaty of February 14, 1967, concerning the prohibition of nuclear weapons in Latin America is of no assistance. It creates an "organism" which amounts to an international organization, the General Conference of which establishes a system of control which the Council sets in motion at the request of a party. Inspectors enter accompanied by the contracting party on whose territory the inquiry is to take place if this State so requests. Their report is sent to all of the other contracting parties by the Secretary-General. The system can lead to the Security Council and the General Assembly of the United Nations being simultaneously seized of a matter as well as the Organization of American

4. The Mexican Government, in 1968, requested that the Agency apply the "guarantees" to all atomic energy activities in Mexico in conformity with subsection A (5) or Article III of the Constitution and Article 13 of the Treaty Prohibiting Nuclear Arms in Latin America. This is the first time a member State has requested that the Agency apply the "guarantees" to all of its nuclear activities (cf. IAEA, *Annual Report of the Council of Governors to the General Conference*, July 1, 1967-June 30, 1968; G.C. (XII) (380).

States. Nor does the Treaty neglect the Agency; its Article 13 requires each party to negotiate multilateral or bilateral agreements with the Agency with a view to the application of its system of guarantee. Thus the permissive, permanent control of the Agency is combined with the compulsory but occasional control of Organism.[5]

Is it conceivable that such a system could be applied to the seabed? It would appear necessary to qualify the answer.

With respect to the continental shelf, an extension of the guarantees of the Agency is conceivable. On the other hand, it does not appear that the great powers envisage the constitution of a specialized organism of the type provided for by the Latin American Treaty; rather, a multilateral control by the signatories of the future treaty is to be expected, along the lines of the Antarctic system.

These cautious approaches are confirmed by the present stance taken with respect to the problem in the United Nations.

Resolution 2340 (XXII) of December 18, 1967, creating a special Committee composed of 35 gave the following mandate: to study "The question of the reservation for exclusively peaceful purposes of the bed and subsoil of the seas and oceans, on the high seas beyond the limits of present national jurisdiction and the exploitation of their resources in the interest of humanity".

On December 21, 1968, the Committee increased from 35 to 42 members and became permanent as a result of the passage of resolution 2467 A. It is worthy of note that in the four resolutions passed under this number, this organism is called "The Committee on the Peaceful Use of the Seabed Beyond the Limits of National Jurisdiction" and although it is required to study all the aspects of exploration and exploitation of the seabed, it is the principle of peaceful use which dominates and provides inspiration for the

5. On the suggestion of the United States the constitution provides for another possibility, the application of guarantees by the Agency at the request of a State to control the peaceful use of atomic energy where there is no question of aid. This clause had been considered so utopian that the constitution provided no means of financing for the application of guarantees following a unilateral request (Art. XIV). However, this clause has been truly successful since it was adopted in the Treaty for the prohibition of nuclear arms in Latin America and its use is foreseen in the proposed non-proliferation Treaty.

work of the Committee in general. However, it should be pointed out, as the delegate from Malta did during the course of the session, that despite the quasi-unanimity with which the members of the special Committee had approved certain principles during the course of the summer session held at Rio de Janeiro, the First Commission had not been able to propose a resolution proclaiming them. In this regard, it should be noted that the resolution directing the Committee "to study the peaceful uses of the bed of the seas and the oceans" does not provide for an exclusively peaceful reservation.

The problem, in fact, is of a complexity which appears at various levels: at the United Nations itself, at the organization level, capability of elaborating the basis of a régime relating to the seabed; at the formal level, the nature of the instrument incorporating it and finally, at the technical level, to what military activities will the prohibition apply and to what maritime zone? In effect, we must distinguish between two series of problems, those relating to the elaboration of the régime and those concerning its scope.

I. ELABORATION OF THE RÉGIME

The creation of a permanent study committee by the General Assembly falls far short of solving the problem of the competent organ and the form of the act reserving the seabed for exclusively peaceful uses. The first question concerns a preliminary decision on the specificity of the problems of non-armament of the seabed as opposed to those of disarmament, as it was examined by the Committee of 18 at Geneva; the second relates to the degree of elaboration of the régime and involves the question of how much time to devote to the preparation of it, there being a certain urgency. Specificity or dilution in relation to the organic components? Elaborate or expedited formulation?

A. *Organic duality*

It is clear that the debate concerning the appropriate organ for achieving the task of reserving the seabed for exclusively peaceful uses involves a substantial question, that of the specificity or non-specificity of the problems of the seabed, from this point of view. Since the first sessions of the Committee in 1968, there have been divergences of opinion as to the procedure to be followed in dealing with the military aspects of the question. Some stressed that the question had already been submitted to the Committee of 18 which is the appropriate body to examine all aspects of disarmament. The Geneva Committee, according to some, should be able to adopt an urgent measure involving the cessation of the arms race on the seabed. However, it has been noted that the Committee could be seen as having only an indirect authority in this area and that the General Assembly should confer on the Committee a more precise mandate to be carried out under its control. This intermediate solution was not sufficient to convince other representatives who had joined the current of thought hostile to any referral of the question to the 18. For them, the problems of the seabed constituted an indivisible whole and by fragmenting the study of it among various organs this unity would be destroyed. Far from gaining time, rather the chances of effective action would be compromised by the use of a body whose workload was already too heavy. Furthermore, taking this approach, the problem is not essentially one of disarmament; it is rather a question of preventing and containing military activities on the seabed.

Finally, the constitution of the Committee of 18 demonstrates that it is only a negotiating body. As well, it is conceivable that it might give opinions to the *ad hoc* committee formed by the General Assembly. It appears that the great powers who are members of the Committee of 18 had a preference for giving this body jurisdiction. Meanwhile, the Soviet Union and the United States first presented proposed resolutions to the Special Committee requesting that the Geneva Committee on Disarmament consider the question.[6] In the final analysis, these resolutions were not adopted by the General Assembly which by resolution 2467 A formed a permanent committee to study the peaceful uses of the seabed, without making a reference to the Committee of 18. It is all the more remarkable that the resolution asks the Committee to work in close collaboration with other bodies which it lists: the specialized organization, the International Atomic Energy Agency and "the intergovernmental bodies concerned with the problem dealt

6. Soviet Resolution A/AC.135/20. American Resolution A/AC.135/24.

with by this resolution in order to avoid duplication or overlapping". This last formulation relates only imperfectly to the Committee of 18, if at all, and only to the extent that the risk of "duplication" should be avoided.

Also, is it not astonishing that, after the Geneva Committee returned to work on March 19, 1969, the Soviet delegate read a message from Mr. Kosygin, while his American colleague read a message from President Nixon? These two addresses, beyond the general problems of disarmament dealt with the demilitarization of the seabed. Furthermore, the Soviets went even further, placing before the Geneva Committee a proposed treaty, which step was imitated by the United States two months later on May 22, 1969, It can thus be said that the problems relating to the peaceful use of the seabed are now in the hands of the Committee on Disarmament. It is to be feared that the preparation of a régime for the reservation of the seabed for exclusively peaceful uses will gain no momentum there.

Nevertheless, the "Seabed Committee" remains seized of this problem which it discussed during the three weeks of the session in the Spring of 1969 (cf. UN Seabed Committee concludes Spring session, the *Department of State Bulletin*, April 21, 1969). The American representative explained there, on the 28th of March last, the position of his Government with respect to this dual competency: "We have always maintained that the ENDC is best qualified to work out the terms of acceptable agreements on arms control. Our Seabed Committee has an interest in the problem as well. But at this juncture, we believe the laboring oar must be filled by the experts in Geneva, while we here maintain a more general overview". That is clearly to say that the effective preparation of an agreement will take place at Geneva.

Also, during the debates of the Special Committee in 1968, certain representatives had suggested that the General Assembly, without delay, make an appeal to the States, and the Government of India lodged a proposed declaration proclaiming the seabed common property of humanity for exclusively peaceful ends. This proposal raised a second aspect of the problem of the elaboration of a peaceful régime, that of the nature of the instrument which should be employed.

B. *Towards a treaty or peaceful reservation*

In the face of the complicity of the problems of the seabed and the risk that time lost may promote an arms race, it appeared highly desirable, at least in the early stages, to proceed with a simple declaration of principle. The Declaration of India (A/AC. 135/21) stated it well: "Convinced that in anticipation of the conclusion of a treaty regulating the administration and use of the bed of the seas and oceans, in the interest of all humanity, it is necessary to enunciate the applicable principle in this regard". Similarly, the United States had lodged with the Special Committee, in 1968, a "proposed resolution containing an enunciation of principles concerning the seabed" (A/AC.135/25). Thus while proposing that the Committee of 18 powers on disarmament define the essential elements of an international agreement which is "practical, permits verification, is efficient, and leads to the prevention of this new domain from being used for the installation of weapons of massive destruction", the American Government suggests that the General Assembly define, in a rather complete declaration more detailed than the Indian proposal, the principal features indicating the solutions to be brought to bear on the various problems raised by the exploration and exploitation of the seabed. It was finally shown that this technique ran the risk of masking serious ambiguities and its adoption raised insurmountable difficulties, the States attaching an overriding importance to certain very concrete aspects of the problem of non-militarization and being unable to permit them to be more or less hidden behind a declaration of principles too vague to arrive at a practical result.

Next, was recourse to the more elaborated technique of the treaty likely to be adopted by the Committee of 18? The Committee found itself seized of two proposed treaties, the first lodged by the Soviet Union on the 18th of March last (ENDC/240), the second by the United States on May 22, 1969 (ENDC/249). The deposition of a proposal by the Soviets led the United States to imitate them quickly. On March 25, Ambassador Smith, head of the delegation to the Committee of 18, declared in his speech: "My delegation does not believe we are quite at the stage where trying to agree on treaty language would be the best way to go about reaching an agreement".

Mr. David H. Popper, the American representative to the Seabed

Committee, declared that there was reason to expect an early agreement at least on the broad outlines and considered in this regard that informal consultations were very useful. It will be necessary to overcome the difficulties revealed by the differences between the two proposed treaties lodged at Geneva; they relate essentially to the extent of the prohibition which they impose.

II. THE SCOPE OF THE PEACEFUL RESERVATION

Certainly the divergences between the two great powers bear essentially on the notion of non-militarization and of the zone on the seabed to which it should be applied.

A. *Denuclearisation or demilitarisation?*

Since 1968 the Soviet Unicn has proposed to the Seabed Committee a prohibition governing all uses for military purposes of the bed of the seas and oceans. On the other hand, during the same period, the United States, in its proposed resolution considered only a limitation of arms. In its proposed amendments, the United Republic of Tanzania (AC.135/20-A/AC.135/26) extended even further the Soviet formulation by proposing that the General Assembly declare that "the bed of the seas and oceans should not be used by any State or group of States for military purposes of any description"; it was also proposed that the Committee of 18 should study, as an emergency measure, a prohibition of the use of the bed of the seas and oceans by nuclear submarines as well as a prohibition of military fortifications and missile bases.

The proposed treaty deposited by the USSR in March, 1969, was inspired by these Tanzanian proposals. In fact, the first article declares: "It is forbidden to place on the bed of the seas and oceans or their subsoil installations equipped with nuclear arms or any other type of weapon of massive destruction or to establish there military bases, installations, constructions, fortifications or other elements designed for military purposes". Thus all military activity is prohibited; on the other hand the United States has a much more limited conception of the prohibition; we find the following in the first article of the proposal lodged last May 22:

"each State party to the present treaty agrees not to install or place fixed nuclear weapons or other fixed weapons of massive destruction or fixed launching platforms for such weapons . . .".

This concern of the United States not to eliminate all activities of a military nature appeared already clearly formulated in the letter of March 18, 1969, addressed to the Committee of 18 by President Nixon. Moreover, in his statement to the Seabed Committee, Mr. Popper repeated word for word the terms used by Ambassador Smith before the Committee of 18 three days earlier. It is thus confirmed that the United States considers that for certain purposes, such as aids to communication and navigation, the seabed may be used for military and non-military purposes at the same time.

As well, the existence of submarine forces requires States to adopt defensive measures such as warning systems placed on the seabed. Finally, there should be noted scientific research undertaken by military personnel using unarmed equipment. As a result, a complete demilitarization would have the effect of prohibiting certain necessary and desirable activities. The principal danger is that of a possible arms race to place weapons of massive destruction on the seabed, whether they be nuclear, biological or chemical, and of course the platforms for launching them. It should be noted that the American proposal dwells on the fixed nature of the installations prohibited. The message of President Nixon and the declarations of the American representatives to the two committees also stress this. They both stated: "Careful consideration must be given to the exact definition of the words 'emplace or fix'. One of the factors to be considered is whether these words should apply only to permanent installations or should also apply to containers or carriers whose principal mode of deployment or operation require physical contact with the seabed".

The American approach is inspired by a proposal made in the United States Senate by Senator Pell who is also of the opinion that military uses remain possible. It is evident that the problem of nuclear submarines is at the centre of the debate. Certain American military critics have noted that the invulnerability of nuclear submarines is a source of equilibrium in international relations. It is to be observed that the proposed treaty lodged by the Soviets does not specifically require this element of fixity and forbids the placing on the seabed of installations equipped with nuclear arms without however taking up the Tanzanian formulation of 1968 to the Seabed Committee which tended to prohibit the use of the seabed by submarines.

These divergences appear more serious than the difficulties involved in determining the extent of the zone of application of the future treaty.

B. *The extent of the zone*

It is quite evident that there exists a certain connection between the position taken on the extent of prohibitions of military activities and that taken with respect to the zone affected by the prohibition. While the Soviet and American proposals cover a zone which leaves only a relatively modest band to the coastal sovereignty of States, the absolute prohibition advocated by the USSR is of a considerable scope since it includes the continental shelf on which certain military installations have been in existence for some time, at least for the purpose of information and defence. On the other hand, while the American proposal also provides that only a narrow coastal band should escape the prohibition, since it relates only to the fixed installation of weapons of mass destruction, it therefore permits other installations to be established on the continental shelf.

Since its proposal of 1958 the Soviet Union has demanded that the reservation for exclusively peaceful purposes relates to the beds of the seas and oceans and their subsoil "beyond the limits of the territorial waters of coastal States". The proposed treaty deposed last March with the Committee of 18 declares in Article I, section 1: "The use for military purposes of the beds of the seas and oceans and their subsoil is forbidden beyond the limits of the 12-mile maritime zone of the coastal States". Article 30 adds: "The exterior limit of the maritime zone for the purposes of the present treaty is calculated from the same base lines as those adopted for the purposes of determining the limits of the territorial waters of coastal States". Thus the Soviet Union, in its proposal, adheres to the rule in Article 24 of the Geneva Convention on territorial waters taking no account of claims for more extensive territorial waters.

In its proposal of May 1969, the United States provides that the régime of non-nuclearization will apply beyond a "narrow band" defined in Article 2 which states: "For the purposes of the present treaty, the external limit of the narrow band envisaged in the first article is to be measured from base lines drawn in the manner indicated in paragraph 2 of this article. The width of the narrow band is three miles". The second paragraph is left blank for the moment. However, the third states: "No provision of this treaty is to be interpreted as damaging the position of a State party to it with respect to the rights or claims which the said States could advance or with respect to the recognition or non-recognition of the rights or claims advanced by any other State, relative to the territorial waters or other contiguous waters or to the bed of the seas and oceans".

This provision is inspired by the technique of freezing demands and rights effected by the 1959 Treaty on the Antarctic. It involves a new element when compared to the Soviet proposal which makes no allusion to the freedom of the high seas; the American proposal alludes to this on two occasions, notably in Article 3 where the means of control are set out.

In the two proposals, the forbidden zone is subject to multilateral control. Article 2 of the Soviet Proposal provides that: "All installations and constructions situated on the beds of the seas and oceans or their subsoil are accessible, on a reciprocal basis, to the representatives of States party to this treaty with a view to enforcing the obligations assumed under this treaty by States having placed such elements there.

Article 3 of the American proposal provides that: "In order to promote the objects of this treaty and ensure respect for its provisions, the parties to the said treaty have the right to freely observe the activities of other States on the beds of the seas and oceans without identifying themselves with these activities or without damaging in any other way rights recognized by international law, including the freedom of the high seas. If, in a particular case, this observation is not sufficient to answer any questions relating to the execution of the provisions of this treaty, the parties are to consult and co-operate in attempting to resolve any questions".

Thus, in neither case, as it could be predicted, is there any institutionalization of the system of control comparable to that in the Latin American treaty, nor is there any allusion to the possible co-operation of the International Atomic Energy Agency to which resolution A passed by the General Assembly in December, 1968, expressly made reference.

The only difference between the Soviet and American proposals is in the fact that the latter provides for an obligation, couched, however, in cautious terms, on the parties to consult and cooperate.

All the same, the second section of Article 3 of the American proposal that the "Revision Conference", which, by Article 5, must take place five years after the present treaty comes into force, will be considered whether it is desirable, by way of amendment, to create other rights or procedures. This need for revision is based on the necessity of taking into account any technological progress achieved during the five years. The Soviet proposal, by prohibiting all military activity of any description, covers at the same time those activities which could arise from technological progress.

We should note one point on which the two proposals coincide perfectly; the American provision in Article 6 adopts, word for word, the fifth section of Article 4 of the Soviet proposal providing for the right of each party to withdraw from the treaty "if it decides that extraordinary events relating to the objects of this treaty have compromised the supreme interests of its country. All other parties and the Security Council of the United Nations must be given three months' notice of this withdrawal. The said notice should set out the extraordinary events that the State in question considers to have compromised its supreme interests". The American proposal does not provide for the coming into force of the treaty while the Soviet proposal provides that this shall occur after five governments, including the governments designated as depositaries under the treaty, have deposited their instruments of ratification.

Chapter II

THE PRESENT AND THE POSSIBLE FUTURE RÉGIMES FOR THE SEABED, THE LIVING RESOURCES OF THE SEABED AND THEIR PROTECTION AGAINST POLLUTION CAUSED BY EXPLOITATION OF THE SEABED RESOURCES

A consequence of the appearance of the problems regarding the seabed is that major importance has been attached to the exploration of its mineral resources. The question of the destiny of the living resources of the sea beyond the limits of national jurisdiction is unquestionably less urgent, yet a long-term solution of this question is equally important. It is from now on possible to conceive an exploitation of the mineral resources of the seabeds; the exploitation of the living resources does not for the time being assume the same dimensions. As a matter of fact, in the debates in the UN concerning the seabed, there has been no reference to the living resources except to stress the risks of pollution which may result from the exploitation of the mineral wealths of the seabeds and the oceans. The specific character of the question relating to the living resources of the seabed beyond the limits of national jurisdiction should therefore be examined before we consider the danger of pollution affecting the seabed.

I. THE LEGAL SITUATION OF THE LIVING RESOURCES BEYOND THE LIMITS OF NATIONAL JURISDICTION

It seems appropriate to stress one point immediately. The continental shelf is the natural refuge of the living resources. In the course of the next 50 years the economic exploitation of these resources will, according to biologists, develop essentially there. The 1958 Convention on the Continental Shelf states, Article 2 (4), that the sovereign rights exercised by the coastal State on this area affect the living organisms which, at the harvestable stage, either are immobile on or under the seabed or are unable to move except in constant physical contact with the seabed or subsoil. It may thus be affirmed that the legal status of the actually exploitable resources on the seabed has been resolved subject, of course, to the biological character of the ambiguities resulting from a clause the application of which has, on several occasions, caused difficulties as regards international practice.

This fact, however, draws the attention to certain points the essential importance of which can only be estimated on the background of the characteristic features of these resources and the submarine areas in which they live.

A. *The biological and geological situation of the living resources*

(*a*) These resources may be considered in two categories:

1. The sedentary, or benthonic species that, at their adult stages, live attached to the seabed, or within the subsoil, or move about on its surface, but do not swim in the waters above. The benthonic organisms that are important sources of food to man, as well as to other species, include both plants and animals. However, because of the rapid absorption of light in sea water, the photosynthesis which is necessary for plants or phytoplankton, is halted at depths ranging from 50 to 100 metres depending on the turpidity of the upper layers of the sea, that is to say within the limits of the continental shelf.

2. The demersal species that have an intimate association with the seabed for food or refuge, although they swim about freely in the water above, such as the flat-fishes and various crustaceans.

However, some species in both categories have free-floating or free-swimming eggs (larvae and juveniles) that are pelagic, that is to say, creatures of the open sea not dependent on the bottom. Conversely, some species that are pelagic as adults, such as herring, may deposit their eggs in shallow waters on the sea bottom.

This means that the species dependent on the seabed or in close contact with it constitute, all or part of their lives, a substantially complex environment of a strikingly heterogeneous nature in comparison to the mineral resources of the seabed or subsoil. This also shows how summary Article 2 (4) of the Convention on the Continental Shelf is.

How does the evolution of the living resources appear as we reach greater depths?

Benthonic animals also occur in greater depths of the ocean. However, the abundance of the bottom-dwelling organisms and the associated demersal species that depend on them for food, decrease very rapidly with depths and distance from shore in all oceans. At similar depths, the benthonic organisms also tend generally to decrease in abundance from the temperate latitude to the tropics.

Scientists estimate the general dispositions of the species in the various depths of the sea to be as follows.

(*b*) Traditionally, the benthonic zones are estimated to cover:
1. The littoral and the sub-littoral zones extending within the limits of the continental shelf; the latter differs from the former especially in that seaweeds no longer exist there.
2. The archbenthonic area, which begins at the slope of the shelf and extends into deeper waters; on an average it is estimated to comprise depths between 200 and 1,000 metres.
3. The abyssal benthonic zone which goes from 1,000 metres to the greatest depths.[1]

The distribution of the living species in these various areas have been defined by Professor Milner B. Schaefer (Director of Maritime Resources, University of California): "of the total biomass of benthonic animals in the world ocean, about 83 per cent. is estimated to exist in depths less than 200 metres, about 17 per cent. between 200 and 3,000 metres, and less than 17 per cent. below 3,000 metres. Studies in various parts of the world ocean confirm that the biomass of benthos decreases very sharply in depths beyond 1,500 metres" (extreme limit of the continental slope).[2]

Seen from an economic point of view, it appears that beyond depths of 1,000 to 1,500 metres, benthonic and demersal species are unlikely to be of economic importance. On the other hand, important commercial fishing for these species is being conducted

1. The vivid definition adopted in the United States to compare the continental margin is the following:
(1) The continental shelf, 200 metres (average gradient 0.1°).
(2) The continental slope, 200-1,500 metres (gradient 3-6°).
(3) The continental rise, 1,500-4,000 metres (gradient 0.1-1°).
(4) The abyssal plain, 4,000 metres (gradient 0.1°).

2. Symposium on the international régime of the seabed, Istituto Affari Internazionali, Rome, June 30-July 5, 1969.

at depths of 500 metres. Known under-utilized resources have been located in depths down to 1,000 metres. Due to the rapid improvements of technology, however, many of these deeper resources are rapidly becoming utilizable. At present, the great majority of the living resources, associated with the sea-floor, which are of economic importance are confined to the continental shelf and the continental slope, except perhaps for the tops of seamounts. The resources of the continental slope cannot be considered, in general, biologically separate from those of the shelf and neither can they rationally be treated independently from this point of view as concerns legal and economic regulations to be made.

Two factors should be taken into consideration: on the one hand, the interdependence which, from a "vertical" point of view exists between benthonic and demersal species, with a special view to their dependence for nutrition in the flux of organic matter. On the other hand, the interdependence which, from a "horizontal" point of view, exists between the species living along the continental margin. Then the question arises whether the consequence of the fundamental uniqueness of the sea environment should not entail uniform legal regulations, or whether, on the contrary, the variety of the species should result in complex laws, as has been the case to date.

B. *Living resources and sovereignty conflicts*

Increasing extension of sovereignty appears as a result of claims to exclusive fishing rights, e.g., the claim concerning the continental shelf, and the 1958 Convention of Geneva has partly recognized such sovereignty. This tendency creates a precedent that may influence the future régime of the living resources of the seabed.

1. Firstly, certain claims exceeded the exploitability criterion, which, however, opens large possibilities of expansion of national jurisdiction. This is the case with the tripartite declaration, signed in Santiago on August 18, 1952, by Chile, Peru and Ecuador, which extends the exclusive sovereignty of these States over their coastal sea to a distance of 200 miles and over the underlying seabed and subsoil (Art. 3). In the geological meaning of the term, continental shelf does not exist, and depths are estimated between 2,000 and 6,000 metres which in a foreseeable future will reduce

all possibilities of exploitation of the living resources on the ocean floor beyond present technical and economic possibilities.

On the other hand, the law of December 29, 1966, and the decree of January 5, 1967, which also extends Argentine sovereignty to 200 miles, bring forth more concrete short-term solutions as the Atlantic coast has a continental shelf and a continental slope. Although certain countries like, for instance, France and Brazil, have protested, it is known that a Soviet flotilla has accepted to pay a fee of 400,000 pesos to the Argentine Government for the right for 40 trawlers to fish 40 miles from the Argentine coasts. It is difficult to draw any conclusions from this precedent as the Soviet Government, by disavowing the captain, has objected to the Argentine interpretation that this should be a recognition of a unilateral extension.

2. Owing to the force of circumstances, however, the number of negotiated solutions concerning the continental shelf increase and moderate this unilateral trend.

Such solutions have become necessary where geographical factors, like continuity and adjacency, occur. Three agreements may be an illustration of this. The agreement between Great Britain and Norway, signed in London on March 10, 1965, which agreement, by the way, also relates to mineral resources. The agreement of October 6, 1965, between Great Britain and the Netherlands, relating to the exploration and the exploitation of the natural resources of the North Sea, and the agreement between Great Britain and Denmark of March 3, 1966. These agreements are in accordance with the Continental Shelf Act of April 15, 1964, by which rights of exploitation of the natural resources of the seabed and the subsoil in the area surrounding British coasts have been conferred upon the British Crown. They all relate to the seabed and the adjacent waters and roughly apply the rule of the median line.

In its decision of February 20, 1969, the International Court of Justice has not considered that the principle of equidistance should automatically be applied and, by inviting the parties to negotiate, the Court encourages a generalization of the rules acquiesced in.

Still, the agreements concerning the North Sea are of no greater interest with respect to the problems of the seabed beyond national jurisdiction, as the depths of the North Sea never exceed

200 metres and, therefore, fall within the uncontested criterion of the shelf only, whereas the depths of the major part of the world oceans and seabeds are located between 2,000 and 6,000 metres.

As a matter of fact, claims of States have two trends. The first one regards States having few technical means at their disposal, who try to assert their rights over very large areas extending from their coasts; the second one leads technologically advanced States to invoke the principle of the freedom of the seas with respect to the ocean floor, in order to ensure the continuation of the exploitations as, for example, the exploitation of lobsters. This, however, does not exclude the possibilities of these States to claim exclusive rights to sedentary fisheries, whether such rights are acquired or to be acquired.

Here again we find the question of the scope of the concept of the continental shelf and the ambiguities of the concept that result from the exploitability criterion.[3]

If the criterion of exploitability is utilized and applied on the continental shelf and the slope is, thus, "grabbed from", the applicability of Article A (4) of the Convention on the Continental Shelf will, at the same time, be extended. Now, the difference established by the Convention between benthonic and demersal species has been highly criticized and has caused international controversies. The "lobster war" is an illustration of this.

Already at the 1958 Conference (Doc. off., Vol. VI, p. 68), the Japanese delegate, Mr. Tsuruoka remarked: "It is extremely difficult to establish a distinction between pelagic and benthonic species because certain fish among the swimming species rest on the seabed during certain periods and others live most of their lives on it as adults . . . it would be even more difficult to establish a distinction between mobile and sedentary animals".

When France ratified the Convention on June 14, 1965, it made a declaration as to the interpretation of Article 2 (4). The wording of the declaration is as follows: "The Government of the Republic

3. At the 24th General Assembly, the first Commission has elaborated a resolution requesting the Secretary-General to make inquiries about the opinion of member States as to the timeliness of convening a conference to interpret or revise the 1958 Convention on the Continental Shelf, in order to adopt a more precise definition of the limits of the region of the seabed over which coastal States exercise sovereign rights as regards exploration and exploitation of the natural resources.

of France interpret the expression 'living organisms belonging to the sedentary species' as excluding the crustaceans, with the exception of the species of crabs called barnacles".

A more comprehensive conception of the rights of the coastal States over crustaceans appears in the exchange of notes between the United States and Japan on November 25, 1965, renewed November 1966 (*UNTS*, No. 7,730), according to which "The Government of the United States of America considers the Alaska king crab a natural resource of the continental shelf over which the coastal State (in this case the USA) exercises exclusive jurisdiction, control, and exploitation rights", whereas the Japanese Government considers it a resource of the high seas. The agreement authorizes Japanese citizens and vessels to conduct fishing of this crab, without taking into consideration the positions as to the principle of ownership. On the other hand, the agreement of February 5, 1965, between the United States and the Soviet Union, renewed February 1967, by stating its conformity with Article 2 (4) of the Convention as ratified by both signatories, recognizes the American claim.

It thus appears that the vagueness of the Article is, in practice, the subject of unilateral or conventional interpretations.

However, ambiguities of another nature also must be taken into consideration. They result from the complexity of the biological environment dependent on the seabed. At present, fishing gear used on the seabed catch both sedentary and mobile demersal animals simultaneously, although with different degrees of efficiency. Even if a gear catches mainly one type it will naturally affect the other—for example trawling for demersal fish over mussel beds. It is now a question whether the equivocal distinction in Article 2 (4)[4] can be maintained and extended beyond the shelf proper. In case this distinction would eventually be abandoned, several hypotheses must be taken into consideration.

(*a*) The modification might relate to the living resources of the shelf. It might just concern those living beyond a shelf as it would be after a revision of the 1958 definition, as well as a fixed limit with respect to depth and extension would have to be established.

4. L. F. E. Goldie, "Sedentary Fisheries, and Article 2 (4) of the Continental Shelf Convention", 63 *AJIL*, 86 (1969).

(*b*) In any case, two opposite solutions are conceivable: assimilation of demersal resources with benthonic resources or, inversely, assimilation of benthonic resources with high sea fishery resources.

Then the question of a future régime of the seabed arises.

1. One solution would be to recognize the coastal State's appropriation of the benthonic and the demersal species, provided that exploitability should be the criterion for considering the seabed to be an extension of the continental shelf.

2. If, on the contrary, a separate régime for the seabed beyond a precisely defined shelf were adopted, still two options would be available.

(i) The "*res nullius*" with grant of preferential rights to the "first comer". This would favour technologically advanced nations. However, a clause similar to that of Article 13 of the Convention on Fishery and the conservation of the biological resources of the high seas with respect to sedentary fisheries would moderate such primacy by granting other nations access.

(ii) The "*res communis*" which will require an international regulation of the exploitation of the living resources of the seabed. As a matter of fact, this world-wide system does not consider these resources. The propositions put forth during the last 18 months with a view to the creation of a regulating and operational Seabed Agency only consider the mineral resources. The fishery field is traditionally subject to a decentralized and regionalized régime; the exploitation of the resources of the seabeds and the ocean-floor is likely also to be subjected to regional régimes.

However, this does not mean that solutions of general importance could not be achieved. Important initiatives are now being taken by the institutions of the United Nations.

In order to facilitate exchange of information between members, the Unesco has, for example, created an International Oceanographic Commission (IOC) in 1960 to further scientific research on the resources of the oceans. This institution is sometimes considered to be likely some day to be transformed into a new specialized institution. The Committee on Fisheries of the FAO plays a very active role, as do the regional organisms[5] of the organisation.

5. D. S. Cheever, "The role of International Organization in Ocean Development", *Int. Organization* 1968, p. 629; Marine Science and Technology

The Unesco and the FAO have set up a joint advisory Committee for research on the resources of the sea. The International Atomic Energy Agency is making a study of the pollution of the sea resulting from nuclear waste, whereas IMCO has undertaken the study of the pollution resulting from hydrocarbons, as well as its endeavours to establish a global regulation of the question. Lastly, the UN Economic and Social Council, which devotes special attention to the study of the sea, has in 1966 requested the Secretary-General to make a survey of the mineral and the biological resources of the sea.[6] It should be noticed, however, that the documentation on "food resources of the sea beyond the continental shelf, excluding fish", submitted by the Secretariat in implementation of the ECOSOC resolution deals virtually exclusively with the pelagic resources of the superficial waters, and not with the benthonic resources.

Mention should also be made of the work of the Economic Commission for Asia and the Far East. In fact, the regional plan is of considerable importance. If, on the one hand, the struggle against pollution of the sea environment may be the subject of general regulations, the exploitation of the resources, on the other hand, rather require localized and specialized solutions.

II. THE PROTECTION OF THE LIVING RESOURCES OF THE SEABEDS AND THE OCEANS

As with respect to the other species of the sea-environment, protection has two aspects, viz. the struggle against lawless and abusive exploitation and the struggle against pollution.

A. Protection against abusive exploitation falls under various intergovernmental bodies which are not especially intended for the seabed resources[7] and which, on the whole, deal with the pelagic species.

---

of the Sea-Surveys and Proposals, Report of the Secretary-General, UN Doc. E/4447, April 24, 1968.

6. ECOSOC res. 1112 (XL), Doc. E/4449 and Add. 1-2.

7. Cf. a list of these organisms in the study of Carroz and Roche: "The Proposed International Commission for the Conservation of Atlantic Tunas", *AJIL*, Vol. 61, 1967, p. 675.

The regulations concerning the resources of the seabed are bilateral because, to this day, they relate exclusively to the continental shelf. Mention should be made of the "provisional régime for the regulation of the fishery of pearls by Japanese nationals", signed on May 24, 1954, which provides a solution to conflicts which throughout decades have opposed Japan and Australia. Immediately after the last World War, the Japanese started to exploit the pearls of the Australian continental shelf on their own behalf. Before then, Japanese divers had worked for Australian companies. In 1952 the Pearl Fisheries Act regulated these fisheries beyond Australian territorial waters. A proclamation of September 11, 1953, made by the Governor-General, declared the extension of Australian sovereignty over the seabed of the continental shelf. After some protest from Japan, an agreement was eventually reached.

The shrimps of the Mexican Gulf, on the coasts of Cuba and Florida, have been the object of an agreement signed on August 15, 1958, and put into force on September 4, 1959, between the United States and Cuba. A Commission for the conservation of the shrimps of the eastern Gulf of Mexico has been set up. Its mission is to further and co-ordinate research as well as to adopt regulations on the basis of scientific information with a view to the conservation of the stocks and an optimum production to the benefit of both countries. The regulations will come into force unless a veto is exercised.

With regard to the Alaska king crab, three kinds of provisions in the above-mentioned agreement between the United States and the USSR provide for the protection of these species. Firstly, by fixing a quota (Art. 2) and forbidding the catching of female crabs, smaller crabs, whose shell-size is less than 14.5 cm., and crabs with soft shells, the agreement states a quantitative and qualitative limitation of the rights of Soviet trawlers to fishery. Any catch of crabs of this kind shall immediately be thrown into the water, with the maximum precautions. The agreement also defines which gear should be used. Furthermore the agreement establishes a control machinery: on the request of one of the signatories, the other shall be ready to contribute to a correct fulfilment of the clauses of the agreement and, to this end, allow that the other contracting party's officials board crab-fishing vessels and draw up a report. Finally, the agreement provides for an intensification of the study of the resources, an annual exchange of results, viz. information of a biological nature (sex, size, place of capture, breeding, nutrition, migrations), statistics of catch (annual bulk for each area), statistics concerning fishing operations (number of gear and flotillas) and statistics of production (canned and frozen crabs).

It will be realized that these agreements should be considered a part of scientific research because a great deal of work in this field still remains to be done and great results may be expected from the International Decade of Ocean Exploration, launched by the United Nations in December 1968.

It may be expected that such arrangements will increase with technical progress and the increasing exploitation of the resources of the continental slope. A regional model seems to be preferable, i.e., adapted to a well-defined geographic zone, although the States concerned may not necessarily have other connections with the zone than their participation in its exploitation. The régime may concern one or all species dependent on the seabed.

A certain number of points must therefore be defined by the Statute:

1. The zone to which the régime would apply, comprising the continental shelf or only beginning beyond the limit of the continental shelf as defined by the Convention. The agreements might very well contain a clause the aim of which would be to "freeze" disputed claims and to state, as do some conventions [8] that no Article should be interpreted as affecting the contracting parties' rights or claims to any of the zones in question. It is, in fact, hardly to be expected that future conventions will be concluded without the participation of the coastal States who intervene either as co-operators or, if the country in question is a developing country, to assert its rights. The resolution of the United Nations recognizing nations' rights to avail themselves of their natural resources must, in fact, be taken into account. It may even be expected that the non-participation of the coastal States in a convention will lead them to challenge the legality of the agreement by qualifying it as a violation of the principle of *jus cogens*.[9]

8. Cf. the above-mentioned study on the Atlantic Tunas, *AJIL*, 1967, Vol. 61, p. 681.

9. Cf. G. Fischer, "La Souveraineté sur les ressources naturelles", *AFDI*, 1962, pp. 516-528.

2. The institutional régime, which may assume the classic form of a Commission with a permanent Secretariat. The aim of the Commission would be to deal with and develop scientific research and determine a conservation policy, like the very detailed ones of the Soviet-American agreement relating to the Alaska king crab. The Commission might either be endowed with determinative power or could simply assume the role of a co-ordinating body by recommending appropriate solutions. Such recommendations would be likely to develop a binding force if they are not rejected by the members within a certain time-limit.

3. If the Commission does not avail itself of its own, recognised, means of control (and to my knowledge this has not been the case in previous fishery agreements), the control would be entrusted to the contracting States themselves according to a very common reciprocity procedure which enables the concerned States' officials to hail, examine, and attach vessels of States signatories to the Convention, although the vessels may be delivered back to the State whose flag it bears and which has the sole competence to apply punitive sanctions.

Relations based on co-operation agreements between these future commissions and other institutions as, for example, the FAO, should be taken into consideration. Such relations will also prove very valuable as regards pollution preventions.

B. The pollution of the seabeds.

The problem of the pollution of the sea in general will not be examined here. The present study concentrates entirely on the pollution affecting the seabed. Another limitation of the subject is necessary: only the bottom of the continental slope and the continental shelf in so far as these are closely connected is dealt with.

Having made this point, it can be stated that living resources dependent on the seabed (benthonics and demersals) may be injuriously affected by two sets of pollution effects. The first, nonspecific, ones coming from the surface, the second ones resulting from the exploitation of the seabed itself.

1. Industrial waste (solid alumina and bauxite residues[10]) or ra-

10. In France, a decree of January 4, 1966, declared solid residues dumped into the sea to be public property. By a sentence of March 15, 1966 (Commune de Cassis), the Conseil d'Etat has rejected the appeal against the

dioactive waste[11] are well known. It will be remembered that the Geneva Convention of April 29, 1958, relating to the high seas lays down that the signatories, observing all rules and regulations elaborated by competent, international organisms, should take all necessary steps to avoid such pollution.[12] Pollution by hydrocarbons has been the subject of various well-known conventions, e.g., the London Convention of May 12, 1954, which prescribes that hydrocarbons should not be discharged in zones situated, in principle, less than 50 miles from shore; the Convention of April 11, 1962, the aims of which are to fill in the gaps of the former. Known also are the draft articles prepared by the IMCO concerning the rights of a coastal State to intervene in case of accidents occurring in the sea beyond the coastal State's territorial waters and resulting in, or which may result in, pollution of the sea with hydrocarbons. If these hydrocarbons float on the surface of the water, the detergents spread, as was the case after the catastrophe of the *Torrey-Canyon*, will sink, and their effects on the living species of the seabeds are not predictable at the present state of knowledge.

2. The risks of pollution resulting from the exploitation and exploration of the seabed and the subsoil are considerable. The above-mentioned 1954 London Convention invited States to adopt an adequate regulation so as to avoid any risks of pollution which may result from such operations.

At the present time, the production of submarine petroleum, which already forms 20 per cent. of the production of the Western world, constitutes a serious danger to the sea environment and especially to the benthonic and demersal species, by the mere fact of the drilling which entails a throwing up of muds, by explosion

---

decision. It is peculiar to see that a typical action of pollution has thus been covered.

11. J. P. Quenaudec, "Le rejet à la mer de déchets radioactifs", *AFDI*, 1965, pp. 750 and following; "Les aspects juridiques de l'évacuation des déchets radioactifs dans la mer", *Revue internationale d'océanographie médicale*, C.E.R.B.O.M., Vol. II, 1966, pp. 5 and following.

12. The international institutions themselves may, to this end, supervise certain operations. Under the sponsorship of the European Agency for Nuclear Energy, 11,000 tons of radioactive waste, which concerned Germany, Belgium, France, Great Britain and the Netherlands, were in 1967 immersed to a depth of 5,000 metres in containers considered to be proof against corrosion. The method, however, has been criticized.

of charges, not to speak of the possible explosion of shafts resulting in an evacuation of petroleum which it is difficult to restrain. An example of this is *Sea Quest*'s accident in January 1968 which caused an escape of gas into the North Sea. States exercising sovereign rights, recognised by the 1958 Convention, extend as regards the continental shelf the principles of mining rights applying to their territory,[13] the oil companies are by a public utility concession subject to the administrative régime of the coastal State. The French Law for the shelf contains provisions concerning security and repression of pollution effects likely to have been caused by installations.

As concerns the zone beyond national jurisdiction, provided the zone has been sufficiently precisely defined, the problem is still standing and is being considered by the United Nations in the activities now being carried on.

Since the beginning of the work of the special Committee on the seabeds and the oceans, established in 1968, Iceland (A/AC. 135/31) has filed a proposal regarding the study of the means of obtaining a maximum reduction of the risk of pollution of the sea environment which may result from the exploration and the exploitation of the seabed and its subsoil. The proposal has been warmly welcomed and fully supported. During the debates on the proposal, the necessity of avoiding overlapping of the work of the organizations studying the problems (AIEA, IMCO) has been emphasized.

Special attention has been paid to the specific risks of pollution which may be caused by the exploitation of the seabed. It has been pointed out that turbidity caused by an intense exploitation of sea sediments may, because of dragging techniques and the use of explosives and chemicals in the course of the recovery and enrichment of the sea minerals, bring about a shrouding of the benthonic fauna and have harmful effects on the other biological resources. Likewise, importance has been attached to the necessity of improving present knowledge in order to obtain correct evalua-

13. J. Devaux Charbonnel, "Régime juridique de la recherche et de l'exploitation des hydrocarbures en mer", *Revue française de l'energie*, October 1964; P. Reuter, "Le plateau continental", étude pour l'association de droits miniers et pétroliers, Paris 1960; E. Sharf, *La plateforme continentale et son statut juridique*, thesis Paris, 1952.

tions of the possible effects on living resources of the exploitation of the mineral resources.

The draft resolution introduced by the United States (A/AC. 135/25) containing a statement of the principles concerning the ocean floors, provided that States adopt "adequate measures to reduce to a minimum the pollution of the seas and the disturbance of the existing biological, chemical, and physical balance processes". A draft declaration introduced by 15 States to the mentioned Committee (Doc. A/7230, p. 67) contains a similar provision.

Lastly, on December 21, 1968, the General Assembly has adopted a resolution B (United Nations report, January 1969), which instructs the Secretary-General to enter, "in co-operation with the appropriate and competent organism(s) carrying on co-ordinated activities relating to the field of pollution prevention", upon a study of all problems connected with the protection of the biological resources of the seabeds and the oceans and the limitation of the "interference between the various means to be used to harvest the wealths of the oceans".

Resolution B is thus devoted to the study of pollution problems, but the study is also provided for by a resolution A creating the "Committee for the peaceful utilization of the seabeds beyond the limits of national jurisdiction", which Committee is composed of 42 States charged with the elaboration of the principles and rules likely to favour international co-operation.

In its report of 1969 to the 24th General Assembly of the United Nations,[14] the Seabed Committee gave a summary of the discussions in the Committee in the course of its sessions concerning the question of pollution and other risks, the question of the obligations and responsibilities of States involved in the utilization, exploration and exploitation of the seabed and the ocean floor. The working group has retained the following elements of the various formulations proposed concerning the activities in the mentioned zone

(i) Necessity of equitable respect of the interests of all States.

(ii) Necessity not to infringe the freedom of the high seas and to avoid unjustifiable hampering of the exercise of this freedom.

(iii) Adoption of adequate protection measures against risk of pollution and other harmful effects on the sea environment. Among

14. UN Doc. Sup. No. 22 (A/7622).

the harmful effects mentioned in the propositions, the following can be found,

(*a*) contamination by radioactive substances;

(*b*) modification of the ecological or other processes or of the equilibrium of the sea environment;

(*c*) deterioration of the flora and the fauna.

(iv) Adoption of adequate protection measures with a view to conservation and protection of the biological resources of the sea environment, or obligation not to hinder the conservation of biological resources.

(v) Adoption of security measures concerning all activities in the mentioned zone.

(vi) Assistance in case of accident, distress or danger.

(vii) Damages caused by activities in the mentioned zone (undertakings without adoption of adequate protection measures) will involve responsibility.

(viii) The coastal States nearest to the zone where these activities take place shall be consulted in order to avoid that their legitimate interests be injured.

(ix) Rights of coastal States to take appropriate measures in order to protect their coasts and their territorial waters against pollution appearing in a zone beyond their national jurisdiction.

(x) Procedure to be followed when it is estimated that certain activities may be harmful to other activities.

In the synthesis of its debates, the Committee points out that it can be taken for granted that the concepts of equitable respect of the interests of all States and of necessity not to infringe the freedom of the high seas and to avoid unjustifiable hampering of the exercise of this freedom do not give rise to disputes. Moreover, the necessity of adopting adequate protection measures against risks of pollution is generally accepted. On the whole, no objections have been raised as regards adoption of adequate measures with a view to protection of the biological resources of the sea environment and protection measures concerning activities in the mentioned zone.

For the time being, no agreement has been reached as to the extent of the rights of coastal States with regard to activities undertaken in the zone, including scientific research and exploration. The question of responsibility incurred for damages caused by activities undertaken in the zone is still being examined.

Chapter III

LEGAL ASPECT OF THE DEVELOPMENT OF THE MINERAL RESOURCES OF THE CONTINENTAL SHELF

The Geneva Convention on the Continental Shelf of April 29, 1958, recognizes, in Article 2, the sovereign rights of the coastal State over the continental shelf for the purpose of exploring it and exploiting its natural resources. These exclusive rights do not depend on occupation, effective or nominal, or on any express proclamation. In these circumstances, it is for the coastal State to allocate mining rights to companies, State or private, national or foreign, wishing to explore and exploit the mineral resources of the shelf. These resources fall into two broad categories: hydrocarbons and solid minerals.

1. *Hydrocarbons*

At the moment, hydrocarbons satisfy half the world's requirements in energy, and supply the chemical industry with a very important raw material. As is known, they were first exploited in terrestrial deposits, and it was only relatively recently that man began to work them offshore. The problems created by underwater hydrocarbons therefore stem from the world petroleum question as a whole. In this respect, they fit into the enormous framework of the international co-operation that has proved so necessary in this field, and which is carried out by various organizations.

The United Nations, one of whose tasks it is to stimulate economic co-operation, has taken up the question of hydrocarbons in a number of contexts. In its resolution 1803 (XVII) of December 19, 1962, it proclaimed "... the inalienable right of all States freely to dispose of their natural ... resources in accordance with their national interests, and with respect for the economic independence of States ...". In the same resolution, and both earlier and later, in resolutions 1515 (XV) of December 15, 1960, and 2158 (XXI) of November 28, 1966, the General Assembly also recommended various norms applicable to the search for and working of hydrocarbons, especially standards for safeguarding foreign capital, the conditions governing the nationalization, expropriation or requisitioning of foreign companies, and the protection of producing countries.

Against this international background, the development of deposits of hydrocarbons in the subsoil of the continental shelf has made great progress over the last few years: one-sixth of world production now originates offshore. The operations concerned cover the exploitation of crude oil, natural gas, gas condensates and any associated gas or substance; 22 countries are now working underwater oil deposits lying off their coasts; while the continental shelf is being prospected in more than 75 countries. The legal aspects of the development of offshore hydrocarbons are determined by a mining law enacted by the coastal State, which must take account of the rules of international law as defined in the Geneva Convention, with a view, in particular, to safeguarding freedom of navigation on the superjacent waters.

2. *Solid minerals*

Offshore solid minerals are not of the same international importance. However, such resources may be of considerable interest to some countries; and so far as developing countries are concerned, they sometimes form the object of leases assigned to foreign companies. Such minerals are worked either by conventional underground mining methods, the deposit being entered from land—as is the case when working mineral deposits within bedrock (coal and iron, nickel, copper or tin ores)—or by dredging, by means of which such materials as sand, gravel, lime shells, diamonds, gold, tin, iron and other heavy mineral sands can be recovered from the surficial layers of the sea floor.

Whether we are dealing with hydrocarbons or with solid minerals, exploitation by nationals or foreigners postulates the existence of adequate administrative machinery (bureau of mines, fuel directorate, ministry of power or of public works, depending on the country concerned). The department in question is responsible for applying the laws and enforcement orders relating to search for and exploitation of mineral resources in general, some of which will deal specifically with the resources of the continental shelf. Here the following national legislation may be mentioned: the French Law of December 30, 1968, on the continental shelf, which includes precise provisions covering the conditions on which the resources of the French continental shelf may be explored and exploited; the Norwegian Law of June 21, 1963; the Italian Law of January 11, 1967, on search for and exploitation of liquid and gaseous hydrocarbons; and the United Kingdom Continental Shelf Act, promulgated on April 15, 1964.

All such administrative and legal machinery gives effect to a genuine mining policy. This policy becomes specially important where the exploitation of hydrocarbons is concerned. As a rule, when entering into association with private operators and financiers, governments make every attempt to give priority to national over foreign companies, and, so far as is possible, to independent enterprises over the great international consortia, whose power they fear. These considerations, valid for the exploitation of hydrocarbons on land, do not always hold for offshore hydrocarbons: the price of exploration or exploitation being very much higher than on land–largely because of the cost of the boreholes–giant enterprises, usually belonging to a "cartel", alone are in a position to work on the continental shelf.

Thus, when entrusted to foreign enterprises, the exploitation of the mineral resources of the continental shelf gives rise to a number of problems bound up with respect for the sovereignty of the host country and the latter's development. This is a typical problem of what is now known as international development law. First, the general problem posed by the exploration and exploitation of the resources of the continental shelf, no matter what the capabilities and standing of the operator, must be considered, followed by specific issues raised by the participation of a foreign enterprise.

I. SEARCH FOR AND EXPLOITATION OF CONTINENTAL SHELF DEPOSITS: LEGAL POSITION

States are free to lay down in their mining legislation the principles applicable to this maritime zone, either by extension of the laws applicable on their terrestrial territory or by enacting special legislation for the shelf. Often, as in the United Kingdom, the United States of America and Norway, the government of the coastal State delineates, as necessary, the maritime areas to which the legislation shall apply.

Two groups of questions arise: those relating to the grant of mining rights to operators; and those relating to the latter's obligations.

1. *Grant of mining rights*

Procedures for the grant of mining rights often involve not only the mining authorities proper, but also other departments concerned with maritime affairs.

A. *Role of the authority empowered to allocate rights*

Mining rights are always allocated by an administrative authority, individual or collective, the nature of which varies from one country to another: the ruler in person; the ministry of public works, the ministry of power or the ministry of economic affairs; the national bureau of mines; or an expert government body. Whatever the authority, he or it must discharge various functions, which have been very well defined in United Nations document A/AC.138/21,[1] of January 27, 1970, in the following terms:
(*a*) to define the offshore areas in which the Government wishes to promote research and development;
(*b*) to invite tenders relating to the exploration, evaluation and/or exploitation rights over such areas;
(*c*) to grant such rights, extend their duration when desirable and approve their transfer as may be appropriate;
(*d*) to provide for arbitration in cases of disagreement over matters relating to rights granted; and
(*e*) to terminate, cancel or otherwise take appropriate action in

1. *Government measures pertaining to the development of mineral resources on the continental shelf*: Review prepared by the [United Nations] Secretariat, pp. 7 and 8.

respect of the rights of operators not observing the conditions and obligations contained therein.

Normally, the administrative authority concerned is required to maintain an official register of rights granted (permits, licences, concessions or mining titles), together with maps showing their location; to enforce the laws governing conduct of operations, safety of personnel and equipment, and the safeguarding of the interests of third parties; and to maintain statistical records and economic reviews of the operations carried out under the rights granted.

B. *Content of the rights allocated*

Legislation governing search and exploitation has as its aims: to encourage exploration and to strike a reasonable balance between the rights and obligations of licence holders. States have discretionary powers to grant either exclusive or non-exclusive exploration rights and exclusive or non-exclusive operating rights. The arrangements vary from country to country and from area to area. The technical and financial credentials of bidders are subject to very close scrutiny, and the conditions on which mining titles are granted are sometimes less generous for the continental shelf than for land operations. However, as the facilities for and cost of seismic surveys carried out to locate deposits of hydrocarbons underwater are more favourable than those for work on land, it is easier and quicker to choose from vast areas those which seem to be of real interest. This is why the legislator often provides for the grant of non-exclusive, short-term licences covering all the areas designated for search. The licence holders in turn can apply, after a short time, for prospecting rights covering a smaller area, over which they will enjoy exclusive rights, and in due course acquire the right to exploit any deposits discovered.

Speaking generally, it may be said that where exploration rights are granted they lead to an exclusive right of exploitation.

The laws and regulations stipulate, with a view to speeding up discovery, that annual expenditure shall exceed a specified minimum and that the areas for which licences have been granted shall be progressively reduced. Thus, for example, Article 3 of the Italian Law of January 11, 1957, provides that ". . . the prospecting licence may not be granted in respect of an area greater than fifty thousand hectares".[2] It is also usually laid down that the licence holder must embark upon geological and geophysical survey operations within periods fixed in the licence, and that he shall notify the mining authorities of any discoveries he may make, and provide them with such economic and technical information as they may request.

When rights are granted, the concessionary State collects certain fees. In most countries, the laws provide that the grant of prospecting rights gives rise to the collection of fees. The main object of this is to cover administrative costs, and the fees are therefore moderate, especially in the case of solid minerals. Cash bonuses, sometimes called "signature bonuses", although also associated with the granting of exploration and evaluation rights, are not of the same nature as concession fees. They comprise the generally large sums of money paid when operators apply for licences in areas where development possibilities are deemed to be very favourable. By *exploration* is to be understood the process of prospecting by reconnaissance surveys—usually geological, geophysical, hydrological and topographical—together with certain more detailed studies, and possibly scout drilling and sampling, to determine whether or not a mineral deposit exists in the area examined. By *evaluation* is to be understood the process of determining, by detailed studies, sampling, drilling and testing, the possibilities of working a mineral deposit commercially. These two series of operations form as a rule, part of the search programme, and obviously entail fairly heavy expenditure, which warrants the checking of both the financial standing of the bidder for the concession and his technical operational resources. It is also the rule for the concessionary State to levy charges on such activities.

Search licences are themselves limited in space and in time. In the first place, exploration rights are granted for areas very much larger than those covered by evaluation or exploitation rights. Moreover, the duration of tenure of exploration rights is usually short (one year in Nigeria, Italy and Morocco), though it may be extended from year to year. Combined exploration and evaluation rights are also known; their tenure (initial term plus extensions), may vary between 5 years—e.g., in Panama—to 17 years, as in the Union of South Africa if the operator is prospecting for hydro-

2. Unofficial translation.

carbons. Exceptionally, there is no limit on the life of such rights in Australia, where renewal may be obtained indefinitely subject to certain conditions. For solid minerals, rights are valid for 4 years in India and for 10 years in Indonesia.

These various problems will crop up again, though on a larger scale, at the phase, no longer of the grant of the exploration licence, but of definitive exploitation.

2. *Operating conditions*

Operating conditions are the result, on the one hand of the general conditions that constitute their legal background, and on the other hand of the various obligations imposed on the operator.

A. *General operating conditions*

The mining laws and regulations lay down the extent and duration of exploitation and its fiscal framework.

(*a*) The first step in fixing the extent and duration of operations is to delineate the zone, the area of which can vary greatly. Article 14 of the Italian Law provides that the operating concession may not cover an area of more than 3,000 hectares and that the zone in question must be square or rectangular in shape, except where part of the perimeter coincides with the State frontier. If the zone is rectangular, the breadth may not exceed one-quarter of the length. In addition, Article 15 stipulates that exploitation areas totalling more than 80,000 hectares may not be allocated, directly or indirectly, to one and the same person, body or company.

These examples, which relate to hydrocarbons, cannot be considered as of universal applicability. In the major petroleum-producing countries exploitation rights apply, as a rule, to the extent of the producing fields. There are however, exceptions, notably in the United States of America, where combined evaluation and exploitation rights are obtained by competitive bidding, covering blocks of approximately 23 square kilometres. It is noticeable that highly industrialized countries tend to grant licences for smaller areas than do countries still in course of development. It is also noteworthy that in other countries, the average area covered by operating rights appears to be about 300 square kilometres, both for hydrocarbons and for solid minerals. It should also be noted that in both the cases quoted the operator may generally hold more than one evaluation and/or exploitation right.

So far as the duration of the operating rights allocated is concerned, the period of tenure runs for much longer periods than those fixed for exploration pure and simple. Exploitation rights are usually designed to allow the deposit to be completely worked out. In the case of hydrocarbons, the duration of operating licences is, for example, 35 years in Argentina and the Ivory Coast, 45 years in the Persian Gulf and Indonesia, 60 years in Libya and 63 years in New Zealand. For solid minerals, tenure ranges between 20 and 50 years, though it should be noted that, where there is provision for renewal, it may total as much as 75 years.

In principle, when the concessionaire wishes to proceed from the phase of exploration or evaluation to that of exploitation, he is required to relinquish a substantial part of the area initially granted to him. Application of this rule of relinquishment, which will normally already have come into play in the exploration phase (when the initial tenure expired), will further reduce the extent of the area when the operating phase is entered. However, in some cases, the concessionaire may retain the part of the area he should have relinquished by paying higher royalty. In some countries, where the contract type of combined exploration, evaluation and exploitation right exists, the operator is obliged to relinquish, every five years, part of the area–up to 25 per cent. of the total– until it is reduced to the size of the workable hydrocarbon field. The legislation of some countries, including Libya and the Netherlands, goes so far as to require that the area covered by the concession granted be reduced by some one-half or two-thirds within a period of 10 years.

Lastly, the right of the operator to surrender voluntarily, before the due date, some parts of the area covered by his right, where they turn out to be less promising than had been hoped, must be recognized. However, it is necessary that the operator should have fulfilled the conditions attaching to the rights granted to him, in particular the payment of royalties, charges, fees and taxes, up to the time of surrender.

(*b*) As regards the fiscal framework, the concessionary State expects to derive certain benefits from the concessions it grants in respect of underwater mineral resources of its continental shelf. In addition to the concession fees, such benefits flow from rentals, royalties, profit taxes and profit-sharing.

(i) Concession fees and cash bonuses (signature bonuses), already mentioned in connection with exploration rights, are also collectable on licences to exploit. It is not uncommon for the cash bonuses paid to acquire combined evaluation and exploitation rights for hydrocarbons to amount to several million dollars, as in for example, Abu Dhabi, Indonesia, Iran, Kuwait and Nigeria. In the United States of America, the sums paid for a lease with a good production potential may run into tens or even hundreds of millions of dollars.

(ii) Rentals are regarded as a form of taxation based on the surface area. Payable annually, they are usually moderate, being designed to cover administrative costs. They may, however, rise substantially during the closing years of validity of an operating licence, to ensure that the operator continues adequately to work the areas allocated to him. It should also be mentioned that in the case of solid minerals, rentals are usually of the order of a few hundred dollars a year per square kilometre.

(iii) Royalties: overall operating costs being very much higher offshore than on land, mainly because of the high cost of drilling, the royalties levied by the coastal State on output are often assessed at lower rates than on shore. They are often calculated on the wellhead value of hydrocarbons, or on the minehead value of the solid minerals. Although different in concept, they have the same effect as the production taxes levied on offshore minerals in most countries. Usually, the operator is required to sell, at the current market price, the amount of production that corresponds to the royalty rate and to pay the proceeds to the government in cash. However, in some cases royalties are payable on a "posted price" basis. The posted price is higher than the current market price, and might be described as a sort of list price that the market price does not usually reach. Royalty rates on the production of hydrocarbons vary rather widely around an average of 12 per cent. Thus it is 12.5 per cent. of the posted price in Abu Dhabi, Kuwait and Libya, whereas it fluctuates between 8 and 10 per cent. in Nigeria, depending on the distance from the coast. In France, the rate varies from 5 to 14 per cent. depending on the rate of production, the distance between the oilfield and refining facilities, and whether crude oil or gas is being produced.

As in the case of hydrocarbons, royalties on solid minerals are always payable in cash; but rates vary much more widely. They are levied on a flat-rate basis or as a percentage of profits.

(iv) Taxes on profits: operators are subject to taxes on profits accruing from their output. These taxes may be the same as those levied normally under company law; or they may be the subject of special stipulations. The way in which they are levied varies from country to country, and they are often designed to encourage the development of the deposits. Provision is often made for tax rebates by abatement or a system of allowances, which may take the form of deductions for depletion of reserves. Thus, in the case of hydrocarbons, depletion allowances may be as high as 27.5 per cent. in France and the United States of America; in the same way, it may be permissible to deduct capital expenditure when taxes are being assessed. It may also be decided that taxes shall not be imposed until development charges have been recouped.

In the same spirit, proceeds from the production of solid minerals may sometimes be free from profit taxes for an agreed period from the date on which exploitation begins, as an incentive to operators to develop new resources vigorously.

(v) Profit-sharing differs from the foregoing practices in that it is not strictly speaking a fiscal measure, being based on a direct sharing in the profits accruing from production. It is usually confined to the exploitation of hydrocarbons, and results from negotiation between operators and oil producing and exporting countries. The bargaining also makes it possible for the concessionary State to impose certain specific obligations on the operator.

B. *Operating obligations*

In pursuance of the applicable laws and regulations, operating obligations are usually laid down in the articles and conditions of the contracts concluded between the government department granting the rights and the operator. They cover the conditions under which the work is to be carried out (work performance); safety of personnel and equipment; and the protection of the interests of third parties.

(*a*) *Obligations relating to work performance*

The obligations imposed on operators apply equally to hydrocarbons and to solid minerals; but it should be noted that they are more onerous in the case of the former.

In order to get an exploitation concession, the applicant must have submitted in advance, within a period laid down in his contract, a detailed work programme. This programme must describe the geological and geophysical surveys to be conducted, and the test wells to be drilled and completed for the purpose of assessing production prospects. The performance of the work is governed by the concept of "good oil-industry practice", a principle the operator must bear in mind in his production operations and to which he must adapt his methods and norms. He must carry out the work on a continuing basis and install the facilities needed for production, storage and transportation. In addition, he must ensure proper conservation of the deposit, especially by eschewing a production programme aimed at "highgrading" the deposit—which would lead to its more rapid depletion—without attempting to work the lower-grade parts.

Concession contracts therefore provide that the concessionaire shall undertake to employ, in bringing the deposit into production and exploiting it, sound engineering methods, in such a way as to avoid wastage of power or industrial supplies; to ensure due conservation of the deposits; and to maintain the economic yield of hydrocarbons at optimum level, especially by using secondary recovery methods where necessary. It is also laid down that the concessionaire shall inform the authority responsible for issuing the licence of the means he intends to deploy, giving the reasons for his choice. He must also provide the authority with samples, drill cuttings and other useful information about the operations carried out in the performance of his contract. In addition, he must notify the competent authorities of any damage to the oilfields or installations and of the steps he has taken to stop it and make it good.

All contracts also impose certain obligations designed to safeguard the safety of operations.

(*b*) *Obligations relating to safety of operations*

Although these obligations are identical to those attached to land operations, they also include special provisions relating to the marine environment; in particular, the interpretation of such obligations may be endowed with some degree of flexibility, having regard to the fact that conditions at sea are much less stable than those pertaining to a terrestrial environment.

Over and above the obligation to ensure the safety of personnel and equipment, it is also incumbent upon the operator to respect the marine environment itself.

(*c*) *Obligations relating to the protection of the marine environment*

Generally speaking, these obligations are aimed at respect for the freedom of the seas, the principle of which remains valid for the superjacent waters in pursuance of the terms of Article 5, clauses 1 and 7, of the Geneva Convention on the Continental Shelf, which provide that exploration of the continental shelf and the exploitation of its natural resources must not result in any unjustifiable interference with navigation, fishing or the conservation of living resources.

The operator must discharge these obligations from the moment at which prospecting starts, especially in the case of seismic surveys, which constitute a threat to the marine fauna because of the explosions involved; seismic sounding is therefore subject to very strict regulation in areas rich in fish, and is sometimes forbidden altogether. On the other side of the picture, trawling may cause serious damage to underwater installations, some natural-gas producers operating in the North Sea having been obliged to bury their pipelines under the sea floor to enjoy complete protection.

The plant and equipment required to work offshore deposits of hydrocarbons present obstacles to navigation, and the danger to which they give rise is heightened by the fact that a collision would be liable to cause a blow-out of crude oil or gas, which would seriously pollute the marine environment. Hence the precise instructions for marking the whereabouts of such installations (see, for example, Chapter 2 of the French Law of December 30, 1968, referred to earlier). Apart from accidents, drilling itself may pollute the sea. In this connection, attention must be drawn to Article 24 of the Geneva Convention on the Law of the Sea, which lays down that "Every State shall draw up regulations to prevent pollution of the seas by the discharge of oil from ships or pipelines or resulting from the exploitation and exploration of the seabed and its subsoil, taking account of existing treaty provisions on the subject". In these circumstances, in many countries the law requires the operator to provide the equipment necessary to stop the flow of petroleum in the event of a blow-out or of a break in the drillpipe or pipelines. Here reference may be made to Article 28 of the French Law of December 30, 1968, or to the United States Rules and Regulations of August 18, 1969 (Section 250.43, paragraphs (*a*) and (*b*)). The latter make the operator liable for damage to third parties and require him to take a number of preventive measures.

Having regard to the need to respect the exercise of the freedoms attaching to the use of the superjacent water, the question arises: what is the legal statue of offshore drilling installations, and is it necessary to distinguish between fixed and floating platforms?

In the case of a collision between a floating platform and a ship, the running-foul rules take effect, and the conventions on rendering assistance at sea apply.

But where the drilling platform stands on the floor of the sea, it is assimilated to fixed installations on shore, and any damage caused or suffered by it is dealt with according to the rules of private international law on civil (third-party) liability (see the French Law of December 30, 1968, Articles 3 and 5, and Chapter 2).

Lastly, States are bound to take specific steps to protect fishing, and national laws provide for penalties ranging from fines to imprisonment for infringement of the regulations in force.

Performance of these several obligations is always subject to supervision by the competent authority, which may, where necessary, go so far as to cancel the licence to exploit. Disagreements between the authority and the operator may be settled either in the national courts of the coastal State or by arbitration, the latter procedure being more particularly resorted to where the operator is a foreign enterprise.

II. PROBLEMS ARISING OUT OF PARTICIPATION BY A FOREIGN ENTERPRISE

We cannot here go into all the problems of the protection of investments that may arise in the case of a foreign enterprise. No matter how important such problems may be in international economic relations, especially for developing countries, they go beyond the scope of our subject.

Confining ourselves to problems of mining concessions, we first note that in a number of countries it is mandatory that the operator be wholly or partly national, or associated with national concerns. The concessionary State is therefore free:

(*a*) to establish a company under local (national) law, with its registered offices in the country, of which the company will accordingly possess the nationality, even though the majority of—or even all—the shares will be held by foreign shareholders. Such an arrangement may be not entirely devoid of interest for the concessionary State, especially since, on 5 February 1970, the International Court of Justice handed down its judgment *in re* the *Barcelona Traction, Light and Power Company Ltd.*, according to which, under international law, diplomatic protection cannot be invoked on behalf of shareholders, the national State of the company concerned alone being entitled to lodge an international claim; or

(*b*) simply acquire a share of a foreign company's capital.

(The operating company can, of course, be completely foreign and the concessionary State have no shareholding in it.)

Three types of problem must be considered:

(*a*) problems arising out of the nature of mining contracts;

(*b*) problems arising out of the applicable law; and

(*c*) the problem of the permanence of agreements.

1. *Nature of contracts for the exploitation of mineral resources*

Contracts covering the exploitation of mineral resources fall into two main groups:

(*a*) Many contracts concluded with foreign public enterprises, such as supply contracts and public works contracts let in preparation for the exploitation of mineral wealth (solid minerals and hydrocarbons) are, both in their purpose and in their content, of the nature of concessions let for the performance of a public service. They are regulated by common law and contain clauses setting forth the prerogatives of the government authority party to the contract.

But as a rule, in the case of the exploitation of hydrocarbons, having regard to the scale of the works to be carried out, the arrangements are made more formally contractual than straightforward public service concessions, with a view to attracting foreign companies to come to work in the country concerned; in other words, a greater part of the arrangements to be set up may form the subject of bargaining.

Anyway, the concession is a contract by which the State hands over to a foreign individual or company the exploitation of a source of national wealth in return for a share in the profits (royalties), playing no direct part in the operator's activities, apart from supervising his performance of the obligations imposed on him under the contract.

(*b*) Since the Second World War, a new type of contract has made its appearance, known as the "economic development agreement" or "establishment convention". These agreements do not simply entrust the exploitation of a source of national wealth to a foreign company; they also seek to secure the latter's participation in the country's development. The contractual nature of such agreements is obviously even more marked, laying down as they do in a wealth of detail the methods to be used in carrying out the operations envisaged. The arbitral award delivered on 23 August 1958 in the dispute between the Government of Saudi Arabia and the Arabian-American Oil Company (ARAMCO) stressed the contractual nature of the oilfield concession granted to the company.

This contractual technique makes it possible for the host country to deal with large international corporations on an equal footing. For their part, foreign investors display great confidence in the method, despite the fact that no legal judgment is enforceable against the contracting State.

Such economic development agreements are very important for the host country, first because of their purpose, namely, to promote, through the investment of substantial amounts of capital and technical assistance, the country's economic development by a variety of operations over and above those involved in the exploitation of the oilfields: the making of roads, the equipment of ports, the construction of railways, the installation of electric power stations and distribution systems, and so on and so forth. On top of all this, such agreements, concluded as they often are for periods covering as many as 50 years, imply long-term collaboration between the parties. In exchange, the private party to the contract is granted certain customs facilities or some fiscal relief.

The drafting of such agreements is invariably a delicate process: the contracting State seeks to protect its political and economic sovereignty, whereas the investor endeavours to secure safeguards against the risks involved in the performance of the contract, especially the risk of a change in national legislation that would increase his obligations. These problems are very closely bound up with the problem of determining the law applicable to the agreement.

2. *Law applicable to agreements*

This problem is of the utmost importance because of the number of oil agreements concluded in all parts of the world, and because the concessions are very often granted by developing countries which have only recently acquired their independence and are understandably anxious to safeguard it. Many opinions have been aired on the subject. In practice, they can all be proved by reference to the type of contract to which they apply.

(*a*) *Application of the municipal law of the concessionary State*

As a general rule, the national laws of the contracting country govern contracts concluded between the State and private persons and performed on the State's territory, to which there is a tendency to assimilate the continental shelf, although, according to the Geneva Convention of 1958, the riverain State simply enjoys sovereign rights over the continental shelf without the latter's being strictly assimilated to an extension of its territory. This view has been borne out by international case law: in its award of 12 July 1929 *in re Serbian and Brazilian Loans,* the International Court of Justice declared: "Any contract which is not a contract between States in their capacity as subjects of international law is based on the municipal law of some country". The Court reached the same conclusion in the case between Iran and the Anglo-Iranian Oil Company after the nationalization of the Iranian oilfields in 1961. For the Court, the agreement involved was "... nothing more than a concessionary contract between a government and a foreign company".

In these circumstances, the agreement belongs to the category of administrative contracts, in other words, contracts defining the important privileges reserved to the concessionary administration, the settlement of disputes between State and concessionaire being a matter for the local courts.

(*b*) *Application of international law*

For some years now a tendency to internationalize agreements concluded between States and private parties has been apparent.

The private party to the contract may feel that he is in an invidious position, and at a disadvantage, if his sole possibility of redress in a dispute lies with the local courts, for, on the one hand, he may be penalized by having to conform to a local procedure with which he is imperfectly acquainted, and, on the other hand, in some countries municipal law might prove insufficiently sophisticated to allow of the settlement of a dispute arising out of the performance of a highly complex contract bringing into play a multiplicity of legal and technical considerations. The application of international law may result from various procedures adopted by the parties by common consent, either by direct reference to international law, or through the medium of an economic development agreement, or, finally, by the conclusion of an umbrella treaty.

A. The contractual ties can be internationalized in either of two forms of legal text. Both relate to the settlement of disputes and concern respectively recourse to arbitration and the possibility of the tribunal's deciding on the applicable law on the spot.

(i) Many agreements make provision for recourse to arbitration; they are always deemed to imply that international law applies, even in the absence of specific clauses to that effect. Hence recourse to arbitration has a two-fold effect. In the first place, so far as rules and procedures are concerned, the institution of arbitration is the same as that hallowed by classic international law, as was made clear in the ARAMCO award: "The arbitration, as such, can only be governed by International Law". But, over and above this, so far as the law applicable to the substance of the dispute is concerned, the inclusion of arbitration clauses often leads to invocation of the rules of international public law.

This trend has been confirmed, not only in bilateral agreements concluded between States or between a State and a private company, but also in international agreements of more general scope, such as the Convention of the International Bank for Reconstruction and Development (IBRD) of March 18, 1965 (Art. 42). The flexibility of arbitral procedure seems to make it particularly suitable for settling some disputes arising out of the application of contracts concluded between State and private company. This explains the success this procedure has known in recent years, whether in the form of *ad hoc* arrangements or in that of an institution recognized in an antecedent bilateral or multilateral treaty.

But arbitration has also met with some opposition, some States considering that it would be more compatible with respect for their sovereignty were the dispute referred to their national courts. This is clearly a matter for negotiation between the parties, anxious on the one hand to safeguard to the greatest possible extent their investment in a foreign country, and, in the case of the State, to attract foreign capital while at the same time safeguarding its sovereignty. It should be noted that at its 16th Conference held in Vienna in 1968 OPEC (Organization of Petroleum Exporting Countries) adopted a resolution declaring that "except as otherwise provided for in the legal system of a Member Country, all disputes arising between the Government and operators shall fall exclusively within the jurisdiction of the competent national courts or the specialized regional courts as and when established". OPEC's resolution has not yet led to any noteworthy change in international practice. There are many agreements in force which still provide for recourse to arbitration between State and the private person, or which (as a compromise) limit its use exclusively to the settlement of disputes between foreign companies and a specific State body, even though the latter is normally a public corporation of the host country. The clauses providing for arbitration are usually rounded off by a reference to the application of general legal principles.

(ii) This reference to general legal principles is considered in practice as a typical internationalization clause.[3]

Many economic development agreements, similar to those we have in mind, and in which the reference to general legal principles has been interpreted as such, can be quoted, in particular: Kuwait and the Kuwait Shell Petroleum Company of January 15, 1961 (Art. 35); Iran and the Consortium, of September 19, 1954 (Art. 46); Iran and AGIP Mineraria, of August 24, 1954 (Art. 40);

3. Cf. Delaume, G., "Des stipulations de droit applicable dans les accords de prêts et de développement économique et de leur rôle" ("Legal provisions applicable in loan and economic development agreements, and their role"), *Revue belge de droit international*, 1968, p. 337.

and the United Arab Republic and Pan-American UAR Oil Company of October 23, 1963 (Art. 42).

Similar provisions are to be found in the Agreement between the National Iraqi Oil Company (NIOC) and ERAP (Art. 35); in Article 46 of the Agreement with the Iranian Consortium; in Article 40 of the Agreement concluded in 1957 between the National Iranian Oil Company (NIOC) and the Italian company AGIP-Mineraria, and in other petroleum agreements concluded by Middle Eastern countries. International law is also mentioned in the agreement concluded in 1966 between NIOC and ERAP (Art. 41 provides that the arbitrator shall be entitled to base his award on considerations of equity and on generally accepted rules of law, especially international law).

Although the reference to international law may be more or less explicit from one agreement to another, that to general legal principles is always deemed an adequate criterion of internationalization; and international case law supports this contention. The arbitral award delivered in 1958 in Sapphire International Petroleum Ltd. *v.* National Iranian Oil Company (controlled by the Iranian State itself), may be quoted in this regard. Many other arbitral awards to the same effect have been handed down: Lena Goldfield(s) *v.* USSR, 1930; Petroleum Developments (Trucial Coast) Ltd. *v.* Abu Dhabi, 1951; and International Marine Oil Company *v.* the Ruler of Qatar, 1953.

B. Economic development agreements are similarly to be considered as calling for the application of international law. Moreover, they often refer to arbitration and general legal principles. The attachment of such agreements to international law is often doctrinal, because of their nature (they are sometimes called "quasi-international treaties").[4] The scale of their subject-matter, the foreign origin of the parties and the powerful forces involved on each side indeed make these agreements real treaties. It is deemed that this type of agreement entails the application of an international economic law now in process of formulation: international contract law. It is in this sense that some arbitral awards, like that rendered in the ARAMCO case, or that handed down in the

4. Schwarzenberger, G., *International Law as Applied by the International Court and Tribunals.* 1957, Vol. I, p. 157.

Sheikh of Abu Dhabi *v.* Petroleum Development Ltd.,[5] are to be interpreted. This analysis comes close to the third way of denationalizing relations between concessionary State and foreign operator.

C. Under *lex contractus* (transnational law) the agreements can be given their own system of law. In these circumstances, in the case of economic development agreements, both the application of municipal law and that of international law must be set aside. Such agreements are governed both by the maxim *pacta sunt servanda* (or of the principle of respect of treaties) and by the general rules of law. According to some authors,[6] we are here dealing with a transnational legal system of mixed nature, deriving its rules in part from municipal law, in part from the provisions of the contract itself, and, finally from general legal principles, the last named having a field of application much broader than those of international public law and deriving from domestic public and private law. Thus, one would be faced with a complex system of international administrative law.

The interest of all our discussions is essentially bound up with the question of the immutability of agreements.

3. *Problems arising out of the permanence of agreements*

Here we find two main, conflicting, theories:

(*a*) the State has the power to amend or terminate agreements unilaterally, by virtue of its sovereignty. Termination need only be justified by considerations of national interest and provide for the payment of compensation. Various judgments support this theory, particularly that in the case of the Delagoa Bay Railways. The difficulty for the arbitrators lies in verifying the motive of national interest invoked to justify unilateral termination or revision. Financial returns poorer than those counted on would not, in constructive law, constitute adequate reason.

(*b*) According to another view, based on the "sanctity of contracts", the agreements would be subject to absolute intangibility,

5. *International Law Quarterly*, 1952, p. 247.

6. *See* Lalive, P., "Recent Version: Abrogation or Alteration of an Economic Development Agreement Between a State and Private Foreign Party", *Business Lawyers*, 1962, pp. 434 *et seq.*

based equally on international law and the permanence of treaties, and on the concept of the *lex contractus* stipulating that the contract, constituting as it does the unique law of the parties, is unassailable unilaterally. This theory, which seeks to safeguard the principle of respect for acquired rights and postulates strict performance of the terms of the agreement, is itself an extreme case.

(*c*) In fact, practice is more flexible than either of these theories:

A. Some agreements include stabilization clauses relating to certain of their provisions.

B. Apart from such clauses, a State's powers to modify an agreement must not be discriminatory or exercised in such a way as to put one particular company at a disadvantage. The State's action shall not challenge the procedure laid down for the settlement of disputes or, in particular, go back unilaterally on the principle of arbitration if this has been agreed to by common consent. Finally, no unilateral revision shall impair the financial provisions of an agreement: financial guarantees, profit-sharing, or fiscal or customs relief. The financial balance of the contract must be respected, a principle which, incidentally, is recognised in municipal administrative law. Any measure susceptible of affecting this balance must be the subject of negotiation.

Third Part

Regional problems

Chapter I

THE EFFECT OF EXISTING LAW OF THE SEA ON PLANNING FOR THE DEVELOPMENT OF THE MEDITERRANEAN REGION AS AN ECOLOGICAL UNITY

With respect to the ecological unity of the sea, man developed a heterogeneous body of law very early. After the 12th century,[1] a principle was affirmed in the Mediterranean, that of a sea adjacent to coasts on which the riparian States demand private rights in order to assure the security of navigation; this principle has been used to justify the establishment of commercial monopolies.

Such were the claims of Genoa on the Ligurian Sea and the Gulf of Lions[2] and those of Venice on the Adriatic.[3]

In France, along the coasts of Nice County from the 15th to the 18th century, rights to the sea were exacted in a zone situated between the mouth of the Paillon and the present Cape Ferrat.

Although the extent of this adjacent sea remained highly variable[4] under the influence of Italian jurists, notably Bartole, the national jurisdictions crystallized in a zone with an exterior limit of 100 miles.[5]

It was contrary to these claims that Grotius formulated the principle of the freedom of the high seas in "le Mare Liberum"[6] in 1609. However, it was not until the 18th century that the extent

1. The ecological and economic unity of the Mediterranean Basin was respected by the peoples of antiquity. Thus the Romans never made a closed sea of the "Mare Nostrum". They respected the right to fish which belonged to all.

2. In 1174, Raymond V, Count of Toulouse granted a charter conceding to the Genoans a monopoly of maritime trade from La Turbie to Narbonne.

3. After 1269, Venice levied a tax on all boats navigating the Northern Adriatic.

4. In France, Jean Bodin limited the territorial sea to 90 miles.

5. The Italian mile equals 1,478 metres. The distance of 100 miles appears frequently in Roman Law; for example, in Rome, the Prefect Urbain exercised his jurisdiction up to 100 miles around the city.

6. Extract from *De jure Praedae* written in 1605.

of the territorial sea was fixed at three miles, following the wishes of the maritime powers.[7]

In the Mediterranean, the territorial sea was limited to six miles by custom. After the failure of the conferences in The Hague in 1930 and Geneva in 1958 and 1960 where the Nations were unable to agree on a universal limit to the territorial sea, national demands have continued to increase. This general phenomenon, exaggerated by the accession to independence of numerous former colonies, has not been absent in the Mediterranean, although exorbitant claims such as those of the Latin American countries have not been possible.[8]

A similar evolution, although more recent,[9] can be observed for the seabed. Since the Truman Proclamation of 1945 the seabed has shown itself to be an inestimable reservoir of natural riches, both living and mineral, particularly on the continental margins which have been the object of demands by riparian States. Under the Geneva Convention of 1958 on the continental shelf, riparian States exercise sovereign and exclusive rights on the seabed up to a depth of 200 metres and even beyond if exploitation is proven possible.

However, in the Mediterranean, the demands are much less pronounced because of the nature of the coast of the Mediterranean Basin with its extraordinarily limited continental shelf. Besides, many of the riparian States are still developing and are scarcely aware of the importance of these riches which sometimes seem inaccessible to them.[10]

Consequently, today, there is a great diversity in the law of the sea depending on the region involved. To the traditional horizontal

7. According to Galiani this limit corresponds to the range of a cannon in that era.

8. Since 1952, Chile, Ecuador and Peru have fixed their territorial waters at 200 miles.

9. However, since the Middle Ages, riparian proprietors have benefited from property rights in the seabed within the limits of exclusive fishing zones granted to them. In this manner claims on the continental shelf began, but only by individual right. In the Mediterranean, these rights were granted, notably, by Byzantine at the beginning of the Middle Ages.

10. However, in the goal of solidarity with the Third World and equally for the preservation of the future, these countries, at the different maritime conferences and presently in the Committee on the Seabed, support the propositions which extend territorial waters to 200 miles with respect to the continental shelf.

division, interior water, territorial water and high seas, a vertical division is now added: seabed and surface waters in each zone, the notion of freedom of the seas, is in conflict with the notion of sovereignty, the basis of national claims. This tension has not proven to be beneficial for the preservation of the resources of the sea nor for the rational development of them.

Free utilization leads to contamination of the milieu and the exhaustion of its resources; the national approach leads to the absence of appropriate measures or to anarchy in the regulation. Also, only a broad collective action of riparian States can develop the Mediterranean Region and maintain its ecological unity.

Finally, in the Mediterranean as elsewhere, there exists a contradiction between positive law based on individual appropriations and the necessity for development which postulates collective action.

It is fitting, then, to treat in a first part, the individual behaviour of the Mediterranean with respect to the oceanic milieu seen as a reservoir of living resources before examining in a second part the possibilities of a joint homogeneous action.

I. THE INDIVIDUAL APPROACH: A REALITY

The riparian State is projected into the sea and the zones thus created fall within its national jurisdiction. We will treat successively the zones under national jurisdiction and the corresponding judical régimes.

A. *The extent of zones under national jurisdiction*

The riparian State exercises rights at the same time on the surface and on the seabed.

(1) *The surface water*

The extent of surface water under national jurisdiction in the Mediterranean, as elsewhere, is characterized by a veritable "Anarchy of Sovereignties"[11] which has its origins in the failure of the

11. G. Scelle, *Course in Public International Law*, 1948.

conferences of The Hague (1930) and Geneva (1958, 1960). From the surface water the riparian States claim territorial waters and fishing zones.

(*a*) *Territorial waters*

Let us now deal with each of the numerous States, of which France practises the 6-mile rule for the most part employing the customary method. It is always tempting to arrive at a specific rule which exemplifies the phenomenon of regionalization of international law.

Custom tends today to be splintered, the 12-mile rule often being substituted, in a written form, for the former practice, without it being possible to find a common approach among the newly independent States (Tunisia claims territorial waters of 6 miles); some States simply develop their own rule (France has just extended its territorial waters to 12 miles [12]).

The extent of territorial waters presently claimed is the following: [13]

- 3 miles for Malta;
- 6 miles for Spain, Greece, Israel, Italy, Turkey and Tunisia;
- 10 miles for Yugoslavia and Albania;
- 12 miles for France, Monaco, [14] Algeria, Cyprus, Libya, Lebanon, Morocco, UAR and Syria.

(*b*) *Fishing zones*

Although for certain States the limit of fishing zones reserved for their nationals coincides with the limit of their territorial waters, [15] other States exercise their monopoly on waters adjacent to

12. Law No. 71-1060 of December 24, 1971, concerning the extent of French territorial waters.

13. According to the limits and status of the territorial waters, exclusive fishing zones, zones of fisheries conservation and continental shelves–FAO, Rome, 1971. Besides, following the same document, it appears that only 4 States are parties to the Convention of 1958 on territorial waters and the contiguous zone; they are Spain (February 2, 1971), Israel (September 6, 1961), Italy (December 17, 1964) and Malta (September 21, 1964).

14. By a "Declaration concerning the limits of territorial waters of the Principality of Monaco" signed at the "Quai d'Orsay" (April 10, 1967) by the representatives of France and the Principality, Monaco, which declares that the limit of its territorial waters is identical to that of France.

15. Notably the case of France since the law of December 24, 1971,

their territorial waters.[16] One of the arguments which militates in favour of the generalization of the 12-mile rule is incontestably the unification of the space over which the riparian State exercises its competence. This has been realized by France with the law of December 24, 1971, cited below.[17] However it is to be feared that new demands will be made beyond 12 miles. Besides the customs zones indicated in note 16, it is in the domain of fisheries that riparian States tend to demand special rights, fisheries being a natural riches indispensable to the Third World countries which is easily accessible to them. Thus the representative of Lebanon at the Committee on the Seabed has estimated that, as concerns fisheries, the riparian State should have an exclusive competence of from 0 to 24 miles and preferential rights from 24 to 48 miles.[18]

---

cited below which by a decree of June 7, 1967 (modifying the law of March 1, 1855) fixed at 12 miles the zone reserved for national fisheries.

16. Notably the case of Spain and Italy who possess territorial waters of 6 miles and a fisheries zone of 12 miles (according to the FAO document cited below). As concerns customs zones a strong heterogeneity exists with national competence being exercised up to 20 miles. Notably the case of Lebanon; the UAR and Syria have limited the customs line to 18 miles; France, Spain and Italy, to 12 miles; Greece and Libya to 10 miles. We should recall at this point that the extension of a contiguous zone beyond 12 miles is contrary to the Geneva Convention on territorial waters and the contiguous zone (Art. 24).

17. Law of July 31, 1968—customs line fixed at 12 miles as in the case of fisheries. It is to be noted that the unification of the customs and reserved fisheries zones was one of the arguments advanced in preparatory work for the law of December 24, 1971. The other arguments are:
—extension of police power to fight hydrocarbon pollution;
—installation of works permitting the reception of tankers;
—security measures on the occasion of nuclear experiments in the Pacific.

Moreover, at the international level, "conciliation between the interests in protection of the riparian State and the interest of the international community in the matter of maritime and aerial navigation has been invoked. Preparatory works:
—National Assembly: legislative project No. 2,020; report of Mr. Jamot in the name of the Commission on Foreign Affairs No. 2107.
—Senate: legislative project adopted by the National Assembly No. 85 (1971-1972); Report of Mr. Taittinger in the name of the Commission on Foreign Affairs No. 97 (1971-1972).

18. Committee on the Seabed, Geneva, July 19-August 27, 1971, according to FAO document COFI/72/7, Supp. 1, November 16, 1971. Lebanon has also proposed a territorial limit of 12 miles.

(2) *The seabed*

According to Professor Bourcart,[19] the Mediterranean continental shelf with the exception of the Gulf of Lions is extraordinarily limited especially along the Riviera and the Oranian coast. The areas of high seabeds such as the Sicilian-Tunisian shelf, the Northern Adriatic and the Aegean cannot be considered as true continental shelves.

This paucity[20] explains the lack of interest on the part of most Mediterranean countries with regard to the continental shelf. Only five of them have ratified the Geneva Convention of 1958: France (June 14, 1965), Israel (September 6, 1961), Malta (September 21, 1964), Spain (February 25, 1971) and Yugoslavia (January 28, 1966).

The definition of continental shelf adopted by the Convention[21] has been contested by France which has reservations about the criterion of exploitability.[22] This notion is equally contested by Greece, Lebanon, Tunisia and Turkey.[23] On the other hand Italy, Syria[23] and the UAR are committed to the double criteria of depth and exploitability.

At present, an agreement seems to be in the process of realization in the Seabed Committee on a fixed limit of 200 miles measured from the low-water mark although no country is seeking to impose this. The adoption of such a rule would result in a division of the

19. Bourcart, *Geography of the Seabed*, Payot.

20. However, following research, effected notably by the specialized ship *Glomar Challenger*, it has been established that the floor of the Mediterranean contains a thick sedimentary layer favourable to the accumulation of oil. In fact, certain interesting discoveries of petroleum have been made, notably by ENI which has found more than 80 million cubic metres of natural gas in the Adriatic.

21. According to Article 1 of the Convention, the expression continental shelf is used to designate:
(*a*) the seabed and underground of underwater areas adjacent to coasts but situated outside of territorial waters up to a depth of 200 metres or beyond this limit as far as the point at which the depth of adjacent waters permits the exploitation of natural resources in the said regions;
(*b*) the seabed and the underground of similar underwater regions adjacent to island coasts.

22. For France, the term "adjacent regions" implies a geophysical, geological and geographic dependence which excludes by itself an unlimited extension of the continental shelf.

23. Declarations of delegates at the Geneva Conference.

Mediterranean, the areas falling outside of national jurisdiction being practically non existent.[24] In any case, the regulation of zones under national jurisdiction would remain in question.

B. *The regulation of zones under national jurisdiction*

Within the limits of its reserved zones the riparian State exercises rights based on national regulation.

(1) *Judicial nature of rights demanded*

In the Mediterranean, the claims of the coastal States arise more from the exercise of recognized rights than from territorial acquisitions.[25]

In the more specialized question of the continental shelf according to Article 2 (1) of the Geneva Convention, "the riparian State exercises sovereign rights". Many Mediterranean countries attach a great importance to this phrase which implies the respect of the principle of freedom of adjacent waters to which they are committed. This attitude is shared not only by the countries which are parties to the Geneva Convention but also by countries such as the UAR and Tunisia for whom access to the live resources of the continental shelf is of considerable importance.

Besides, according to Article 2 (2), of the same convention, sovereign rights exercised by the riparian State on the continental shelf are exclusive in the sense that non-exploration or non-exploitation does not result in extinction.[26] By the same article, the ripar-

24. In its wide part, between Algeria and France the Mediterranean is scarcely 700 kilometres wide. The riparian States could thus be led to generalize delimiting agreements such as that concluded between Italy and Yugoslavia, January 8, 1968, on the line of partition between their respective continental shelves.

25. Notably the case of national fisheries zones situated beyond territorial waters. In some cases, it even happens that the exterior limit of a reserved fisheries zone takes the place of the exterior limit of territorial waters. Thus the territorial waters of Morocco, of which the exterior limit is fixed at 12 miles arise from a fishing convention with Spain signed on January 4, 1969. On the other hand, the French territorial waters arise from the public property régime.

26. The exclusivity of State competence takes on all of its significance in the Mediterranean where, for most riparian States, it is not possible to exploit

ian State can exploit mineral resources as well as live resources belonging to sedentary species. In its instrument of adhesion, France interpreted the expression "live organisms which belong to sedentary species" as excluding crustaceans with the exception of a species of crab called "barnacles".[27]

While the States party to the Geneva Convention, as well as the UAR, exercise sovereign rights on mineral and live resources with the exception of swimming species, other States prefer to limit their rights exclusively to mineral resources. This is notably the case of Greece and Italy who invoke the freedom of fisheries as a corollary of freedom of the seas. The case of Syria is peculiar in that only the exploitation of natural resources is envisaged.[28]

(2) *Judicial status of reserved zones*

The judicial status of territorial waters, fishing zones and continental shelves can only be determined by the national regulation of the riparian State.

As concerns the more specific question of the protection of live species, the national legislation of the Mediterranean countries on the pollution of water "important as it is, does not appear to be sufficient", "the first concern of States being to preserve (above all) their interior waters".[29]

Nevertheless, the riparian States are beginning to be preoccupied by hydrocarbon pollution. For example, the French law No. 68-1181 of December 30, 1968, concerning the exploration of the continental shelf provides as a punishment a fine of 2,000 to 20,000 francs and in the case of a former offender, imprisonment from 6 days to 6 months and a fine of 5,000 to 50,000 francs or one of the two penalties for whoever, in the course of exploration or

---

the possible riches of their continental shelves when these exist. Consequently, the petroleum companies are obliged to solicit from the riparian State the grant of permits in conformity with national offshore legislation.

27. This reservation by France points up the ambiguity of the Geneva Convention raised by the distinction between species attached to the seabed and swimming species living on the seabed.

28. The law on territorial waters of November 28, 1963, employs the very general expression "natural products".

29. See our study concerning four Mediterranean countries–Pacem in maribus–Malta, July, 1971.

exploitation of the natural resources of the continental shelf, discharges or allows to escape into the sea . . . some products set out in (1) of Article 3 of the international Convention for the Prevention of Pollution of the Oceans by Hydrocarbons, signed at London on May 12, 1954.

As regards the conservation of species, the national legislation appears too complex in certain countries while insufficient and even non-existent in others.[30] For example, the regulations relative to fishing in French maritime waters[31] include a considerable collection of texts.

The dispositions ensuring the conservation of maritime species have as a legal basis the law of January 9, 1852, on the exercise of maritime fisheries. Besides, there exist in most Mediterranean ports, professional organizations called "Prud'homies de pêche" which, by virtue of local customs, take special measures. Finally, besides the texts applicable to the entirety of the coastline some special texts are applicable solely in the Mediterranean.[32]

The multiplicity of national regulations does not permit that the effective maintenance be assured of the ecostructure of species which are protected by the conservation rules of one State, but not protected by the laws of neighbouring States. To the extent that live species are ignorant of maritime boundaries created artificially by man, only a general regulation at the regional level can preserve the ecological unity in the maritime environment. The necessity for a joint approach is indeed affirmed.

II. THE JOINT APPROACH: A NECESSITY

The struggle against pollution and the rational exploitation of stocks should be arrested, applying the general principle of prohibition in order to preserve the nutritive character of the seas. More-

30. Notably the case of Greece.

31. Complete dossier established by the maritime fisheries management (No. 1363 P4) for the purposes of communication to the office of the Commission of the EEC applying Article 2, § 2, of EEC regulation No. 2141/70 of October 20, 1970.

32. Examples of texts concerning the Mediterranean: law of May 29, 1954, regulating the use of "Lamparo"; law of July 31, 1969, regulating eel fisheries; law of November 30, 1970, forbidding deep sea trawls and trawling "en boeuf"; decision of November 20, 1970, on the use of trawling.

over, this principle should be generalized to include the totality of maritime regions, live species, like pollutants, being prone to considerable migrations.[33] In this regard the decision of IMCO[34] concerning the convocation of an international conference in 1973 with the goal of promoting an international agreement which would impose limits to the contamination of the sea, the land and the atmosphere by ships, boats and any other material exploited in the marine environment is very encouraging.

By the same token, it can be hoped that the conference on the environment to be held at Stockholm in June 1972 will succeed in drawing the outlines of such an agreement.[35]

However, today, the collective action of riparian States acting at the regional level remains very fragmentary. This is the case in the Mediterranean, moreover, where the prevention and control of pollution has a special importance because of the position of a sea, partly closed.[36] Furthermore, a regional policy on the exploitation of species has been shown to be particularly necessary in the Mediterranean which is poor in nutritive elements with the result that the stock could easily be exhausted.

Positive law contains certain useful elements, some relating to agreements between States; others, to institutional structures.

A. *The conventional base*

Besides bilateral agreements between riparian States, multilateral conventions at the international level affect the Mediterranean.

33. No marine region is sheltered from hydrocarbon pollution. It has been established, notably, that petroleum spilled in the Atlantic, and carried by marine currents, can enter the Straits of Gibraltar and deposit itself on Moroccan and Algerian beaches. See *Le Monde* of June 3, 1967, relating the experience of "des messages à la mer".

34. Assembly of IMCO, resolution A. 176 of October 21, 1969.

35. Note that 10 Mediterranean States have prepared a proposed convention to be submitted to the conference in June 1972. See note on the advisability of a regional agreement on the control of marine pollution in the Mediterranean by the representatives of Cyprus, Spain, France, Italy, Malta, Morocco, Turkey, Yugoslavia, Algeria and the United Arab Republic—Pacem in Maribus—Malta, July 1971.

36. On the other hand, the riparian States of the North Sea have reacted more rapidly before the urgency of the situation. An agreement was signed at Bonn on June 9, 1969, concerning co-operation in the fight against hydrocarbon pollution of the waters of the North Sea.

(1) *Bilateral agreements*

These concern, essentially, mutual rights of access to national fishing zones.[37]

Foreign fishermen are bound to conform to national regulations concerning maritime fisheries and are sometimes obliged to respect certain special conditions such as the prohibition of certain types of fishing or of certain zones. These agreements do not establish a true policy of conservation of species and have shown themselves to be as completely insufficient as national regulations.

(2) *Multilateral agreements*

These agreements include not only general conventions, but also more specific conventions:

(*a*) *General conventions*

Three Mediterranean States are party to the Geneva Convention (1958) on fisheries and conservation of biological resources of the high seas.[38] In view of the fight against over-exploitation, the convention provides in Article 7 the possibility, for all riparian States, "in order to maintain the productivity of biological resources of the sea, of the unilateral adoption of appropriate conservation measures . . . in any part of the high sea adjacent to its territorial waters" following the failure of negotiations with other interested States.[39]

37. For example:
–Agreement between Tunisia and Italy of February 1, 1963, authorizing Italian boats to fish in Tunisian waters;
–Agreement between Morocco and Spain of January 4, 1969, authorizing nationals of the two countries to fish in the territorial waters of the contracting parties;
–Agreement between France and Spain of March 20, 1967, by which fishermen of the two countries have access to a zone between 6 and 12 miles of their respective national waters;
–Agreement between Italy and Yugoslavia of April 16, 1969, authorizing Italian ships to fish in Yugoslav waters for a period of 3 years.

38. The States are Spain (February 25, 1971), France (September 18, 1970) and Yugoslavia (January 28, 1966).

39. It should be noted that, under § 2 of Article 7 of the convention, these measures must be justified by urgency based on appropriate scientific conclusions and, in no way discriminatory, to foreign fishermen.

It is evident that these can only be emergency measures preliminary to an overall regulation which alone can be effective given the homogeneous nature of the marine environment.

This is also the case in the struggle against pollution with respect to measures taken in application[40] of the limited provisions of the Geneva conventions on the high sea and the continental shelf.[41]

(*b*) *Special conventions*

These conventions deal with the fight against pollution, to which people are more sensitive than to the protection of over-exploited species.

The international convention for the prevention of pollution of the seas by hydrocarbons was signed May 12, 1954, in London on the initiative of IMCO.

In the Mediterranean, ships of contracting parties[42] are obliged to avoid the dumping of hydrocarbons within 100 miles of coasts. But only the flag State, in conformity with national legislation, is

40. The French law No. 64-1331 of December 26, 1964, curbs hydrocarbon pollution of the sea. Although passed in application of the international convention for the prevention of the pollution of seawaters by hydrocarbons signed at London, May 12, 1954, this law, however, gives effect indirectly to Article 24 of the Geneva convention on the high seas which it should be noted, France has not ratified. It should equally be noted that French law No. 68-1181 of December 30, 1968, concerning the exploration of the continental shelf and the exploitation of its natural resources is cited below.

41. By Article 24 of the convention "Every State is obliged to enact rules with a view to avoiding pollution of the seas by hydrocarbons spilled by ships or pipelines or resulting from the exploration of the seabed or the underground of the seabed taking account of the relevant existing conventional dispositions".

By Article 25, § 1, every State is obliged to take (in co-operation with competent international organizations) measures to avoid pollution of the seas by radioactive wastes.

In the Mediterranean, the parties to this convention include Spain (February 25, 1971), Israel (September 6, 1961), Italy (December 17, 1964). France, Lebanon and Tunisia have signed but not ratified.

According to Article 5, § 7, of the convention on the continental shelf "the riparian State is obliged to take all measures in security zones for the protection of the biological resources of the sea against harmful agents".

42. Four Mediterranean States are parties to the convention: Algeria, Spain, France and Greece.

competent to curb infractions[43] committed on the high seas.

By a resolution of October 21, 1963,[44] the Assembly of IMCO amended the constitution of 1954 repealing, notably, the annex concerning forbidden zones. The present principle is thus, that of a prohibition relating to all maritime areas.[45]

The international convention on intervention on the high seas in the case of an accident resulting in or which could result in hydrocarbon pollution was signed at Brussels on November 29, 1969, also on the initiative of IMCO. Under Article 1 (1), the States linked by the present convention can take the necessary measures on the high seas "to prevent, diminish or eliminate the damaging consequences of pollution of seawater by hydrocarbons".

In contrast with the IMCO convention, the riparian State, can take measures with respect to ships not flying its flag.[46] However, these measures remain subject to substantive and formal conditions.[47] By Article 11, the convention will become effective 90 days after the date on which 15 ratifications or adhesions have been deposited.

B. *The institutional base*

For the survival of the Mediterranean ecology an institutional approach is needed. Although scientific and research organizations exist in sufficient numbers, subordinate organizations with the power to set compulsory regulations for the riparian States should be created. Certainly, a model exists, the EEC; but it is limited to two Mediterranean States, France and Italy. Besides, it does not presently appear to be in a position to promote an ecological regulation of the maritime environment.

43. See, for example, French law No. 64-1331 of December 26, 1964, curbing hydrocarbon pollution of seawaters, cited below.

44. Resolution A. 175 (VI).

45. The convention, however, provides that certain dumping in the sea is legal. See amended Articles 3, 4, 5 of the convention.

46. The convention does not specify whether these measures concern all ships or only ships of contracting parties.

47. See J. P. Queneudec, "The Brussels Conference of 1969 on the Damage Caused by the Pollution of Ocean Waters", *AFDI*, 1969, pp. 747 and following.

(1) *Co-operative organization*

We will treat successively "the general council for Mediterranean fisheries" and the other organizations concerned with the ecology of the Mediterranean.

(*a*) *The "general council for Mediterranean fisheries"*

The CGPM (French initials) is an intergovernmental organization created in 1949 by an international agreement concluded within the framework of Article 14 of the constitution of the FAO,[48] which, according to the preamble of the agreement, favours "co-operation between States having a mutual interest in the development and appropriate utilization of the resources of the Mediterranean Sea and adjacent waters".[49]

The agreement forming the CGPM came into effect on February 20, 1952, and presently involves 16 countries, all Mediterranean riparians with the exception of Great Britain.[50]

According to Article 7 of the agreement, the functions of the CGPM include, notably: to expose problems, encourage, co-ordinate, undertake research work and development projects, promote standardization, complete comparative studies on fisheries legislation and prepare reports on special problems.

Different from certain international fisheries commissions which have a regulatory power, the CGPM has only a consultative role. However, because of the seriousness of its work on Mediterranean ecology, the CGPM appears to be in a position to create general regulations concerning the protection of the Mediterranean environment.

48. Article 14, lines 1 and 3, foresees the possibility for States forming the organization to hold a meeting or to get together during a technical conference with the goal of establishing an agreement or convention concerning food or agriculture.

The CGPM is the second fisheries council to be established following the procedure of Article 14, the first being the "Indo-Pacific fisheries council". A third "The Latin American fisheries council" (1951) has not yet come into effect lacking the required number of adhesions.

49. The expression "adjacent waters" includes the Black Sea which constitutes with the Mediterranean an ecological unit. On the other hand the CGPM is not concerned with the Red Sea which has more affinity with the Indian Ocean.

50. These States are: Cyprus, Spain, France, Greece, Israel, Italy, Lebanon, Libya, Malta, Morocco, UAR, Tunisia, Turkey and Yugoslavia.

During its tenth session which took place at Rome from December 8 to 13, 1969,[51] the work group on the evaluation of the exploitation of the swimming species living in close association with the seabed recommended that rational measures on legislative, administrative and technical plans be taken by member States and transposed on a regional Mediterranean plan with a view to assuring the protection and reconstitution of threatened stocks.

Moreover, member States could transform the CGPM into a subordinate organization if that is what they want.

(*b*) *Organizations with a special interest in the development of the ecology of the Mediterranean*

International Commission for Scientific Exploration in the Mediterranean sea (CIESMM, French initials): created in 1919,[52] the "CIESMM" promotes oceanographic and biological studies in the Mediterranean. Originally the "CIESMM" appeared to be the sole institution for Mediterranean research; with the creation in 1949 of the CGPM, the possibility of useless duplication appeared.[53] This dual competence could be avoided if the CGPM became an organization with an economic emphasis while the "CIESMM" remained an organization exclusively scientific.

Intergovernmental Oceanographic Commission (COI, French initials): it is through the offices of COI[54] that Unesco shows its interest in the marine environment. Originally, the COI was scarcely interested in the Mediterranean region except for the presence of observers at the CGPM. In a 1967 resolution,[55] COI decided to adopt a joint study of the Mediterranean as an official programme to be carried out jointly with CIESMM and the CGPM from 1969.

Presently 15 States are participating in the joint study of the Mediterranean ("ECM")[56] (ECM stands for "Etude en Commun

51. See CGPM report on the 10th session, Rome, 1970.

52. Text of the agreement in Bulletin No. 1 of the CIESMM, 1920, Monaco.

53. All the more, since, with the exceptions of Algeria and Rumania, all members of CIESMM are also members of the CGPM.

54. Among the 58 member countries of COI are 12 Mediterranean countries: Algeria, France, Greece, Israel, Italy, Lebanon, Monaco, Morocco, Spain, Tunisia, Turkey and the United Arab Republic.

55. COI resolution V-4.

56. The countries are Algeria, France, Greece, Israel, Italy, Lebanon, Malta, Monaco, Morocco, Spain, Syria, Tunisia, Turkey, the United Arab Republic and Yugoslavia.

de la Méditerranée" which means "joint study of the Mediterranean").

ECM is a very structured international programme[57] which could be transformed with few modifications into an intergovernmental organization.

The goal of ECM is to permit a systematic study of the marine environment in order to aid in the development of resources and to permit a rational marine policy for the riparian States. The Mediterranean zone can serve as a model for the development of resources in other maritime regions. The participation of the USSR and the USA in the ECM is evidence of this universal orientation.

(2) *The case of the EEC*

To the extent in which the EEC Council regulation[58] No. 2141/70 of October 20, 1970,[59] establishing a common policy in the fishing sector, has introduced in its Article 2, § 1, the principle of freedom of access of fishing vessels flying the flag of one member country in waters under the sovereignty or jurisdiction of other member countries;[60] the problems of excessive exploitation are reinforced and protection of the seabeds becomes an urgent matter. In this regard, Article 5 of the regulation stipulates that when fishing in maritime waters of member States exposes certain resources to the risks of over-exploitation, the council,

57. See bulletin of ECM No. 1, Monaco, 1970.

58. On the competence of the Community to enact this regulation, see D. Vignes, *Fisheries Regulation in the Common Market as Community Law.*

59. JOCE, L 236 of October 27, 1970.

60. The question of freedom of access to waters claimed by member States has been reopened by the negotiations on the enlargement of the Common Market. The English, Irish, Danish and especially the Norwegians have claimed preferential rights contrary to the community regulations. After tough negotiations, the Community has accepted, until 1983, the principle of coastal fishing zones within the 6-mile limit, with Norway obtaining even 12 miles for most of its coast. The Community has insisted on the exceptional and transitory nature of these measures, the principle to attain, remaining that of free access for all fishermen of the EEC in waters reserved to member States.

In the Mediterranean, the consequences appear to be the following: until 1983, community fishermen will not have access to French and Italian waters except in the area between 6 and 12 miles. After 1983, the same fishermen will have access to the 0-6 mile zone except for special dispensations granted by the Community.

acting on the recommendation of the commission, can take the necessary measures to ensure their conservation. These measures can include, notably, restrictions relating to the capture of certain species, zones, periods, methods and fishing equipment.[61]

The existence of the Community could equally affect fisheries zones situated outside waters reserved by member States, notably, the fate of species attached to the continental shelf. However, the application of the EEC treaty to the continental shelf of member States could lead to the same problems of over-exploitation as those noted with regard to fishing in national waters.[62]

The Commission of the European Community has, nevertheless, prepared a memorandum favourable to the applicability of the EEC treaty to the continental shelf.[63]

Finally, it would appear that the EEC with its limited geographical range can scarcely provide a solution for the entire Mediterra-

61. Already, in Article 6 of its proposed regulations concerning structures, the commission has proposed to enable the council to lead all international action necessary for the exploitation and conservation of the biological resources of the sea. As a result of the opposition of member States, the commission deleted Article 6.

62. There is also the problem of compatibility with the Geneva Convention which reserves to the riparian State a monopoly with respect to exploration and exploitation.

63. See the memorandum of the Commission SEC (70) 3095 final, Brussels, September 18, 1970.

In this memorandum, the commission arrives at a highly questionable assimilation between notions of territory and the continental shelf. Applying the formula, employed by the ICJ in the matter of the continental shelf in the North Sea, the shelf is certainly "the prolongation of territory under the sea"; however, this does not necessarily mean that its judicial status is that of territory. This is explained in the preamble to the French law of December 30, 1968, concerning the exploration of the continental shelf and the exploitation of its resources which does not claim the status of public property as opposed to the rights conferred on the riparian State by the Geneva Convention.

Nevertheless, it does not follow that the continental shelf falls outside the community competence. The EEC treaty confers on community institutions, functional economic competence corresponding perfectly with the judicial nature of rights exercised by member States on the continental shelf. Following the pertinent argument of Mr. Mathijsen, "The treaty contains rules for the exercise of power by States, not within determined territories, but rather within determined domains".

Finally, the continental shelf of member States could always be placed under community competence on the basis of Article 835 of the EEC treaty which provides for gaps in the treaty.

nean region. Moreover, the EEC could cause a duplication of powers if the CGPM, for example, was transformed into an organization with regulatory power for the entire Mediterranean region. Only an integrated model can prove useful to the extent that Mediterranean States, aware of the urgency of the ecological problem are resolved to act within an institutional framework.

The Mediterranean has always been a world of conflict dominated by strategic and political factors and the Arab-Israeli conflict hardly contributes to making the region a peaceful zone. It can be hoped that the necessity of economic development could result in a community effort with a view, not to suppressing, which would be illusory, but to "placing in parentheses" the political contradictions such as the opposition between rich countries and developing countries. This attempt can only be realized by a collective action of all riparians, either within a conventional framework or within an institutional framework. Present efforts in the struggle against pollution are within the conventional framework: a regional agreement relating to all maritime areas should be rapidly concluded. On the other hand, the institutional approach appears more adequate for the promotion of regulations for the conservation of species and it should be noted that the CGPM is incontestably equipped to become the competent Mediterranean organization. Only if the Mediterranean countries renounce their national political divergences and act at the regional level, can true ecological regulation assure the development of the Mediterranean basin.

Chapter II

NATIONAL LEGISLATIONS RELATING TO WATER POLLUTION IN FIVE MEDITERRANEAN COUNTRIES

Sea pollution is a problem which mostly concerns countries on the coasts of enclosed seas. This is a particular problem in the Mediterranean, centre of civilizations, the meeting point between East and West, due to the intensity of populations who live on the coasts.

Of course, the Mediterranean is not a sea completely enclosed by land: there is a certain flow of current between it and the Atlantic Ocean on one side, and through the Suez Canal with the Red Sea on the other side.

This exchange of waters delays pollution. If it is therefore false that the Mediterranean will be entirely dead in ten years, it is nevertheless true to say that important parts of this sea will become dead. We realize the danger because of the fact that the industry of the greater number of the countries which lie on the coasts depends to a large extent on fishing and tourism. It is therefore time to take the necessary measures in order that "ce toit tranquille où marchent les colombes" of which Paul Valéry speaks will not become a lake of hydrocarbon and acid.

Is it not significant that the Centre of Studies and Research in Biology and Medical Oceanography of Nice has been invited to study the problems of pollution on Moroccan and Greek coasts by their respective governments?

Such are the reasons which justify a study of the existing legislations to prevent pollution of Mediterranean countries, in five examples: Spain, Italy, France, Tunisia and Israel.

These national legislations are more preoccupied with the protection of internal waters than with the sea at large. In fact, this is the first historical record of legislative preoccupation. Early national legislations contain rules which prohibited dumping in the water of harmful substances. At first the law sought to control the right of good relations between neighbours, easements, and public hygiene. Secondly, the law concerned itself with certain particular types of pollution (industrial waste, hydrocarbons, etc. . . .) and the legislator had the problem to create a real water policy. Finally, the States have turned to the protection of the sea water itself.

It is useful to speak of legislation relating to internal waters since all waters flow inevitably to the sea. Let us remember the famous affair of Minamata in Japan. Dozens of people fell ill, and others died, due to copper poisoning after having eaten fish taken from the sea. But in fact the factories responsible for the presence of copper were not to be found on the seaside but at several kilometres from the coast on the side of a small river. Nature is no respecter of frontiers and territories.

In this domain, as in many others, States prefer to take recourse in national legislations rather than in international law. Of the five countries named, four adhered to the London Convention of May 12, 1954, and Tunisia seems disposed to do so in the near future. But the States have taken too long to ratify the Convention. Only to give one example, the amendments made in 1962 to the London Convention of 1954 were published in France in the *Journal Officiel* of December 20, 1967, that is to say after the catastrophe of the *Torrey Canyon* incident and, without doubt, thanks to it.

Internal legislations are still not sufficiently complete. If it is normal to find a lack of legislation in Tunisia, a country which has little industry, it is nevertheless surprising that effective legislation does not exist in Italy.

I. PROTECTION OF FRESH WATER

Very early the legislation wished to prohibit and punish certain activities resulting in pollution. To day, it seeks to define an efficient water policy.

A. *Traditional protection*

It concerns primarily the question of hygiene, the protection of public health, and regulating the problems of relationship between neighbours and the preservation of the fishing industry.

For instance in Italy, Article 913 of the Civil Code treats the problem of water concerning existing easements between the property owner and the beneficiary of the rights of easement. We note particularly, regarding the question of pollution, the text of Article 1033 which says that the property owner "is obliged to allow passage on his property to waters of all kinds for the benefit of he who has the right, even of a temporary nature, to utilize them for vital needs or for agricultural and industrial needs". The expression "waters of all kinds" is to be stressed and to be taken in 'ose connection from the text of Article 1043 which prescribes that this charge "can be demanded even for impure water, on condition that sufficient precautions be taken in order to avoid harm".

The Penal Code forbids in Article 439 the dumping in water destined for drinking purposes any substances harmful to the human body. Finally, a decree of July 27, 1934, published sanitary laws protecting water utilized for the cultivation of rice and well-water, forbidding the use of polluted, industrial or unsanitary water for domestic purposes unless after complete purification. Even the return of water used for industrial purposes to rivers which cross inhabited areas or in canals without the necessary purification is forbidden.

The Prefect and the Provincial Council of Health must take appropriate measures and make enquiries.

–In Tunisia, a municipal decision in the town of Tunis of July 5, 1908, prohibits by Articles 11 and 66 the dumping, in the sewers and canals, of wastes, liquid or solid, of garbage, of manure and of substances which give off unpleasant vapours, and dangerous or inflammable gases.

Article 68 prohibits "the direct or indirect dumping in rivers of all waste or injurious substances, without special authorization".

Finally, a decree of July 26, 1951, prohibits by article 12 "the dumping of waste water or residues in the sea or the part of large rivers, streams and canals situated downstream at the point where the water is no longer salted by contact with the sea, without previous authorization by the Director of Public Works".

Finally, one must note dispositions of Article 310 of the Penal Code which prescribe that all persons who knowingly throw insanitary or infected substances in water destined for human or animal consumption will be punished by one year in prison.

That is all and that is not enough. Moreover these texts date from the Protectorate period and nothing else has been done in this domain.

On the other hand, two other Mediterranean countries have more complete legislation on the subject.

–To begin with Spain undertook to protect its internal waters at the end of the last century. In fact, a law of June, 13, 1879, called the law of water, empowers in Articles 219 and 220 the Governor of the Province to close temporarily an industrial establishment which dumps substances injurious to health or vegetation in the water in so far as the person responsible does not adopt necessary measures. If these measures are not followed in the lapse of six months, the proprietor is supposed to have given up the exploitation of his industry.

The perpetual use of public water is permitted, but if this water becomes injurious to health or vegetation further utilization is prohibited without a right to indemnity.

A decree of November 16, 1900, has completed these dispositions by forbidding the dumping in streams of water which has been used to wash minerals or industrial preparations (Art. 1). The discharge of water is only allowed if the said water does not in any respect disturb fishing, navigation or all other uses.

Factory owners are obliged to inform the Civil Governor of the Province for approval of the system they use for the purification of water.

Finally, Article 13 forbids all dumping in public water of all residuary substances, resulting from industrial fabrication, without authorization from the Governor, who can refuse this authorization after consultation with the Director of the Public Works and the Provincial Health Council.

On the other hand, a decree of April 6, 1943, modified by the decree of August 13, 1966, giving approval to fishing regulations, forbids in Article 15 all dumping of residues, all fabrication or exploitation harmful to aquatic fauna or flora without previous purification approved by the Fishing Service and the Administrative Council of Mountains, Hunting and River Fishing.

Finally, a decree of November 14, 1958, gives approval of a regulation to the water police, forbidding the dumping of residuary water which results in a danger to public health because of its chemical composition or harmful bacteria. The Hydraulic Service can demand the purification of water and the factories are obliged to show a purification project established by an authorized technician which will be given a public enquiry and studied by the Provincial Health Administration. All industrial establishments, sanatoria, poor-houses, hotels, etc. . . . are obliged to be the object of an enquiry by the Provincial Health Administration, by the Fishing Service Administration and by the Hydraulic Service. These establishments should be authorized by the Hydraulic Service.

We can draw from this legislation two conclusions. There are two different objectives: protection of health, and of the fishing industry, etc. . . .; water is not considered as a source of riches which must be preserved for its intrinsic value. On the other hand, this diversity of objectives constitutes a multiplicity of competent organs.

These characteristics exist equally in French legislation.

Concerning the protection of public health, the system most frequently used in France is the system of zones of protection.

Article L 20 of the Code of Public Health, modified by Article 7 of the law of December 16, 1964, prescribes that "in view of the protection of the quality of water, the act giving birth to the declaration of public utility services to remove water destined for human consumption, puts a limit around the point of removal, an immediate zone of protection of which the soils must be acquired in full property, a neighbouring zone of protection inside of which all activities, deposits or installations are forbidden or controlled by regulation if they are harmful directly or indirectly to the water quality and, if necessary, a zone of protection a bit further on inside of which activities, installations and deposits therein indicated may be subject to regulations".

Article 47 of the Code of Public Health contains punishment for "anyone who by negligence or carelessness permits the introduction of excreta or all other substances which may contaminate springs, fountains, etc. . . .". The punishment is increased if the act is wilful. On the other hand, Article 434 I of the Rural Code prescribes that "anyone who throws, dumps or allows the entry in rivers, directly or indirectly, of all substances which may produce an action or reaction resulting in the destruction of fish, of their nutrition, of their reproduction or of their nutritive value, will be punished by a fine of 50,000 to 500,000 francs and with imprisonment for ten days to a year or of one of these prescribed punishments.

Installations of the water system are especially protected (Article 70 of the new departmental sanitary regulation) which resembles the institution of the zones of protection.

Finally, one must mention the law of December 19, 1971, on dangerous, unpleasant and unhealthy establishments. This text was not elaborated in direct function of the risk of pollution; however the "alteration of water" is considered in several instances as a dangerous or an unhealthy action. The establishments are divided in three classes following the degree of danger that they represent. To open such an establishment the authorization by the Prefect is necessary. The Prefect fixes the conditions which control the authorization, and he can modify them during the exploitation if he thinks fit.

The law of finance for 1968 instituted in Article 87 a tax on classified establishments. The sum furnished by this tax is used for the recruitment of administrative officials charged with the control of these establishments.

These texts, in spite of their importance, do not permit the complete control of pollution. To cite only an example, the law of 1917 is of no interest other than to industrial establishments and leaves completely aside dumping by urban towns.

These texts are always in force, but are enforced to day in a real policy of prevention of pollution.

B. *New protection*

In France, a law of December 16, 1964, governs the subject. First of all, as regard the institutions, the problem of the water policy was the subject of a decree of April 5, 1968, causing a concentration of efforts by the various ministers concerned.

The delegate concerned with territorial planning administration was designated by the Prime Minister to ensure this concentration of effort and to execute the decisions stated. The law of 1964 created on the other hand a consultative organ: the National Water Committee, composed of local delegates, consumers and representatives of the State.

At regional level, France is divided into zones in which a financial agency is charged to facilitate actions of common interest and which is helped by an advisory zone committee.

The law recalls the role that the departments and communes are obliged to play.

The law foresees, on the legal level, the possibility of prevention of the dumping of certain products, of limitations of sale and the right to give effect to these limitations. Expropriation can be given effect to permit factory owners to acquire the necessary lands for the construction of stations for water purification.

And what is more, the law gives to local councils, which create an organ against pollution, and to financial agencies, the right to receive taxes not only charged on private persons but also on institutions. This tax is calculated relative to the quantity and quality of water utilized.

Finally, the law imposes the establishment of a general inventory of water pollution. The project of river classification in different categories according to the degree of pollution has been abandoned. Meanwhile the law prescribes a series of steps governing not only the prevention of water pollution but also its regeneration (improvement of methods of purification, etc. . . .). The problem of solving the definition of a veritable water policy was given birth by the creation of a new ministerial post on January 7, 1971. There exists now in France a Ministerial Delegate charged in function by the Prime Minister for the protection of nature and the problems of environment.

–In Spain, the same problems are being examined. The ordinance of September 4, 1959, obliges the hydraulic services to classify rivers in four categories: protected rivers, controlled rivers, normal rivers and industrial rivers.

Dumping is equally classified as inoffensive, suspect, dangerous. Certain of these dumpings are authorized, others are authorized under certain conditions, the rest are forbidden.

A decree of October 8, 1959, created Water Commissioners who are now competent to deal with all matters relating to pollution. After the decree of March 23, 1960, they became empowered to authorize dumpings, to control rivers and to deal with law-breaking. By an ordinance of October 9, 1962, the powers of commissioners were completed and increased enabling them for example to visit and control industrial installations.

—No kind of such legislation exists in Italy.

Article 37 of the bill of January 11, 1957, prescribes certain measures for protection against oil and petrol-wells.

Article 49 of the model regulation which was approved on January 19, 1959, forbids in particular the dispersion of oil, salt water, residues, etc. . . . on soils. It is on the other hand forbidden to do research or to exploit petrol at less than 50 metres from the springs, waterways and rivers and at less than 100 metres of installations for water protection. The Prefect is competent to apply this legislation.

In Italy, a decree of the President of the Republic enacted on February 13, 1964, concerns control of radioactivity.

However, Parliament is examining a project on control of radioactivity.

In this domain, Italian law is dangerously insufficient, like Tunisian law which does not deal with anything more than the classical protection already mentioned.

—In Israel a law passed by the Knesset in 1959, called "Water Law" determines the water policy in this State. The purpose of this law is the drawing up of regulations concerning all kinds of water.

Water resources are public property (springs, streams, rivers, lakes. etc. . . .).

Water is subject to the control of the State and is destined to meet the requirements of inhabitants and the development of the country.

Chapter 2 gives a definition of pollution of water. Pollution means: "whatever makes water less fit for the use for which it is intruded, and includes salination and deterioration of the properties of water".

This law takes also strong measures for the preservation of water. More especially, section nine provides that:

"A person shall

(1) deal efficiently and sparingly with water coming under his control;

(2) keep any water installations under his control in proper condition, so as to prevent waste and pollution of water;

(3) refrain from blocking up, depleting and polluting any water resource;

(4) prevent the blocking up, depletion and pollution of the water

resource from which he produces water".

And in its section 22 A (amendment No. 4 of July 7, 1965) it provides that a person shall not establish any installation designed for the production of water or for the diversion of water save under an established licence and in accordance with the conditions of the licence the following authorities have competence in the matter of pollution:

–the Minister of Agriculture who may prescribe rules concerning protective strips, give order to water producers for the regulation of production, prescribe all norms and rules for the quantity, quality, price, conditions of supply and use of the water, declare water rationing, prescribe tariffs for water charges, etc. . . . ;

–the Water Board advises the Minister of Agriculture on questions of water policy. It consists of not less than 27 and not more than 36 members including the Minister of Agriculture who is the chairman, the Water Commissioner, who is the vice-chairman and representatives of the public and of the Government and a representative of the World Zionist Organization;

–the National Water Authority is a corporation empowered by the Minister of Agriculture the functions of which are to establish and manage the National Water System, to supply water, to maintain it in proper condition, to improve and enlarge it, and more generally, to do any other act necessary for the supply of water;

–the Water Commissioner is appointed by the Government to manage water affairs in the State. He submits to the Water Board a report on his activities at least once a year. He sees to it that the provisions of section nine are observed. He may prescribe protective strips, do inspections, and order regulation of the productions. He gives production licences and may cancel or modify them;

–the Tribunal of Water Affairs receives the objections from persons who consider themselves aggrieved by an order, it has also the powers of a district court in the scope of its jurisdiction. It consists of three members: a judge and two representatives of the public.

Moreover in accordance with the Streams and Springs Authorities Law, the Minister of the Interior and the Minister of Agriculture may establish an authority for a particular stream or spring or any other water resource.

The function of this authority is to plan and carry out certain operations and more especially the pulling down of sanitary nuisances connected with pollution of the stream or water resource or with the changing flow of its water, the preservation of the landscape and amenities of nature along the stream and the preparation of those areas for the purposes of gardens, recreation and sports.

Internal water is therefore more or less well protected. What is being done for sea water?

II. PROTECTION OF SEA WATER

The States study the prevention of pollution both of internal waters and of territorial seas.

A. *The protection of internal waters*

–In France, there are too many competent authorities.

In the commune, the Mayor has the power to take steps, in the interest of public health, in the public domain of which the beaches are a part. A circular of May 19, 1964, of the Minister of Public Health established several recommendations to prevent the dumping in the sea of all sorts of residues, particularly petrol residues, and to prevent the soiling of beaches. It recommends in particular the creation of purifying stations which are often lacking in number.

Article 66 of the Code of Ports also gives authority to the Administration of Public Works, in the event of deterioration of the coasts, ports and internal waters.

Finally, the maritime administration is equally competent to examine incidents rendered unlawful by regulations taken by a maritime prefect, who is equally competent in questions of control of the coast.

A decree of August 31, 1926, deals with precautions to be taken inside ports concerning the cleaning of the holds of ships, and the Code of Maritime Ports of May 27, 1956, modified by the ordinance of January 7, 1959, prohibits with a penalty of a fine the throwing of rubbish in the water of ports. The simple refusal to obey orders given by officers and port-masters constitutes a crime against the highway code even in the absence of any wilful damage.

–Similar measures were taken in Tunisia during the Protectorate period. They are still in force.

To cite for example the decree of July 26, 1951, which prohibits in Article 12 "the dumping of waste water or residues in the sea or the part of large rivers, streams and canals situated downstream at the point where the water is no longer salted by contact with the sea, without authorization by the Director of Public Works", and the decision of the Director of Public Works of August 10, 1953, creating regulations in particular concerning the port of Tunis-La Goulette which prohibits in Article 14 the throwing of rubbish into the water of the ports and which controls the transport of certain dangerous substances.

–In Israel the first problem is naturally oil. An ordinance enacted by the high Commissioner in Palestine in 1936, amended by the Knesset on June 20, 1966, decides that if any oil is discharged, from vessels or land or from apparatus used for the purpose of transferring oil, in waters, the owner or the master of the vessel, the occupier of the land or the person having charge of the apparatus is guilty of an offence and liable to a fine of ten thousand pounds. However, there is no occasion to prosecute if the escape is due to the vessel being in collision, causing damage to the vessel and also if all reasonable means were taken to prevent the escape.

This ordinance prohibits also transfers of oil at night without written permission from the Officer in charge of the Port.

Moreover every vessel must have a record of all operations in connection with transfer of oil, that can be inspected by the Officer. If any person required to keep such a record fails to do so, he is liable to a fine.

–In Spain, an ordinance of June 1, 1963, obliges within ten months petrol-refining companies or petrol-utilizing companies to establish in ports fixed or floating installations enabling the collection of residues resulting from cleaning the tanks of ships. In addition, these companies must within a period of three months present a report explaining the methods they plan to use to collect such residues. They are dispensed from those obligations if the port is already equipped with such installations. In return for payment, they can use these installations.

An ordinance of May 27, 1967, forbids factories and mills of all categories to dump petrol residues or contaminated products in the sea. The Maritime, Public Works, Industry and Trade Ministries are competent to sanction law-breaking.

What is more, an ordinance of August 24, 1967, obliges oil-refineries and industries which are situated on the coast to have at their immediate disposal a certain quantity of detergents and absorbants.

To cite finally a resolution of April 23, 1969, of the General Direction of Ports which prescribes norms applicable to purification stations.

This text, which is composed of not less than 25 articles, attempts to deal with the problem of coastal pollution in its totality.

It does not only, in effect, regulate the construction of purification stations but it fixes as well the dimensions and material to be used for the construction of septic tanks, and the rules applicable to the construction of submarine pipes; it examines the different processes for purification (treatment, decantation, etc. . . .); it fixes equally the mathematical formula to be used in order to determine the degree of pollution. Finally, it obliges industrialists who discharge industrially used water in the sea to present a report on the nature of these rejects and the method of treatment.

Periodically, however, the administration undertakes an analysis to ensure that this discharge is not harmful either to submarine flora or fauna and does not disturb the utilization of the beaches.

There exists, on the other hand, since June 13, 1962, a National Commission for the Study and Prevention of sea-water contamination by hydrocarbons. Its competence has been extended by an ordinance of July 11, 1963, to cover industrial pollution.

These reports and studies have given birth to the legislation formally noted. They concern not only internal waters but also territorial sea.

B. *The protection of the territorial sea*

By a report of the Spanish National Commission, an ordinance of June 1, 1963, regulated the construction of oil-tankers.

All oil-tankers of more than 20,000 tons must have a tank in order to store water which has been used to clean the holds.

All ships of more than 500 tons must have a system for water purification in order to separate hydrocarbons from water.

–In Italy law 363 of July 14, 1965, forbids the deposit of polluting substances into the sea directly or indirectly.

A Permanent Interministerial Commission for Pollution studies all problems relative to pollution.

–In France, a bill of December 16, 1964, provides: "it is forbidden to dump or immerse in sea water substances of any nature, in particular of industrial or atomic waste, liable to cause harm to public health as well as submarine fauna and flora and to disturb economic or touristic development of coastal areas.

As far as existing dumping is concerned, the Prefect determines the period of time at the end of which the present interdiction will be applicable".

Decrees by the State Council determine the condition which can regulate or forbid: "the dumping or discharge, throwing, depositing, directly or indirectly, of water or substances and more generally everything likely to alter the quality of surface or subterranean water and of *sea-water within territorial limits"*.

The regulation of the fishing police foresees special sanctions, similar to these foreseen by Article 434 I of the Rural Code.

The texts applicable are different for every five maritime regions.

Finally, the bill of December 26, 1964, brought French legislation in conformity with London Convention of May 12, 1954, amended in 1962. The law foresees penal sanctions applicable in internal and territorial waters against French and foreign ships, even ships of a State not bound to the London Convention which discharge oil in the sea.

We know that the London Convention is also applicable to the high sea; theoretically, national legislation is not applicable. But, there is an extension in the field of the application of national law by the regulation for the exploration and exploitation of the riches of the continental shelf.

The State has generally extended to the continental shelf the mining régime in force in its territory. Drilling concessions and public service concessions are covered by the same administrative rules as drilling in territories.

It is rare for States to organize a system to evade this kind of pollution (Great Britain, Denmark, Netherlands).

In France, a bill of December 30, 1968, punishes by a fine of 2,000 to 20,000 francs and, in case of repetition of the offence, imprisonment from 6 days to 6 months and of a fine of 5,000 to 50,000 francs "anyone who, in course of the exploitation or exploration of the natural resources of the continental shelf, dumps or allows to escape" products covered by paragraph 1 of Article 3 of the London Convention of 1954. However, this infraction is not committed if the dumping took effect in order to ensure the security of installations or in order to prevent damage or to save human life in the sea, or if the discharge results from damage or a leak unforeseen or impossible to prevent, and all necessary measures have been taken after the discovery of the damage or the leak to prevent, stop or reduce this leakage. French law punishes only wilful infraction.

One can only hide the deception at the end of this enumeration of these numerous laws in certain domains, not sufficiently numerous in others. The States have treated as the first problem the protection of the internal waters. These mentioned legislations, while being important, are not in fact sufficient. The mouths of rivers are often real dumping grounds, uncovered sewers coastal towns seldom ever have purification stations, they take advantage of their site so as to evade the construction of expensive purification stations; ships do not respect regulations concerning the discharge of oil within specified regions: why should they, since the cost of discharge in ports is more expensive than the fine. Finally, governments hesitate to penalize their industries. Only complete international legislation can solve the solution of the problem of sea pollution on a regional basis.

Unfortunately, the Mediterranean was always a world of conflicts. It still remains so: industrial countries and developing countries, Israel and Arab countries, petrol conflicts.

Will the Mediterranean governments be capable of surpassing these political and economic tensions so as to safeguard their common heritage?

Chapter III

TOWARD A CARIBBEAN REGIONAL REGIME?

The regionalism can be understood in two ways, which are sometimes complementary.[1]

1. Firstly, in the narrowest sense, the regionalism is capable of co-ordinating and harmonizing the national claims.

In this sense, the regional concert could avoid the legislative chaos and the escalation of counter-measures, and could favour the emergence of a legal community facing common problems.

But this first stage stops the regionalism at the conciliation of State interests which are sometimes opposed to each other.

2. Secondly, on the contrary, the State wills may converge in an international realization and give birth to a regional interest. In this case, the regionalism crystallizes at this level a part of international aspirations of States. This stage is particularly interesting, because the whole body of different problems and situations give birth to a regional community more well-knit than the concept of international society understood on the level of mankind.

I. THE REGIONALISM, A CO-ORDINATING FACTOR IN THE NATIONAL CLAIMS

It appears from different declarations, especially in the United Nations Seabed Committee, that the national appropriation of the maritime space must be finalized, limited and flexible, or rigid enough to be changed on the basis of reciprocity.

1. The term regionalism used in the context of the Caribbean in fact is employed to simplify the language, because in reality it is *sub-regionalism.*

A. *Appropriation for economic purposes*

One of the major reasons why the economic aspects rather than the political ones have been emphasized in the appropriation of zones can be explained by the direct or indirect presence of the big powers in the Caribbean.[2] In an heterogeneous system, the negotiation on the division of riches raises less problems than the consensus on political options.

The major concern of certain concerned western countries, like France, in the appropriation of zones is geared to economic ends. For this reason, *the territorial sea*, as far as it is a manifestation of the sovereignty of the State, must not be extended beyond certain limits. And the limit of 12 miles appears to be a true reflection of the present-day international claims.

The Caribbean countries are ready to negotiate in this spirit, because, except Panama (claiming 200 miles as territorial sea), the claims of other Caribbean States on the territorial sea *stricto sensu* range from 3 to 12 miles.[3]

As far as France is concerned, the interpretation of Article 24 of the 1958 Geneva Convention on the territorial sea and the contiguous zone limits to 12 miles the maximum extension of *prerogatives of sovereignty*. These prerogatives of sovereignty are the principal legal element of the territorial sea.[4] The legal motivation of this limit is clear: the régime of the territorial sea is not mainly aimed at protecting the economic interests.

As a consequence, and also not having participated in the ministerial reunion of the Special Conference of the Caribbean countries on the sea problems (June 7, 1972), France cannot but approve the Declaration of Santo Domingo which declared: "Every

2. France by Guadeloupe and Martinique. But equally the United States which provides protection for the autonomous Commonwealth of Puerto Rico and administers the Virgin Island. Similarly, the United Kingdom provides protection for the six associated, autonomous States of Antigua, Dominica, Grenada, St. Christopher Nevis, St. Lucia and St. Vincent (cited by R. D. Hodgson, "The American Mediterranean, One Sea, One Region?", The geographer, Department of State, 1972, *Report on the Proceedings of Caracas*, p. 7). Finally, the Soviet Union is capable of exercising an influence indirectly through Cuba.

3. Cf. United Nations *Legislative Series* ST/LEG/SER. B/15.

4. Declaration on this matter by M. Yvon Bourges, Foreign Secretary, in the National Assembly, JORF, A.N. Débats, December 8, 1971, p. 6517.

State has . . . the right to fix the breadth of its territorial sea up to the limit of 12 nautical miles from the base line" (UN Doc. A/AC.138/80, p. 3).

Consequently, it appears that France may negotiate an international legal régime, recognizing *special economic rights* to the coastal States beyond 12 miles and in the sense of the concept of "patrimonial sea" developed by several Latin American States.[5]

Now, different economic studies have demonstrated that the Caribbean Sea is an important reservoir of biological riches, but especially mineral resources, and in particular oil and manganese nodules.[6] A regional co-ordination of the claims is therefore envisageable to achieve the optimum exploitation by the coastal States. This may be the beginning or the complementary factor to the Caribbean organization managing an *indivisum* territory between member States.

B. *The protection of the freedom of navigation*

If it appears that France is favourable to the extension of zones *based purely on economic grounds*, particularly in the seabed, a legal distinction must be clearly made: the *political* and administrative *rights* traditionally belong to the territorial sea and the State sovereignty, whereas the patrimonial sea reflects only the *economic rights.*[7]

Thus, inside this functional economic zone, not only the *right of innocent passage* which characterizes the régime of the territo-

5. The views concerning France expressed in the present study are the personal views of the author and cannot in any respect commit the French Government. As far as the appropriation of the *seabed* is concerned, the French position is still more precise, because the Government accepts in principle the limit of *200 miles* (cf. the declaration of the French representative in the UN Seabed Committee, UN Doc. A/AC.138/SC.II/SR.27, p. 39).

6. Cf. on these problems D. D. Arden, Jr., "Petroleum Prospectives in the Caribbean Area", UNESCO-FAO Symposium, FRm/R. 71.1, pp. 205-211.

7. This distinction equally justifies the uniqueness of the French legislation on this matter: ". . . Article 5 (of the Bill of December 24, 1971, concerning the delimitation of territorial waters) maintains the principle of the *necessary unity of the legal régime of territorial waters in the whole domain subject to the French sovereignty*. In this field, there cannot be derogatory laws applicable to such and such region, because, I insist, the régime of territorial waters is not aimed at protecting the economic interests". (Declaration by the Foreign Secretary, *op. cit.*, note 8, p. 6517).

rial sea must be recognized, but also *the freedom of navigation.* [8] The right of free navigation is particularly important in the context of half-closed seas, such as the Caribbean. This character of "mediterranean" emphasizes the utility, if not the necessity, of a regional co-ordination between coastal States.

C. *The flexibility of the régime based on the reciprocity of agreements*

An 80-mile fisheries zone is envisaged for the French Guyana. The interesting aspect of this provision lies in the fact that it shall not be applicable to the nationals of the States having a territorial sea less or equal to 12 miles. On the contrary, it shall be applicable to the States which, like Brazil, have extended territorial waters to 200 miles.

In the context of the Caribbean, the regional negotiation could avoid this type of measure which is susceptible to inviting retaliation. In this way, the French position reflects the will to reciprocate aimed at balancing the economic interests in question. [9]

But the principle of reciprocity must be equally envisaged in the regional context from a positive point of view: in order to have a healthy administration of the biological resources, the Caribbean States establishing patrimonial economic zones could conclude regional agreements on fisheries. Thus opening the different patrimonial seas to the nationals of Caribbean States.

The interpenetration of the national and regional appropriation would thus benefit the common interests of the region. A solution of this type was adopted by the European Economic Community [10] and cannot but develop by this integration a new type of

8. The Declaration of Santo Domingo, *op. cit.*, recognizes in the patrimonial sea this right of free navigation and overflight, adding, however, "without other restrictions than those which may result from the use of its rights upon the said sea by the coastal State".

9. This reciprocity is indirectly manifested in Article 55 of the 1958 French Constitution, stipulating the supremacy of the treaty on the internal laws on the condition that the opposite party puts the agreements into effect.

10. Thus, regulation No. 2141/70 of the Council of the European Communities (*JOCE*, L 236 of October 27, 1970) stipulates in its Article 2, § 1, the principle of the freedom of access of the fishing boats, flying the flag of one of the member States, in the sea waters subject to the sovereignty or the jurisdiction of the other member States.

regionalism which will be more elaborated, and integrate the international aspirations of its members.

II. THE REGIONALISM, INTEGRATING FACTOR OF THE INTERNATIONAL ASPIRATIONS

The passage of a State to the universal international community poses multiple difficulties. Thus, a uniform legal régime is of course not desired, because the multiplicity of situations and particular needs necessitates local adaptations.

The regionalism avoids a high degree of abstractions and can serve as a stage between the State and mankind, whose heritage on the seabed beyond national jurisdiction has been recognized by the United Nations.

A. *The Caribbean and the notion of common heritage of mankind*

The concept of common heritage of mankind is difficult to analyse legally, particularly in its legal and geographical context.

The Declaration of Santo Domingo of June 7, 1972, affects the position that the Caribbean seabed, beyond the patrimonial sea and the continental shelf which is not covered by the said sea, is the common heritage of mankind.

It may be asked if the French position, even though not officially declared in distinguishing between the oceans and the "mediterraneans", might not be different. "Mediterraneans" are half-closed seas creating from this fact close relationships between riparians. [11] From this fact, two propositions may be deduced from this distinction:

On the one hand, the coastal States according to the principle of the patrimonial zones may envisage an appropriation based on the fact that the "mediterraneans" are half-closed and small in size. On the contrary, as far as the oceans are concerned, the fact that the distances are very large between the coastal States render them a common heritage of mankind. The Caribbean seabed is not, from

11. The theory of the "mediterranean" was put forward in 1968 by Italy in the first Seabed Committee. Cf. UN Doc. A/AC.135/I Add. 9.

this geographical point of view, a necessary part of this heritage because the national appropriations are possible.

On the other hand, the community of interests between the coastal States has pushed certain States, such as Uruguay (in the context of Latin America), to propose an American regional organization to exploit the seabed, dedicated "to the promotion of the economic, social and cultural development of the Latin American peoples". [12]

In the Caribbean, France might adhere to such a regional organization.

B. *The geographical necessities in the choice of a régime of property*

Supposing that some half-closed seas are not part of the totality of the régime based on the common heritage of mankind, two kinds of property are negotiable in the regional context.

When the geographical and geological data is sufficiently simple, the coastal States may divide the seabed through bilateral or multilateral agreements. The *Mediterranean* is a good example of this theory and hence an extension of patrimonial jurisdictions up to 200 miles may be envisaged.

The regionalism, in this case, has a limited scope and brings us back to the first level of co-ordination of national claims.

However, when geographical data is complicated, the physical necessities may contribute to the birth of a legal regional régime and even to a machinery.

Thus, it is envisageable that some countries interested in the region may think impossible the division of the Caribbean Sea because of the multiplicity of islands. Consequently, a system of *property in indivisum* is capable of overcoming this difficulty, giving at the same time a body to a regional system of exploration and exploitation. The Caribbean seabed beyond a certain limit would be hence assimilated to a *common heritage of riparians of this sea.* [13]

12. Cf. declaration of M. Legnani (Uruguay) in the Seabed Committee, UN Doc. A/AC.138/SR.47, p. 35.

13. This solution has equally the advantage of safeguarding the future: in the case of a legal international régime applicable to the common heritage of

The advantage of the system of *indivisum* as compared to the separate national appropriations is to answer better the development needs of the coastal States. In effect, the division of the regional heritage leads every State to assume individually its "economic salvation".

To the contrary, the management of the system of *indivisum* would help accomplish a regional strategy of development. Consequently, an Agency would be necessary.

C. *The characteristics of a regional Agency*

In the light of French declarations concerning an international machinery, the regional Agency must be *intergovernmental*, in such a way that the States would act as intermediaries between the Agency and the enterprises in charge of exploration and exploitation of the seabed.

Hence, France is not favourable to the exploration and exploitation of mineral riches directly by the Agency, which might put her in opposition to the draft treaty presented by several Latin American countries in the Seabed Committee. [14] The French argument is based on the *necessity of attaining economic efficiency*, which, according to her, is not realizable by the direct management.

In this context, it would be interesting to institute a legal framework relating in some respects to Chapter VIII, part II, of the Treaty establishing the European Atomic Energy Community (EURATOM).

A distinction would be made between the Community of the Caribbean States, possessing the seabed property through the system of *indivisum*, and the regional Agency, having the legal personality and playing the role of a commercial instrument. This

---

mankind, a regional system based on *indivisum* might furnish a fund more easily acceptable by the coastal States than an individual contribution by each State, as the Maltese draft treaty envisaged.

14. Chile, Colombia, El Salvador, Ecuador, Guatemala, Guyana, Jamaica, Mexico, Panama, Peru, Trinidad and Tobago, Uruguay, Venezuela. This draft treaty provides in its Article 33, the establishment of an *Enterprise*, "an organ of Authority which is capable of exercising all the technical, industrial and commercial activities for the purposes of exploration of the zone and exploitation of its resources (by *itself* or jointly with the legal persons duly patronized by the States)". UN Doc. A/AC.138.49.

juridical distinction would thus enhance the system of *indivisum* and the regional character of the property. Similarly, it would facilitate the quantitative control of mineral resources extracted in order not to strongly disturb the rates of the same raw materials extracted from the continent.

So, it appears in conclusion that the juridical position of Martinique and Guadeloupe is the position of France. However, it is in a position to introduce changes in its "départements d'Outre-Mer" according to regional needs, bearing in mind especially the economic nature of the new law of the sea [15] and the freedom of navigation.

The system of *indivisum* may appear to affect the common heritage of mankind. However, the progressive awareness of a more and more vast international community is capable of changing the regional system in the future as a decentralized element of the universal régime.

15. Cf. on this matter the declaration of the French representative in the Seabed Committee, 54th Meeting, UN Doc. A/AC.138/SR.54, p. 108.

SELECTIVE BIBLIOGRAPHY OF RECENT PUBLICATIONS

A. *Evolution of the Law of the Sea*

(1) *Books*

Bowett, D. W., *The Law of the Sea*, Manchester UP, 1967, 117 pp. (Victoria University of Manchester, Melland Schill Lectures).

British Institute of International and Comparative Law, *Developments in the Law of the Sea, 1958-1964*, London 1965, 208 pp.

Brown, E. D., *The Legal Régime of Hydrospace,* London, Stevens (for) London Institute of World Affairs, 1971, 236 pp.

Colombos, Constantin John, *The International Law of the Sea*, 6th rev. ed., London Longmans, 1967.

Friedmann, Wolfgang, *The Future of the Oceans*, NY Braziller, 1971, 132 pp.

MacDougal, Myres S. and Burke, W. T., *The Public Order of the Oceans; A Contemporary International Law of the Sea*, New Haven, Conn., Yale UP, 1962, 1226 pp.

(2) *Articles*

Alexander, Lewis, "The Law of the Sea; International Rules and Organisation for the Sea", *Proceedings of the Third Annual Conference of the Law of the Sea Institute*, June 24-27, 1968, edited by L. M. Alexander, Kingston, University of Rhode Island (1969), 464 pp.

Beesley, J. A., "Some Unresolved Issues on the Law of the Sea", *Natural Resources Lawyer*, Chicago, July 1971, pp. 629-638.

Brown, E. D. , "The 1973 Conference on the Law of the Sea; the Consequences of Failure to Agree", in Alexander Lewis ed.: *Law of the Sea: a New Geneva Conference*, Proceedings of the

Sixth Annual Conference of the Law of the Sea Institute, Kingston RI, 1972, pp. 1-37.

Burke, William T., "Comments on Current International Issues relating to the Law of the Sea", *Natural Resources Lawyer*, Chicago, July 1971, pp. 660-667.

Burke, William T., "A Contemporary Legal Problem in Ocean Development", *International Lawyer*, Chicago, April 1969, pp. 536-559.

Butte, W. L., "The Law of the Sea: Breakers Ahead", *International Lawyer*, 1972, pp. 237-257.

Dupuy, R. J., "Les contradictions du droit de la mer", *Revue française de l'énergie*, February 1973, pp. 186-194.

Engo, Paul B., "Current International Issues relating to the Law of the Sea", *Natural Resources Lawyer*, Chicago, July 1971, pp. 622-628.

Essen, M. M van der, "L'évolution du droit de la mer depuis 1958", *Chronique de politique étrangère,* Bruxelles, November 1970, pp. 657-689.

Friedmann, Wolfgang, "The Law of the Sea; Past, Present and Future", in Logue, John, ed.: *The Fate of the Oceans,* Villanova UP for the World Order Research Institute, 1972, pp. 100-113.

Friedmann, Wolfgang, "Selden Redivivus: Towards a Partition of the Seas", *American Journal of International Law*, October 1971, pp. 757-770.

Goldie, L. F. E., "Geneva Convention of the Law of the Sea: the Need for Future Modifications", *The Law of the Sea: Off Shore Boundaries and Zones*, ed. by L. M. Alexander, Colombus, Ohio, 1967, pp. 273-293.

Griffin, W. L., "Emerging Law of Ocean Space", *International Lawyer*, Chicago, July 1967, pp. 548-587.

Hargrove, John L., "New Concepts in the Law of the Sea", *Ocean Development and International Law Journal*, Spring 1973, Vol. 1, No. 1.

Henkin, Louis, "Changing Law for the Changing Seas", in Gullion, E. ed.: *Uses of the Seas*, Englewood Cliffs, N.J., Prentice-Hall, 1968, pp. 69-97.

Levy, Jean-Pierre, "Ocean Management and a New Law of the Sea", *Ocean Management*, 1973, pp. 129-143.

Levy, Jean-Pierre, "La troisième conférence sur le droit de la mer", *Annuaire français de droit international*, 1971, pp. 784-832.

MacDougal, M. S., "International Law and the Law of the Sea", in *The Law of the Sea: Off Shore Boundaries and Zones*, ed. by L. M. Alexander, Ohio State University Press, 1967, pp. 3-25.

Oda, Shigeru, "Some Observations on the International Law of the Sea", in *Japanese Annual of International Law*, No. 11, 1967, pp. 37-50.

Pontavice, E. du, "Les problèmes nouveaux posés en droit international par l'exploitation des mers", *Droit maritime français,* 1971, pp. 323-334.

Voelckel, Michel, "La mutation juridique du milieu marin", *Revue de défense nationale*, Paris, May 1969, pp. 794-810.

B. *Use and protection of the ocean space*

(1) *Economical use*

Alexander, L. M., "Resources of the Sea, National Jurisdiction and the Use of the Sea", *Natural Resources Journal* (Albuquerque, N. Mex.), July 1968, pp. 373-400.

Andrassy, Juraj, *International Law and the Resources of the Sea*, NY Columbia UP, 1970, XVIII, 191 pp.

Askevold, Gerald, "Ocean Mining in Perspective", *Stanford Journal of International Studies*, June 1970, pp. 115-142.

Boasson, Charles, "Resources of the Sea and International Law", *Israel Law Review*, July 1971, pp. 291-308.

Bouchez, L. J., "Deep-Sea Mining", *Report of the Deep-Sea Mining Committee of the International Law Association*, February 21, 1968.

Brooks, D. B., "Deep-Sea Manganese Nodules: from Scientific Phenomenon to World Resources", *Natural Resources Journal*, 1968, pp. 401-423.

Brown, E. D., "Deep-Sea Mining: the Legal Régime of 'inner space' ", *Yearbook of World Affairs*, Vol. 22, 1968, pp. 165-190.

Christy, F. T., "Economic Criteria for Rules Governing Exploitation of Deep-Sea Minerals", *International Lawyer*, January 1968, pp. 224-242.

Craven, John P., "The Challenge of Ocean Technology for the Law of the Sea", *Judge Advocates Journal*, 1967, pp. 8-31.

Dole, H. M., "Ocean Minerals and the Law", *Natural Resources Lawyer*, November 1969, pp. 352-359.

Firth, F. E., ed., *The Encyclopedia of Marine Resources*, NY, Van Nostrand Reinhold Co., 1969, 740 pp.

Garcia Amador y Rodriguez, F. V., *The Exploitation and Conservation of the Resources of the Sea: a Study of Contemporary International Law*; Leyden, Sythoff, 1963, 240 pp.

Jouvenel, Bertrand de, "Vue économique des problèmes marins", *Les futuristes*, T. XIV, 1972, pp. 1046-1086.

Ketchum, B. H., Fye, A., Maxwell, Emery, K. O., "Ocean Science and Marine Resources", in *Uses of the Sea*, ed. E. A. Gullion, The American Assembly, Columbia University, 1968, pp. 16-68.

La Prairie, Yves, "Le CNEXO et les promesses de l'océan", *Revue de la défense nationale*, Paris, August-September, 1969, pp. 1351-1367.

Oda, Shigeru, "International Law of the Sea", Académie de Droit International de La Haye, *Recueil des cours*, 1969, T. 127, pp. 355-484.

Remond, Martine, *L'exploitation pétrolière en mer et le droit: droit maritime, droit de la mer*, Paris, Ed. Technip, 1970, 197 pp.

Sohn, L. B., "Status of Mineral Resources on the Ocean Floor", *California Western Law Review*, 1969, pp. 299-312.

Talbot, R., "L'exploitation du pétrole en mer", *Revue de la défense nationale*, August-September, 1969, pp. 1472-1485.

Talbot, R., "Les débuts de l'exploitation minière des océans", *Revue de la défense nationale*, June 1969, pp. 1071-1079.

Vigne, J., *Le rôle des intérêts économiques dans l'évolution du droit de la mer*, Coll. Institut Universitaire des Hautes Etudes Internationals, Geneva, 1971, 143 pp.

(2) *Scientific research*

Barton, Robert, *Oceanology Today, Man Explores the Sea*, Garden City, NY, Doubleday, 1970, 192 pp.

Behrman, D., *Exploring the Ocean*, Paris, UNESCO, 1970, 89 pp.

Bouchez, L. J., "The Legal Régime of Scientific Research on the

Sea-Bed", Symposium on the International Régime of the Sea-Bed, Rome, 1969, 23 pp.
Burke, W. T., *Marine Science Research and International Law*, Kingston University of Rhode Island, LSI, 1970, 36 pp.
Burke, W. T., *A Report on International Legal Problems of Scientific Research in the Oceans*, Springfield, Va., Clearinghouse for Federal Scientific and Technical Information, 1967, 143 pp.
Emery, K. O., "An Oceanographer's View of the Law of the Sea" in Alexander, L. M., ed.: *The Law of the Sea, National Policy Recommendations*, Proceedings of the Fourth Annual Conference of the Law of the Sea Institute, Kingston, University of Rhode Island, 1970, pp. 211-225.
Grousta, F., "Legal Problems of Scientific Research in the Oceans", *Journal of Maritime Law and Commerce*, July 1970, pp. 603-614.
Knauss, John, "Developing the Freedom of Scientific Research of the Law of the Sea Conference", *Ocean Development and International Law Journal*, Vol. 1, No. 1, Spring 1973.
Ringeard, G., Scientific Research from Freedom", *Ocean Development and International Law Journal*, 1973, Vol. 1, No. 2, pp. 121-136.
Schaefer, M. B., "Freedom of Scientific Research and Exploration in the Sea", *Stanford Journal of International Studies*, June 1969, pp. 46-70.
Voelckel, M., "Le statut juridique des systèmes d'acquisition des données océaniques (SADO)", *Annuaire français de droit international*, 1971, pp. 833-854.

(3) *Protection of the ocean space*

Andrassy, Juraj, "Etude des mesures internationales les plus aptes à prévenir la pollution des milieux maritimes", *Annuaire de l'institut de droit international*, 1969, pp. 547-711.
Baskin, J. J., "Questions de Droit international relatives à la pollution des eaux", *Revue générale de droit international public*, April-June 1969, pp. 421-431.
Browning, D. S., *The International Legal Environment for Ocean Exploitation*, First Annual Offshore Technology Conference, Houston, Tex., May 18-21, 1969, Vol. II, pp. 273-295.

Caflisch, L. C., "International Law and Ocean Pollution: the Present and the Future", *Revue belge de droit international*, 1972.

Cristol, C. Q., *Oil Pollution of the Marine Environment, a Legal Bibliography*, Washington, Government Printing Offices, 1971, 93 pp.

Douglas, William, "Environmental Problems of the Oceans: the Need for International Controls", *Environmental Law Review,* 1971, pp. 149-166.

Goldie, L. F. E., "International Principles of Responsibility for Pollution", *Columbia Journal of Transnational Law*, Fall 1970, pp. 283-330.

Krueger, R. B., "International and National Regulation of Pollution from Offshore Oil Production", *San Diego Law Review*, July 1970, pp. 541-573.

Levy, Jean-Pierre, "Le droit de l'environnement marin", *Revue française de l'énergie,* No. 253, May 1973.

Lucchini, L., "Pollution des mers par les hydrocarbures: les conventions de Bruxelles de novembre 1969 ou les fissures du droit international classique", *Journal du droit international*, 1970, pp. 697-795.

Petaccio, V., "Water Pollution and the Future Law of the Sea", *International and Comparative Law Quarterly*, January 1972, pp. 15-21.

Pontavice, E. du, *La pollution des mers par les hydrocarbures*, Paris, 1968, Pichon et Duran-Auzias, 142 pp.

Schachter, O., and Serwer, D., "Marine Pollution Problems and Remedies", *American Journal of International Law*, January 1971, pp. 84-111.

C. *The conflicts in the use of the maritime areas*

Branco, R., "Rational Development of Sea-bed Resources: Issues and Conflicts", *Ocean Management*, 1973, No. 1, pp. 41-54.

Cheever, D. S., "Economic Development, the Great Powers and the Sea-Bed", in Rubinstein, A. Z. and Ginzburg, G., *Soviet and American Policies in the United Nations,* New York, 1971, pp. 95-124.

Craven, J. P., "Western Civilizations and the World Ocean", *Oceans Magazine*, 1, pp. 33-37.

Evensen, J., *The Military Uses of the Deep Ocean Floor and Its Subsoil: Present and Future*, in Symposium on the International Régime of the Seabed, Rome, 1969, *Proceedings*, 1970, pp. 535-556.

Graillot, H., "Les mers, théâtre et enjeu des conflits", *Revue française de science politique*, Paris, August 1970, pp. 720-735.

Henkin, L., "International Law and 'the Interests': the Law of the Seabed", *American Journal of International Law*, July 1969, pp. 504-510.

Hydrospace in International Relations, edited by Lucius C. Caflisch, Annals of International Studies, vol. 4, Geneva, 1973.

Knauss, J. A., "The Military Role in the Ocean and Its Relation to the Law of the Sea", in Alexander Lewis, ed., *Proceedings of the Sixth Annual Conference of the Law of the Sea Institute,* Kingston, RI, 1972, pp. 77-86.

MacDougal, M. S., "Panel: Conflicting Approach to the Control and Exploitation of the Oceans", *American Journal of International Law*, 1971, pp. 104-143.

Martin, L. W., *The Sea in Modern Strategy*, London, Chatto and Windus, 1967, 190 pp. (Institute for Strategic Studies–London.)

Moineville, H., "Les Etats et la mer, aujourd'hui et demain", *Revue de la défense nationale*, June-July 1968, pp. 1062-1076.

Olmstead, C. J., "Conflicting Approaches to the Control and Exploitations of the Oceans", in *Proceedings of the American Society of International Law* at its 65th meeting, Washington DC, 1971.

Pardo, A., *Sovereignty Under the Sea, the Threat of National Occupation*, Round Table, London, October 1968, pp. 341-355.

Ratiner, L. S., "National Security Interests in Ocean Space", *Natural Resources Lawyer*, July 1971, pp. 582-596.

Stevenson, J. R., "Conflicting Approaches to the Control and Exploitation of the Oceans", in *Proceedings of the American Society of International Law* at its 65th meeting, Washington DC, 1971, pp. 107-114.

Weissberg, G., "International Law Meets the Short-Term National Interest; the Maltese Proposal on the Seabed and Ocean Floor–Its Fate in Two Cities", *International and Comparative Law Quarterly,* London, January 1969, pp. 41-102.

Zacklin, R., "Latin America and the Development of the Law of the Sea", *Annals of International Studies,* Vol. 4, Geneva, 1973.

D. *The legal régime of maritime areas*

(1) *Territorial sea and contiguous zone*

Burke, W. T., "Consequences for Territorial Sea Claims of Failure to Agree at the Next Law of the Sea Conference", in Alexander Lewis, ed., *Proceedings of the Sixth Annual Conference of the Law of the Sea Institute,* Kingston, RI, 1972, pp. 37-45.

Florsheim, B. L., "Territorial Seas: 3000 Year-old Question", *Journal of Air Law and Commerce*, Winter 1970, pp. 73-104.

Freeman, R. D., "Possible Solutions to the 200 Miles Territorial Limit", *International Lawyer*, April 1973.

Kolodkin, A., "Territorial Waters and International Law", *International Affairs*, Moscow, August 1969, pp. 78-81.

Oudendijk, J. K., *Status and Extent of Adjacent Waters: a Historical Orientation*, Leyden, Sijthoff, 1970, 160 pp.

(2) *High seas*

Dinstein, Y., "Oil Pollution by Ships and Freedom of the High Seas", *Journal of Maritime Law and Commerce*, 1972, pp. 363-374.

Jennings, R. Y., "General Course on Principles of International Law, Pt. 4. The High Seas, Airspace and Outer Space", Académie de droit international de La Haye, *Recueil des cours*, 1967, II, pp. 387-415.

Simonnet, M. R., *La convention sur la haute mer adoptée à Genève le 29 avril 1958 par la Conférence des Nations Unies sur le Droit de la mer*, Paris LGDJ, 1966, 292 pp.

(3) *Continental shelf*

Alexander, L., "Alternative régimes for the continental shelf", *Pacem in Maribus*, Royal University of Malta Press, 1971, pp. 31-43.

Finlay, L. W., "The Outer Limit of the Continental Shelf", *Ameri-*

can Journal of International Law, January 1970, pp. 42-61.

Goldie, L. F. E., "Where Is the Continental Shelf's Outer Boundary?", *Journal of Maritime Law and Commerce*, April 1970, pp. 461-472.

Krueger, R. B., "The Background of the Doctrine of the Continental Shelf and the Outer Continental Shelf Lands Act", *Natural Resources Journal*, July 1970, pp. 442-514.

Oxman, B., "The Preparation of Art. 1 of the Convention on the Continental Shelf", *Journal of Maritime Law and Commerce*, January 1972, pp. 245-305.

Vallée, C., *Le plateau continental dans le droit positif actuel*, Paris, Pédone, 1971, 359 pp.

(4) *The seabed and the international ocean floor, common heritage of mankind*

Auburn, F. M., "The International Sea-Bed Area", *International and Comparative Law Quarterly*, London, April 1971, pp. 173-194.

Borgese, E. M., "A Constitution for the Oceans", in Logue, John, ed.: *The Fate of the Oceans*, Villanova UP for the World Order Research Institute, 1972, pp. 1-10.

Colliard, Dupuy, Polvèche, Vaissière, *Le fond des mers*, ed. Armand Colin, Coll. U, Paris, 1971, 205 pp.

Eichelberger, C. M., "The Sea-Bed Question in Context, One of Many Issues Massing for the 1973 Conference", *San Diego Law Review*, May 1971, pp. 653-657.

Goldie, L. F. E., "Two Neglected Problems in Drafting Régimes for Deep Ocean Resources", *American Journal of International Law*, October 1970, pp. 905-919.

Ifrin, D., "On the Concept of Common Patrimony of Mankind: the Legal Régime of Submarine Areas Beyond the Limits of National Jurisdiction", *Revue roumaine d'études internationales*, Bucharest, 1970, No. 3-4, pp. 47-85.

Knight, H. G., "The Draft UN Conventions on the International Sea-Bed Area: Background, Description and Some Preliminary Thoughts", *San Diego Law Review*, May 1970, pp. 459-550.

Levy, J. P., "L'ordre international et le développement des fonds marins", *Revue générale de droit international public*, Paris, April-June 1971, pp. 356-391.

Mero, J. L., "A Legal Régime for Deep Sea Mining", *San Diego Law Review*, July 1970, pp. 488-503.

Newton, W. F., "The New Quest for Atlantis: Proposed Régimes for Seabed Resources", *JAG Journal,* December 1970-January 1971, pp. 79-92.

Piquemal, A., *Le fond des mers, patrimoine commun de l'humanité,* edité par le Centre National d'Exploitation des Océans (CNEXO), Paris, 1973, 290 pp.